LEARNING AND TEACHING
Learning Process

LEARNING AND TEACHING
Learning Process

Editors
Monica Tomar
S.K. Sharma

ISHA BOOKS
DELHI-110 033

Learning and Teaching—Learning Process

Rs. 750

ISBN: 81-8205-158-4

Published in 2005 in India by
Isha Books, D-43, Prithviraj Road,
Adarsh Nagar, Delhi-110 033

Laser Typesetting at: Shree Vaishnavi Creations, Delhi
Printed at: Mehra Offset Press, Delhi

PREFACE

Learning can be defined as 'the ability to modify behaviour as a result of experience'. This ability allows us to adapt to changing environmental conditions. Everyone is involved in the learning process for at least a quarter of his life; some are much more than that. Understanding the basic concepts of learning and how the brain actually functions leads to better performance both as a teacher and as a student.

This book describes key learning concepts that are commonly used in explanations of how learning occurs in children and adults. The various approaches to learning, including behavioural, cognitive, humanistic and constructivistic are discussed elaborately. The factors influencing the learning process are comprehensively analysed. Various vital aspects related to teaching and learning process are also covered.

The book will enable the reader to gain a deeper understanding of how the human learns; investigate the theories of learning and apply the information to improve conditions of learning for oneself or for another student. It will help teachers to be more effective and reduce the frustration that most teachers feel. It will help students to develop their own teaching and learning methods from their understanding of these theories. Although the book is written with teachers and students in mind, it will be beneficial to policy makers, school administrators, parents, counsellors and anyone who wants a better understanding of the learning process.

Editor

CONTENTS

1
CONCEPTS OF LEARNING

Learning can be defined as 'the ability to modify behaviour as a result of experience'. This ability allows us to adapt to changing environmental conditions. This chapter describes key learning concepts that are commonly used in explanations of how learning occurs in children and adults.

For all the talk of learning amongst educational policymakers and practitioners, there is a surprising lack of attention to what it entails. In Britain and Northern Ireland, for example, theories of learning do not figure strongly in professional education programmes for teachers and those within different arenas of informal education. It is almost as if it is something is unproblematic and that can be taken for granted. Get the instructional regime right, the message seems to be, and learning (as measured by tests and assessment regimes) will follow. This lack of attention to the nature of learning inevitably leads to an impoverishment of education. It isn't simply that the process is less effective as a result, but what passes for education can actually diminish well-being. Here we begin by examining learning as a product and as a process. The latter takes us into the arena of competing learning theories — ideas about how learning may happen. We also look at Alan Roger's helpful discussion of task-conscious or acquisition learning, and learning-conscious or formalized learning.

LEARNING AS A PRODUCT

Pick up a standard psychology textbook - especially from the 1960s and 1970s and you will probably find learning defined as a change in behaviour. In other words, learning is approached as an outcome - the end product of some process. It can be recognized or seen. This approach has the virtue of highlighting a crucial aspect of learning - change. It's apparent clarity may also make some sense when conducting experiments. However, it is rather a blunt instrument. For example:

— Does a person need to perform in order for learning to have happened?

— Are there other factors that may cause behaviour to change?

— Can the change involved include the potential for change?

Questions such as these have led to qualification. Some have looked to identifying relatively permanent changes in behaviour (or potential for change) as a result of experiences. However, not all changes in behaviour resulting from experience involve learning. It would seem fair to expect that if we are to say that learning has taken place, experience should have been used in some way. Conditioning may result in a change in behaviour, but the change may not involved drawing upon experience to generate new knowledge. Not surprisingly, many theorists have, thus, been less concerned with overt behaviour but with changes in the ways in which people 'understand, or experience, or conceptualize the world around them'. The focus for them, is gaining knowledge or ability through the use of experience.

The depth or nature of the changes involved are likely to be different. Some years ago Säljö carried out a simple, but very useful piece of research. He asked a number of adult students what they understood by learning. Their responses fell into five main categories:

— Learning as a quantitative increase in knowledge. Learning is acquiring information or 'knowing a lot'.

— Learning as memorising. Learning is storing information that can be reproduced.

— Learning as acquiring facts, skills, and methods that can be retained and used as necessary.

— Learning as making sense or abstracting meaning. Learning involves relating parts of the subject matter to each other and to the real world.

— Learning as interpreting and understanding reality in a different way. Learning involves comprehending the world by reinterpreting knowledge.

As Paul Ramsden comments, we can see immediately that conceptions 4 and 5 in are qualitatively different from the first three. Conceptions 1 to 3 imply a less complex view of learning. Learning is something external to the learner. It may even be something that just happens or is done to you by teachers (as in conception 1). In a way learning becomes a bit like shopping. People go out and buy knowledge - it becomes their possession. The last two conceptions look to the 'internal' or personal aspect of learning. Learning is seen as something that you do in order to understand the real world.

A man knowing little or nothing of medical science could not be a good surgeon, but excellence at surgery is not the same thing as knowledge of medical science; not is it a simple product of it. The surgeon must indeed have learned from instruction, or by his own inductions and observations, a great number of truths; but he must also have learned by practice a great number of aptitudes. Learning how or improving an ability is not like learning that or acquiring information. Truths can be imparted, procedures can only be inculcated, and while inculcation is a gradual process, imparting is relatively sudden. It makes sense to ask at what moment someone became apprised of a truth, but not to ask at what moment someone acquired a skill.

In some ways the difference here involves what Gilbert Ryle has termed 'knowing *that*' and 'knowing *how*'. The first two categories mostly involve 'knowing that'. As we move through the third we see that alongside 'knowing that' there is growing emphasis on 'knowing how'. This system of categories is hierarchical - each higher conception implies all the rest beneath it. 'In other words, students who conceive of learning as understanding reality are also able to see it as increasing their knowledge'

LEARNING AS A PROCESS

In the five categories that Säljö identified we can see learning appearing as a process - there is a concern with what happens when the learning takes place. In this way, learning could be thought of as 'a process by which behaviour changes as a result of experience'. One of the significant questions that arises is the extent to which people are conscious of what is going on. Are they aware that they are engaged in learning - and what significance does it have if they are? Such questions have appeared in various guises over the years - and have surfaced, for example, in debates around the rather confusing notion of 'informal learning'.

One particularly helpful way of approaching the area has been formulated by Alan Rogers. Drawing especially on the work of those who study the learning of language, Rogers sets out two contrasting approaches: task-conscious or acquisition learning and learning-conscious or formalized learning.

Task-conscious or Acquisition Learning

Acquisition learning is seen as going on all the time. It is 'concrete, immediate and confined to a specific activity; it is not concerned with general principles'. Examples include much of the learning involved in parenting or with running a home. Some have referred to this kind of learning as unconscious or implicit. Rogers, however, suggests that it might be better to speak of it as having a consciousness of the task. In other words, whilst the learner may not be conscious of learning, they are usually aware of the specific task in hand.

Learning-conscious or Formalized Learning

Formalized learning arises from the process of facilitating learning. It is 'educative learning' rather than the accumulation of experience. To this extent there is a consciousness of learning - people are aware that the task they are engaged in entails learning. 'Learning itself is the task. What formalized learning does is to make learning more conscious in order to enhance it'. It involves guided episodes of learning.

When approached in this way it becomes clear that these contrasting ways of learning can appear in the same context. Both are present in schools. Both are present in families. It is possible to think of the mix of acquisition and formalized learning as forming a continuum. At one extreme lie those unintentional and usually accidental learning events which occur continuously as we walk through life. Next comes incidental learning - unconscious learning through acquisition methods which occurs in the course of some other activity. Then there are various activities in which we are somewhat more more conscious of learning, experiential activities arising from immediate life-related concerns, though even here the focus is still on the task.

Then come more purposeful activities - occasions where we set out to learn something in a more systematic way, using whatever comes to hand for that purpose, but often deliberately disregarding engagement with teachers and formal institutions of learning. Further along the continuum lie the self-directed learning projects on which there is so much literature. More formalized and generalized forms of learning are the distance and open education programmes, where some elements of acquisition learning are often built into the designed learning programme. Towards the further extreme lie more formalized learning programmes of highly decontextualized learning, using material common to all the learners without paying any regard to their individual preferences, agendas or needs. There are of course no clear boundaries between each of these categories.

This distinction is echoed in different ways in the writings of many of those concerned with education - but in particular in key theorists such as Kurt Lewin, Chris Argyris, Donald Schön, or Michael Polanyi.

The Realm of Learning Theories

The focus on process obviously takes us into the realm of learning theories - ideas about how or why change occurs. Here we focus on four different orientations.

— the behaviourist orientation to learning

— the cognitive orientation to learning

— the humanistic orientation to learning

— the social/situational orientation to learning

As with any categorization of this sort the divisions are a bit arbitrary: there could be further additions and sub-divisions to the scheme, and there a various ways in which the orientations overlap and draw upon each other.

These approaches involve contrasting ideas as to the purpose and process of learning and education - and the role that educators may take. It is also important to recognize that the theories may apply to different sectors of the acquision-formalized learning continuum outlined above. For example, the work of Lave and Wenger is broadly a form of acquisition learning that can involve some more formal interludes.

There are many different theories of learning. We will look first at three main categories of learning theory: behaviorism, cognitivism, and the social construction of knowledge. We also discuss some issues arising from these theories, such as cognitive development, student differences, and motivation and engagement in learning.

Behaviorism

At the heart of behaviorism is the idea that certain behavioral responses become associated in a mechanistic and invariant way with specific stimuli.

Behaviorist psychology arose in the 1920s and 1930s from an attempt to model the study of human behavior on the methods of the physical sciences. Therefore it concentrates attention on aspects of behavior that are capable of direct observation and measurement. At the heart of behaviorism is the idea that certain behavioral responses become associated in a mechanistic and invariant way with specific stimuli. Hence a certain stimulus will evoke a particular response. At its simplest, the response may be a purely physiological reflex action, like the contraction of an iris in the eye when stimulated by bright light.

However, most behavior is more complex. Nevertheless, according to behaviorists, it is possible to reinforce through reward or punishment the association between any particular stimulus or event and a particular response. The bond formed between a stimulus and a response will depend on the existence of an appropriate means of reinforcement at the time of association between stimulus and response. Behavior therefore can be modified or controlled by appropriately reinforcing random behavior as it occurs.

This is essentially the concept of operant conditioning, a principle most clearly developed by Skinner. He showed that pigeons could be trained in quite complex behavior by rewarding particular, desired response, randomly occurring, with appropriate stimuli, such as the provision of food pellets. He also found that intervening stimuli to be present, thus linking an initially remote stimulus with a complex behavior. Furthermore, inappropriate or previously learned behavior could be extinguished by withdrawing reinforcement. Skinner also claimed that rewarding behavior was more effective than punishment.

Underlying this approach is the belief that learning is governed by invariant principles, and these principles are independent of conscious control on the part of the learner. Behaviorists attempt to maintain a high degree of objectivity in how they view human activity, and they generally reject reference to unobservable states, such as feelings, attitudes, and consciousness. Human behavior is above all seen as predictable and controllable. Behaviorism stems from a strongly objectivist epistemological position.

Skinner's theory led to the development of teaching machines, measurable learning objectives, computer-assisted instruction, and multiple choice tests. There was also a tendency until recently to see technology, particularly computers, as being closely associated with behaviorist approaches to learning. Today there has been a strong movement away from behaviorist approaches to teaching in higher education, although its influence is still strong in corporate and military training and in some areas of science, engineering, and medical training.

Cognitivism

Behaviorism denies or ignores mental activity as the basis for learning. Learning for behaviorists is determined by external environmental structures that lead to reinforcement of behavior, rather than to mental processing or conscious thought on the part of the learner. Cognitivists, though, insist that there are mental processes "internal and conscious representations of the world" that are essential for human learning. Fontana summarizes the cognitive approach as follows:

> "It sees the individual not as the somewhat mechanical product of his environment, but as an active agent in the learning process..."

> "The cognitive approach holds that if we are to understand learning we cannot confine ourselves to observable behavior, but must also concern ourselves with the learner's ability mentally to reorganize his psychological field (i.e., his inner world of concepts, memories, etc.) in response to experience. This latter approach therefore lays stress not only on the environment, but upon the way in which the individual interprets and tries to make sense of the environment. It sees the individual not as the somewhat mechanical product of his environment, but as an active agent in the learning process, deliberately trying to process and categorize the stream of information fed into him by the external world."

Thus the search for rules, principles, or relationships in processing new information, and the search for meaning and consistency in reconciling new information with previous knowledge, are key concepts in cognitive psychology. Cognitive psychology is concerned with identifying and describing mental processes. In some ways, basic mental processes are often considered genetic or hard-wired but can be programmed or modified by external factors, such as experience.

Cognitive approaches to learning cover a very wide range. On the one hand, attempts have been made through areas such as artificial intelligence to provide mechanical, electronic, and physical representations of mental processes, reflecting very much as objectivist epistemological position. On the other hand, teachers who place a strong emphasis on learners— developing personal meaning through reflection, analysis, and construction of knowledge through conscious mental processing would indicate much more of a constructivist epistemological position. Cognitive approaches to learning "with their focus on abstraction, generalization, and creative thinking" seem to fit much better in higher education.

Social Construction of Knowledge

We have pulled together different theories of learning here under the common theme of the social construction of knowledge.

Both behaviorist and some elements of cognitive theories of learning are deterministic, in the sense that behavior and learning are believed to be rule-based and operate under predictable and constant conditions over which the individual learner has no or little control. However, the trend these days is to recognize the importance of consciousness, free will, and social influences on learning. Although constructivism has become the "flavor of the month" in higher education in recent years, the belief that humans are essentially active and free and strive for meaning in personal terms has been around for a long time. Carl Rogers stated that "every individual exists in a continually changing world of experience in which he is the center." The external world is interpreted within the context of that private world. Knowledge is thus not just about content but also about values.

Individuals consciously strive for meaning to make sense of their environment in terms of past experience and their present state. It is an attempt to create order in their minds out of disorder, resolve incongruities, and reconcile external realities with prior experience. The means by which this is done are complex and multifaceted, from engaging in personal reflection to seeking new information to testing ideas through social contact with others. Problems are resolved, and incongruities sorted out, through strategies such as seeking relationships between what was known and what is new, identifying similarities and differences, and testing hypotheses. Reality is always tentative and dynamic.

For many educators, the social context of learning is critical. Ideals are tested not just on the teacher but also with fellow students, friends, and colleagues. Furthermore, knowledge is mainly acquired through social processes or institutions that are socially constructed: schools, universities. What is taken to be "valued" knowledge is also socially constructed. Knowledge is thus not just about content but also about values. One set of values comprises those around the concept of a liberal education. According to this notion, one of the principal aims of education is to develop a critical awareness of the values and ideologies that shape the form of received knowledge. This aim suggests a constant probing and criticism of received knowledge.

One consequence of theories of social construction of knowledge is that each individual is considered unique, because the interaction of each person's different experiences and the search for personal meaning result in each person being different from anyone else. Behavior is thus not predictable or deterministic, at least not at the individual level (although pollsters will argue that patterns of group behavior is predictable).

The key point here is that learning is seen as essentially a social process, requiring communication among learner, teacher, and others. This social process cannot effectively be replaced by technology, although technology may facilitate it.

Theory of Multiple Intelligences

Human intelligence should not be equated solely with linguistic or logical-mathematical intelligence alone, according to Howard Gardner. As the author of a new way of looking at human intelligences, Gardner, a Harvard professor, identified a total of seven different intelligences that humans may possess. His list includes:

— Linguistic intelligence

— Logical-mathematical intelligence

— Spatial intelligence

— Musical intelligence

— Bodily-kinesthetic

— Interpersonal intelligence

— Intrapersonal intelligence

Gardner is working on more intelligences that qualify as cognitive processes: "Multiple intelligences theory, on the other hand, pluralizes the traditional concept". Gardner's fascination with human intelligence and how the brain works was started with an investigation of people who had experienced brain damage of some sort. He recognized that not all abilities, whether cognitive or motor-sensory, were eliminated from the individual's repertoire despite having endured some form of brain damage. Gardner hypothesized that we possess more than one form of intelligence.

The theory of multiple intelligences provides a more holistic view of the intelligence of humans. Gardner advocates that we may all attempt to develop each of these intelligences to our optimum level. However, we may be more adept in only certain of these intelligences. We may however, aspire through practice and development to improve in the remaining intelligences.

The use of technology appeals to this view of intelligence in that Gardner's theory acknowledges that cognition is not a linear process. The computer as a learning tool has enormous potential in developing the different forms of intelligences of Gardner's theory.

Learning is the process by which we receive and process sensory data, encode such data as memories within the neural structures of our brain, and retrieve those memories for subsequent use. The variety of information stored within such memories is enormous, including such items as: how to control your sphincter muscle until a socially appropriate occasion, how to identify mommy in a crowd, how to ride a bicycle, what is the shortest path to grandmother's house without going near the lair of the wolf, what is the tune for Beethoven's *Ode to Joy*, and what a philosopher means when she says "The cat is on the mat." All learning takes place within the brain, and as our understanding of the underlying structures and processes of the brain increases we can begin to apply that knowledge to improve our construction of learning environments.

Our ability to describe and understand the basic processes by which our brain learns has been enhanced by recent technological developments and by the accumulation of long-term studies in human and animal populations. Of particular benefit has been the development of brain-imaging techniques that allow us to observe the operation of normal human brains during the performance of a variety of tasks. Magnetic Resonance Imaging (MRI) and similar technologies have allowed researchers to map neural activity during sensory data processing and monitor the transfer of information into long-term memory. Researchers have also made great strides in determining the basic mechanisms that underlie the transmission of information within the brain. Such research on brain structure, neural transmitters, and the process by which memories are stored and retrieved have allowed the development of neurophysiological models of learning.

Although neuroscience has provided us with an increasingly rich and accurate descriptive theory of learning within the brain, we still need prescriptive theories of how to maximize the efficiency and capacity of human learning. To some extent all learning theories are prescriptive and seek to minimize the time required to transfer information into memory and maximize the efficiency of retrieving that information. Our current knowledge of the brain, and our speculations regarding the evolutionary function of learning, should assist such prescriptive theories in designing learning environments that provide for maximum learning efficiency.

In particular, prescriptive theories informed by our current knowledge of neuroscience should allow us to evaluate the role of multimedia in learning environments. We should also be able to maximize the impact of multimedia in such environments through application of learning theories and our knowledge of the human brain. Learning environments should not be construed simply as the traditional formal classroom within the context of institutionalized public education. Such environments occur within the workplace, the home, and other social institutions as communication and information technology continues to penetrate Western society. We should also be aware that the use of multimedia will have an impact upon the development of the human brain, particularly when such techniques are used with children and adolescents whose brains are still developing and maturing.

The Brain: The three-pound universe that is our brain consists of more than 100 billion neurons and the associated structures that organize, nourish, and protect their functioning. Each neuron may have between 5,000 and 50,000 connections to other neurons, forming a dense connective mat that allows the storage of enormous amounts of information. It is important to remember that structures within the brain continue to develop until late adolescence and that neurons will continue to grow connections to other neurons throughout adult life.

The basic structures in the brain that are important for bodily functions and for learning and memory are :

— *The brain stem* is primarily concerned with basic survival functions and the regulation of body systems.

— *The cerebellum* is involved in the performance of automatic movement patterns (walking, running, touch-typing, and other physical skills that can become part of automatic procedural memory).

— *The limbic system* is responsible for the processing of short-term memory into long-term memory as well as the generation and regulation of emotions.

— *The cerebral cortex* is the area of the brain in which sensory data is received and analyzed, decisions are made, and behavioral responses are activated.

Information is received from the major sensory organs of the body: eyes, ears, nose, tongue, and skin; and is held briefly in sensory memory. The further processing of that information appears to be dependent upon the state of emotional arousal of the brain and the utility of such information for potential survival. Long-term memories are generated through the growth and spread of neural connections between those modular structures that contain the memory. The more often such structures are activated and the stronger the connections become to associated structures, the more easily such memories are retrieved and used by the brain in decision making and conscious thought.

To some extent the driving forces behind the way our brain processes sensory input and makes decisions are the survival imperatives that accompanied human physical and cultural evolution. Our brains reflect the importance that survival places upon evaluating potential threat situations, making a quick response, and focusing all body resources on support of those functions that may lead to continued survival. In high-threat situations the focus of the brain will be almost exclusively upon what is identified as the potential threat while the body shuts down relatively unimportant systems to concentrate on those involved in the fight-or-flight response.

Low-threat situations allow the brain to sample and evaluate a broader spectrum of sensory input and to analyze such input for future use. Thus a large looming shadow in the cave mouth tends to generate fear, prompting the body to shut down digestion, pump more adrenaline, and prepare the cerebellum to handle the process of running while the cerebral cortex looks for places to hide or make a stand.

Strong negative emotion tends to evoke the fight-or-flight physiological and mental responses that shut down high-level cognition. A premium should therefor be placed upon the reduction of those factors within a learning environment that give rise to negative emotions. At the same time, sensory input that does not receive attention is not available for processing through short-term into long-term memory.

Clearly a balance must be struck between too much and too little stimulation in learning situations. Some stimulation and motivation is necessary for the learner to pay attention to the data that they are required to learn; on the other hand too much stimulation (particularly in a negative context) is liable to create anger or fear as an emotional response, either of which can serve to reduce the amount of learning carried out within the environment.

It appears that the limbic system plays an important part in the process of storing information as long-term memories. Those activities that provide an emotionally supportive environment may well have a positive effect upon the processing of information into long-term storage and subsequent retrieval of those memories. Group activities, co-operative learning, role-playing, and simulations tend to provide emotional support and emotional context for learning.

Retrieval of long-term memories is enhanced when a large number of connections have been established between the neural modules that store such memories. To some extent our growing knowledge about the organization of the brain tends to support those theories of learning that can generally be labeled as constructivist. That is, situated knowledge that is connected to a large number of other memories is more apt to be recalled than is unconnected knowledge that has been learned by rote.

Because the process of creating connections between ideas and memories is essentially carried out through a process of rehearsal and review, learners should be encouraged to review knowledge that is being learned and attempt to build connections to that knowledge that is already easily retrieved from long-term memory. Such cognitive tools as narration, story-telling, constructing metaphors, and making comparisons are strategies that help to build and maintain connections. The construction of knowledge is essentially the growing of connections between the neural modules that contain individual memories.

If the apparent symmetry between contemporary brain-based learning theories and constructivism is accurate, then basic guiding principles of constructivism should be used in designing learning environments. These principles include:

— Learning is a search for meaning. Therefore, learning must start with the issues around which students are actively trying to construct meaning.

— Meaning requires understanding wholes as well as parts. Parts must be understood in the context of wholes. Therefore the learning process focuses on primary concepts, not isolated facts.

— In order to teach well, we must understand the mental models that students use to understand the world, and the assumptions that support those models.

— The purpose of learning is to construct one's own meaning, not to have the "right" answers by repeating someone else's meaning. Learning is inherently inter-disciplinary, and the only valuable assessment of learning is assessment that is part of the learning process and that provides students with information on the quality of their learning.

Such learning environments should also be designed around the ideas that come forward from brain-based learning. That is, they should employ the three instructional techniques associated with brain-based learning: "orchestrated immersion, where learning environments are created that fully immerse students in a learning experience; relaxed alertness, where an effort is made to eliminate fear while maintaining a highly challenging environment; and active processing, where the learner consolidates and internalizes information by actively processing it". Learning environments constructed with these principles in mind will tend to be organized around thematic units featuring knowledge in depth and the exploration of projects that have real meaning for the participating learners

How should we then use multimedia presentations of information to effectively learn in the context of current brain-based learning theory? The communications and information technology that constitutes contemporary multimedia platforms has some significant advantages in creating a learning environment, but there are some pitfalls that must be accounted for as part of the learning process.

Multimedia, at its best, allows us to bring the real world to the learner through the use of sound and video. Such connection to the real world should serve as a factor in motivating students, and as a factor in providing them with additional connections to other knowledge structures. At the same time, multimedia allows students to experience information through multiple modes of presentation. Such multi-modal learning should help to build connections within the learner's brain if only because multiple modes of reception will engage different areas of the learner's brain.

Contemporary multimedia platforms allow a greater degree of learner control and more freedom for the learner to undertake self-directed exploration of the material. Such self-directed learning is likely to be more meaningful and more connected to existing knowledge structures within the learner's brain. Therefore, we should see advantages for learning programs that include multimedia presentations. Learners should also gain from the possibility of self-paced instruction based upon contemporary multimedia learning technology. Whenever possible, immediate feedback should be built into a multimedia program to assist students in forming correct connections prior to reinforcing connections between new and old information incorporated within existing knowledge structures.

Designers of multimedia instructional packages should take comfort in the strengths of multimedia, but they should also be aware of potential problems in using multimedia with learners. Although current multimedia technology allows excellent presentation in both video and audio modes, and provides some tactile feedback through the use of keyboards, there is little to offer students who need tactile experience multimedia is essentially a bimodal presentation strategy unless additional work is done to prepare material for students.

Even the best multimedia programs cannot provide the total stimulation that natural environments provide?we have yet to incorporate smell or taste into such presentations, and tactile sensations are still limited. More importantly, there is a clear danger that multimedia programs may be used to substitute for interaction with other learners. We should not be seduced by technical virtuosity or cutting-edge visual and aural effects, there is still a need for human interaction and emotional support.

Above all else, we should beware of the tendency to substitute passive learning for active learning. Multimedia provides significant advantages in presenting information to learners, particularly if sufficient resources have been invested to create presentations that make full use of current technology. Presentation of information, no matter how technically sophisticated, is not enough; learners must interact with content to construct their own meanings and integrate new knowledge into the dense web of neural connections that is mind and memory.

Cognitive Neo-associationist Theory of Learning

In this section an attempt is made to trace the historical and philosophical foundations of the emerging "cognitive neo-associationist" theory of learning. We begins with the identification of commonalities in Cognitive Developmentalism and Radical Behaviorism: those apparently conflicting perspectives which provide the empirical support and epistemological premises for all modern cognitive learning models in the first case, and for those loosely termed "neo-associationist" in the second.

In-depth study of the two conceptual frameworks reveals a considerable area of agreement, in spite of prevailing opinion to the contrary. Both models are soundly scientific and interdisciplinary. Both resolve the old nature/nurture controversy by demonstrating that any specific human behavior is likely to represent a complex mix of genetic endowment as well as learned acquisitions. Theorists in both camps view learning as an activity of the whole organism, grounded in biology and operating in all animals from the moment of birth, according to a mechanism similar to that governing species evolution. Both explain the process as developmental, and the product of organismic-environmental interaction. Modern cognitive models can be traced back to the pioneering work of Jean Piaget; various versions of neo-associationism to B.F. Skinner.

Each theorist saw his model as a first step in building a comprehensive evolutionary theory of knowledge and culture. The key factor distinguishing the two perspectives is Piaget's principle of "equilibration" as opposed to Skinner's "operant conditioning", with its mechanism of "reinforcement", the first being a refinement of Herbert Spencer's approach to evolution and the second, an extension of Darwinism. Both mechanisms were assumed to operate biologically, psychologically and culturally. "Equilibration" appears to be internally driven — by the active learner's need to maintain harmony with the environment — and "operant conditioning" to be instigated from without by the environmental contingencies of previous action. In order to render the two conceptual frameworks compatible and complementary — and to recognize both as necessary building blocks of the new "cognitive neo-associationism" — we need only interpret Piaget's concept of inborn activity in terms of an innate urge to control incoming experience, while adding to this Skinner's postulated instinctive propensity to be reinforced by the pleasure resulting from satiation of a drive.

Practitioners in broadly conceived, applied fields such as education and therapy, who wish to select the most reliable tools available, now have little alternative other than a "hit or miss" eclecticism. What is needed, instead, is a rigorous interdisciplinary approach to the specific problem areas with which they deal: an approach which focuses on the task of developing — as a prerequisite to building a reliable knowledge base — a common language community among all the scholars involved. It would appear, however, that one of the greatest obstacles to this kind of progress in the social sciences in every era has been the reluctance of leading theorists to read the works of their contemporaries, and to encourage their followers to do so. Jean Piaget was more aware of this than most. He once reported the following comment of a fellow scholar who was laboring in the same vineyard: "There seems to be some similarity... [in our approaches]. But I will never read a work of yours and you will never read a work of mine."

In fact, a regressive custom seems to have developed which encourages scholars to adopt *ideological* positions on the various contending schools of thought. The circumstances under which students are professionally socialized encourage them to commit early in their careers to the models favored by their mentors, and to reject all others out of hand. Practitioners in these studies are sometimes not even aware of other legitimate perspectives capable of shedding light on their area of interest. As a result, the identical research problem is often organized and explained by competing scholars in mutually inconsistent ways and by incommensurable concepts and terminology. This means that research is seldom replicable across schools even within the same discipline, and the possibility of the interdisciplinary testing of common problem areas is virtually nonexistent.

Nowhere is the need for a common language community more apparent than in the study of how people learn. Jean Piaget and B.F. Skinner made remarkable — and quite separate — breakthroughs here but, because of the difficulty in translating their findings into terminology understandable by both, neither was able to benefit from the other's contributions. Piaget was opposed to behaviorism, yet his writings reveal little real familiarity with the concepts underlying that model as it was developed by B.F. Skinner. He usually equated it to the older "blank-slate" sensationalism of John Locke, as reflected in the behaviorism of John B.Watson, of which he was justifiably critical. He thought that his own theory differed from behaviorism chiefly in that it allowed a role in learning for *both* external and internal reinforcements. But a cursory reading of Skinner would have revealed that radical behaviorism does not draw any line between "inner" and "outer" where reinforcement is concerned.

Skinner's opinion of Piaget's cognitive developmentalism was even more starkly negative; but he, too, seems not to have read the works of the chief architect of that perspective. For example, of Piaget's "stages", he wrote, "If developmental stages follow one another, it is because one stage builds the conditions responsible for the next." But that happens to be Piaget's point as well! Skinner also maintained, in an attack on cognitive theory, that "language does not just grow" and neither is it innate. Again, Piaget would have agreed. One cannot help but wonder if educational psychology might been more scientifically productive if these two great scholars had looked for common ground and sought, from there, to build a joint model that could eventually become a guiding paradigm for their shared problem area.

That key problem area is the nature of human learning; of the biological/maturational factors affecting the cognitive development which both results from and furthers it; and of the sociocultural influences shaping the entire process. Because biological and sociological as well as psychological factors are necessarily involved, the entire area is perhaps better referred to as "socialization".

Piaget and Skinner, unarguably the two most influential psychologists of the twentieth century, devoted most of their lives to one or more aspects of this complex subject, and to its implications for related areas of study such as education. Yet these men, with their followers, worked in virtual isolation from one another. Because communication was impossible across the conceptual divide thus maintained, we have largely failed to recognize and benefit from a few powerful insights at which both arrived while following their different paths.

This is particularly tragic in the case of Piaget and Skinner because not since John Dewey has there been anything with as much potential significance for education as can be found in the ideas of these two scholars. Both were aware of this, and of the need for reliable psychological knowledge in the general field of instruction. Piaget deplored the absence of a science of education, and our widespread ignorance of the longtime results of various popular teaching strategies. He thought that any real advance in this field must be based on the kind of interdisciplinary social science research that he was seeking to pioneer.

Contrary to popular interpretations of his theory, Piaget viewed learning not as an isolated process remote from his focus of concern, but as the chief source and defining aspect of cognitive development. "It does seem," he said, that we should accept both these factors [structural maturation and environmental influences] as constantly at work and that development is a product of this continuous interaction... *the child has everything to learn*." He thought of learning as the growth of operational knowledge within the individual, involving "a giving up of erroneous ideas for more current ones, or... a transformation of these ideas into higher-level, more adequate conceptions." And his work had led him to conclude that Athe same learning has a different effect according to the stage of development of the subject." For Piaget this meant that, while learning is all-important, it must be viewed in the context of development, just as development must be viewed in terms of the interaction of maturational and environmental influences that either further or hinder it. Education, in turn, must be understood as a purposefully structured process by which environmental influences are adapted to students' learning requirements — as determined by their developmental level.

Skinner, too, was concerned with education and with the learning process which teaching is intended to further. Humans, he believed, differ from other animals chiefly in their capacity for lifetime modification of behavior, and thus in the proportion of their mature capacities that are due to learning rather than genetic makeup. "In general", he wrote, "the evolution of men has emphasized modifiability rather than the transmission of specific forms of behavior." It is this inherited modifiability that makes the potential for education so great. However, Skinner had little faith in the enterprise as it is presently planned and pursued — in the absence of any scientific base. He felt that "those who have spoken out most vigorously [on the subject] have completely neglected method."

The development of a workable technique for controlling the conditions of learning was, in fact, Skinner's greatest contribution to education — but it has been largely ignored. He defined learning as "the reassortment of responses in a complex action" and identified the possible ways in which a living organism (human or otherwise) can learn as follows: "when a reinforcer (1) accompanies another stimulus or (2) follows upon the organism' own behavior." The first is Pavlovian reflex conditioning and the second is the operant conditioning discovered by Skinner himself. He concluded that it is this second mechanism which explains the complex learning most typical of humans.

As learners, Skinner said, "we are automatically reinforced when we successfully control the physical world." Teaching implies the identification of desired outcomes and precise planning of strategies for facilitating "the arrangement of contingencies of reinforcement which expedite learning." The educator prepares the students for situations not yet risen by bringing discriminant operants under the control of stimuli expected to occur in those situations. The child is forewarned and forearmed with powerful tools for controlling nature, the very exercise of which provides reinforcement. Because of this, the natural payoffs inherent in the subject matter are the teacher's chief allies. Skinner maintained that educators who recommend external means of motivating learning have got it all wrong, noting that "the sheer control of nature itself is reinforcing." As he reminded us, "The motives in education are the motives of all human behavior... We appeal to that drive to control the environment that makes a baby continue to crumple a noisy paper and the scientist to continue to press forward with his predictive analysis of nature."

Given the significance of the work of these two theorists for our understanding of learning, is it possible to find an area of agreement between what we have come to know as the genetic (or cognitive) developmentalism of Piaget and the radical behaviorism of Skinner? Certainly a survey of public and professional perceptions on the matter would indicate the precise opposite. For most people involved in the humanities, social studies and education, the two psychological theories are as different as night and day. This may be related to a phenomenon commented on by many: the fact that Skinner has been the victim of the worst press since Darwin. Examples of this "press" abound in the writings of scholars of the period. Hannah Arendt thought that "behavioral sciences aim to reduce man as a whole, in all his activities, to the level of a behaving animal." Erich Fromm claimed that "neither behaviorism or instinct theory allows human beings the slightest control over their own lives "

On the other hand, cognitive psychology seems to have had an immediate attraction for the general academic community. An example of this is the response of the educational establishment to the two theories. Piagetian concepts are familiar to all teachers, and are referred to by educators throughout the world, whether or not they are correctly interpreted and applied; and Piaget feared that, often, they were not. Yet even carefully designed and tested learning machines based on behaviorist principles were spurned almost wholesale by the same educators, until the advent of the computer introduced identical programs in the new format. This drove Skinner to the wry conclusion that "many people were afraid of programmed instruction just because it worked. They did not fear traditional education because they knew it was ineffective and hence harmless."

There are many apparent differences between the two models, and it is these that are usually noted and used to identify the models as incompatible. Skinner is often accused by Piagetian cognitive psychologists of viewing the individual as merely a passive respondent to environmental inputs, while Piaget is congratulated for his interpretation of the learner as active. Skinner is condemned for equating human learning to the reflex conditioning characteristic of simpler forms of animals, while Piaget is admired for recognizing its essential distinctiveness and complexity. Skinner is reviled for "reducing" humans to their observable behavior; for explaining human relations solely in "mechanistic" terms; and for attempting to destroy our faith in the uniqueness and autonomy of the individual. Piaget, on the other hand, is applauded for making it possible for us to continue viewing humans as moral beings with a consciousness uniquely human.

Behaviorists, in their turn, criticize cognitive psychologists for resorting once more to "mentalism": for creating out of whole cloth a network of unobservable structures supposedly housed in the brain. Some even say Piaget's ideas are a throwback to the "nativism" of Rousseau, and the "vitalism" of Henri Bergson. Skinner himself saw an inevitable conflict between the individual viewed as a storehouse of images (both conscious and unconscious) and the organism seen as operating on the environment and being changed by the process — although he contended that Piaget wanted it both ways. He also saw a conflict between his own approach which "traces human behavior to its genetic and environmental histories, and the cognitive tradition, which traces the same behavior to an initiating self."

In Skinner's opinion, the cognitive psychologists, with their computer metaphor, have moved the environment back inside the head (where Kant had placed it) in the form of autonomous logical structures or "modules" representing concepts and rules. And they have concocted an internal simulacrum of the organism to provide for the storage. This simulacrum is then used, he said, as the basis for inferring the nature of the nervous system that would be required to generate its search for equilibrium. In this way they have sent those physiologists influenced by their theories on a fool's errand. Skinner noted that his own approach would leave the subject of the nature of the nervous system to those equipped to observe it directly — the physiologists themselves. "Meanwhile, the experimental analysis of behavior would give them a correct assignment, whereas cognitive science sent them looking for things they would never find."

For Skinner, it was not good enough to say, as Piaget did, that humans function by actively sampling and organizing environmental cues into a working model of the world, and by storing all this for later recall. None of this, he noted, explains or predicts observable regularities in behavior which, after all, is the goal of a psychological *science*. "Where an organism, exposed to a set of contingencies of reinforcement, is modified by them and as a result behaves in a different way in the future, we do not need to say that it stores the contingencies... What we recall... is a response... The conditions which are said to determine the accessibility of stored memories really determine the accessibility of responses."

Skinner claimed that the cognitive psychologists are confined by their model to verbal reports and instructions that lead nowhere. This is why their findings, although massive in quantity, have not been cumulative. "The contingencies of reinforcement are the missing key, " he concluded. He felt that his own work had provided a comprehensive yet simple theory readily compatible with modern genetics and physiology, and one which has already demonstrated its reliability and fruitfulness in identifying the essential principles for a working technology of human behavior. Yet, he said, for purely ideological reasons, followers of the more politically powerful cognitive school continue to ignore the scientific power of modern behaviorism.

Piaget did most of his work before Skinner rose to prominence, and obviously he was not familiar with the latter's research and writing. Watson's "methodological behaviorism" was probably the version best known to him. Piaget was convinced that behaviorism dealt with only isolated aspects or parts of the individual, while Gestalt psychology erred in the opposite direction by focusing only on unanalyzable "wholes". Piaget saw his own theory as a synthesis of the other two, in that he viewed the individual as an open system in "transaction" with its environment. As the term suggests, he had based his model on John Dewey's idea that meaningful forms of cognition are *constructed* by the learner in the process of acting on, and being acted on by, the environment.

Skinner, on the other hand, thought it was his own model that had restored balance to psychology. He considered that cognitive theory, no less than Freudianism and its offshoots, represented the prevailing mentalist position: one that overemphasized the "inner" person. Watson's behaviorism had done the opposite, he said, focusing exclusively on the environment, while ignoring the genetic and historical programming brought to the current situation — and even denying the very possibility of self-observation. Skinner admitted that subjective perception is, of course a problem to be reckoned with, but what is happening inside the skin is no different in kind from the events without — just less accessible to observation. Inevitably it is one aspect of the behavior under study, but it is not the *source* as Piaget seemed to believe. He suggested that we are misled by self-awareness into a belief in the conscious self as an *uncaused* instigator of action.

Just how justified are these criticisms on both sides of the controversy? How many of them are based on meaningful differences between the two philosophical perspectives on learning, and how many stem from uninformed stereotypes rather than the actual concepts being dealt with in each case? Perhaps we should begin to look for answers in the similarities between the two, rather than in their presumed differences.

There are indeed similarities. For example, Piaget, too, believed that there is no essential line of demarcation between what goes on inside and outside the skin. As he put it, "since the organism is itself also a physicochemical object, its actions and reactions are from the outset transparently dependent on the physical universe, because, through its very inner structure, the organism participates in and obeys the laws of this universe."

In addition, both perspectives are grounded in evolutionary theory, and both are interdisciplinary in scope and methodology. An indication of the widespread recognition of this similarity is the fact that each scholar, at the height of his career, was invited to present the Herbert Spencer lectures at Oxford University. Both theorists were thoroughly scientific in approach, each expecting that his hypotheses would stand or fall on the empirical evidence. Both saw learning in terms of behavior: covert as well as overt. And they saw it as dependent upon individual-environmental interaction. Both were pioneering systems theorists in that they assumed some sort of an adaptive feed-back process by which changes resulting from the individual's operations on the environment in turn shape subsequent thought and action. For both thinkers the process of learning was thus cumulative or developmental. Furthermore, Piaget, no less than Skinner (and Spencer) considered human learning to be governed by the same laws that govern the learning occurring in other species.

Both theorists were convinced that intellectual development, although built upon and limited by genetic propensity, is to a large degree the result of learning from experience. In fact, both considered their work to have resolved the old nature/nurture controversy in general. According to Piaget, his theory did this by presenting "a dialectical solution halfway between empiricism and innatism." It explains how the adaptation of self-regulating structures, at progressively higher states of equilibrium, coordinates the interaction of maturational and environmental effects. For any particular pattern of action, there is no way to measure the relative impact of these effects.

Skinner's theory accomplishes the same end by demonstrating the relationship between the operation of phylogenic contingencies directing biological evolution (through natural selection) and ontogenic contingencies directing learning (through operant conditioning). He wrote, "Successful responses are selected in both cases, and the result is adaptation. But the process of selection is very different and we cannot tell from the mere fact that behavior is adaptive which kind of process has been responsible for it."

Both Piaget and Skinner admired John Dewey, and believed that their work was building on his. Skinner chose "operant" as a more specifically meaningful term than Dewey's "instrumental" to denote the active operation of the organism on the environment which was assumed by both theorists. Sounding much like Dewey, he also maintained that "to say that knowledge is power is simply to say that it is successful action." Another interesting similarity between Dewey and Skinner is that the first article written by both was on the subject of the "reflex arc". Skinner, like Dewey before him, revealed that he preferred the method of functional analysis to the older mechanistic, stimulus-response approach. Also like Dewey (and Piaget as well) he considered the study of behavior and epistemology to be closely related. "Behaviorism was a theory of knowledge, and knowing and thinking were forms of behavior." And, again like Piaget as well as Dewey, he recognized a special value in the scientific pursuit.

Skinner's only criticism of Dewey was revealed by his comment that "what he threw out [of education] should have been thrown out. Unfortunately, he had too little to put in its place." He thought that his own theory, with its principle of reinforcement, provided the grounds for the practical teaching strategy that was missing from Dewey's theories. This was because "operant conditioning" explained learning at all levels and by all animals — including humans of all ages. "By using rate of response as a dependent variable, it has been possible to formulate the interaction between the organism and its environment more adequately," he concluded. All in all, Skinner believed that he had refined and improved upon the Pragmatism of John Dewey and George Herbert Mead. Once he quoted a letter from a Deweyan scholar who said, "Your type of explanation is something I understand one hundred percent... If I had been aware I would have built directly on your procedure".

Piaget, too, was greatly influenced by Dewey. As he explained the tradition which he had inherited, "on the one hand, the work of the pragmatists had revealed the role of action in the constitution of all mental operations... [on the other hand] genetic psychology had increased considerably in scope, particularly with the work of Stanley Hall and J.M. Baldwin. These two trends found their exact point of intersection in John Dewey." And he believed that his own work had built from there. He also claimed that Baldwin had further developed his "genetic logic" from Dewey's work as well as that of Hall — who had also been Dewey's mentor. (Piaget's term "genetic epistemology" was actually borrowed from Baldwin.) Piaget, like Dewey, recommended "active" rather than "receptive" methods of teaching. He was even using Dewey's terminology when he emphasized "the role of action in the transaction between the biological and social factors... [in learning]. This role played by action (or by *praxis*) has been abundantly emphasized by Marx, who quite rightly went so far as to consider perception itself as an 'activity' of the sense organs." Piaget also noted that, "as Dewey demonstrated with such profundity, true interest appears when the self identifies itself with ideas and objects."

In describing his own intellectual journey, Piaget toid of having become disenchanted with Bergson and turning to the writings of the American Pragmatists. Many of Piaget's basic concepts come directly from them. For example, the idea of "the permanent object" (originating with Schopenhauer and subsequently employed by Spencer) had been refined considerably by George Herbert Mead. And Mead had written that "the essence of the self is cognitive; it lies in the internalized conversation of gestures which constitute thinking." Piaget also described his decision to develop Dewey's idea of "action itself admits of logic." He subsequently wrote, "We can get to know objects only by acting on them."

Both Piaget and Skinner saw their theories as immediately applicable to the field of education, and both provided specific teaching methods and techniques for the purpose. Neither was studying how the individual learns as an end in itself, but as the means of arriving at a comprehensive theory of knowledge and of cultural evolution. Both were concerned above all with epistemology, and consequently saw their models as incipient philosophies of science. Both believed that human behavior was rooted in biology. Both were systematic and interactionist in orientation.

As Skinner explained it, people "operate on the world and change it, and are changed in turn by the consequences of their actions." Piaget was interested in developing " a theory of adaptation of thoughts to reality, even if this adaptation at last reveals... the existence of an inextricable interaction between subject and object." Both saw language and thought as types of activity. Both recognized the futility of trying to separate "nature" from "nurture", as do the evolutionary psychologists of today. Both were neutral monists in ontology. They saw the learning organism as "one". Yet neither thought of the learner in "holistic" or "vitalistic" terms. And, finally, both men hoped that their work would provide a revolutionary theoretical foundation capable of incorporating diverse and conflicting schools of thought within a common conceptual framework: one that would eventually integrate all of social science and thus provide, at long last, a sound scientific basis for the practice of education.

With so much in common, one would expect that the basic concepts in each of the two theories might well be similar, in spite of being couched in quite different terminology, and being walled off from one another by current keepers of the conflicting orthodoxies. And in fact, once the issue is posed in these conciliatory terms, something quite exciting begins to happen for the student of both theories. A common ground of considerable significance indeed begins to emerge, where fundamental *ideas* are concerned.

The key principle in cognitive psychology is "equilibration": another term borrowed from Herbert Spencer. Spencer, along with Freud, had assumed that to be scientific was to operate within the Newtonian conceptual framework. These early social scientists had not recognized the implications of Darwin's discovery of the vehicle of natural selection — and the principle of dynamic systems feedback according to which it operates — for their own field of study. Darwinian theory had, in fact, opened the door for the revolutionary understanding that, with the emergence of organic life, contingent causality began to replace the push-pull mechanistic form governing change at the inorganic level of relations in nature. Equilibrium is a central concept in Newtonian mechanics.

Piaget developed the concept of "equilibration" as a way to accommodate organic change processes to what was still seen by many as the prevailing model of science. The new term symbolized what Piaget viewed as the coordinating process synthesizing ongoing physiological maturation with incoming environmental impact, and thereby increasing the viability and comprehensiveness of adaptation. As he explained it, "at each level of development there are two poles of activity: changes in the structure of the organism in response to environmental intrusion (accommodation) and changes in the intruding stimuli due to the existing structure (assimilation)." He thought that the necessary synthesis occurs by means of self-regulating mechanisms operating on the basis of feedback. The process, he said, is common to biological evolution, individual learning and the growth of scientific knowledge. He saw it as fundamental to the understanding of all three, and to any general theory of human development capable of incorporating them all.

Skinner's key principle is that of reinforcement as the means by which "operant conditioning" operates to provide feedback from surrounding contingencies. As with Piaget's "equilibration" Skinner identified the role of reinforcement at all three of the biological, psychological and cultural levels. As he explained it, "Behavior is shaped and maintained by its consequences." Desirable behavior can be strengthened by means of positive reinforcement (reward) or through negative reinforcement (removal of existing aversive effects). Or it can be eliminated simply by the absence of reinforcement, or by allowing aversive effects in nature to operate without interference. Behavior can also be changed by punishment: the deliberate imposition of aversive consequences devised for the purpose. However, Skinner's research indicated that this is the least effective of the ways in which his basic principle of learning works.

From the standpoint of the learner as agent, Skinner said, the only inner compulsion operating initially is a capacity to be satiated by life-sustaining food and comfort and to experience deprivation in their absence. He assumed that all forms of complicated verbal behavior — including thinking — are essentially driven by the deprivation of these basic requirements. This means that any activity resulting in their satiation will be experienced as rewarding, and thus tend to be repeated. Interestingly, Piaget's model relies on just such a requirement — the satiation of curiosity or tension resulting from a lack of "fit" between incoming data and current cognitive patterning. He saw activity as a necessary attribute of living organisms. He believed that adaptation, at any level, begins with explorations or trials into the environment, caused by an impulsion either to re-establish or to strengthen equilibrium.

Equilibrium can thus be understood as the absence of cognitive conflict: a temporarily harmonious state of the system brought about through the integration of incoming stimuli into the learner's current conceptual framework. For this to occur, the learner must impose order on those stimuli. In other words, if environmental inputs are to be experienced, they must be perceived — or assimilated — in a form amenable to accommodation by the learner's cognitive or meaning system. One has only to interpret Piaget's search for equilibrium as an innate impulsion for (cognitive) power — or as a need to control or make sense out of one's surroundings — in order to make Piaget's theory directly compatible with that of Skinner!

It is easy to understand how the tension created by cognitive disjunction could drive human beings — just as does the organic disjunction (resulting from hunger, discomfort and fear) on which it is grounded. This broadened definition of the instinctual urge to control the contingencies governing action, common to all animals, allows us to see both theories in a new light. Most of the complex verbal behaviors distinguishing humans from other animals are rooted in this urge for power over other aspects of nature. It is the drive to adapt to environmental challenge: a challenge manifested, as well, in the deprivation of food, comfort and sex assumed by Skinner — and Freud before him. This inner drive for power over one's environment can readily spiral in the direction of control of *people* rather than *things*. The same tension that generates intellectual development and the scientific process can be readily comprehended as the source of aggression in human beings, as well as political behavior of all kinds.

All this becomes increasingly clear as we observe how children learn. The chief criticism of Skinner's behaviorism has stemmed from the fact that, for the outside observer, it is seldom clear what actually *constitutes* a reinforcement or reward — or, conversely, the withholding of reward. This has meant that critics often fail to register the universality of Skinner's fundamental principle of learning, because it is the child's *feeling* of power that is actually being reinforced, although the observer is unaware of this. More in-depth comprehension of organic and environmental sources of this experience of power in children can be gained by studying Piaget's observations of child development. He recognized four stages of intellectual development : the "sensorimotor", "pre-operational", "concrete operational" and "formal operational". When we interpret these in terms of increasingly powerful breakthroughs in children's ability to manipulate and control their surroundings — spurred on by the natural *reinforcement* that such power offers — we have a superbly simple (and "powerful") explanation for the process so ably documented by Piaget.

A cognitive neo-associationist interpretation of Piaget's observations would agree that the child learns to adapt to the physical environment by maneuvering through the relations of the surrounding space, and by handling objects, but it would point out that this is because the child's behavior is being *reinforced* by experienced regularities in surfaces, dimensions and motions. As Skinner noted, "If we could not find some uniformity in our world our conduct would remain haphazard and ineffective." This can be recognized as the source of the internal construction of rules posited by Piaget.

Many behaviorists have criticized cognitive theorists for confusing an essential distinction between rules and reinforced propensities to act. They maintain that rules are consciously elaborated and learned *descriptions* of contingencies, and that the behavior governed by them is quite different from that shaped by the contingencies themselves, which operate without conscious awareness in the person being affected. But a close reading of Piaget reveals that he viewed the rule-assimilating process somewhat as Dewey saw habit formation; and as Skinner himself saw contingent reinforcement. Only gradually, at a relatively advanced stage of intellectual functioning, is the child able consciously to recognize, apply and infer rules. In fact, it is the critical relationship between unconscious rule-following and the deliberate application of rules that alters as the child develops in a moral and intellectual sense. Abstract (or "formal") thought requires this ability. However, Piaget discovered that the latter will not develop without appropriate feedback from the environment (in other words — *reinforcement*)! In fact, he once noted that "Skinner's machines provide evidence of good psychology, in that they made use exclusively of positive reinforcement." This is one of the many examples of how Piaget's observations can be explained in terms of Skinner's theory. It is also an example of how behaviorism can be enriched by the assimilation of Piaget's insights.

The key concepts of social learning theory can also be interpreted in terms of an equilibration process operating by means of reinforcement. In the case of the baby's first smile it is easy to see how both the adult model and the infant imitator are reinforced by the feedback process set up in the response of the learner and the expressions of pleasure revealed in the adult by that response. Subsequent and more complex imitative reconstructions can be explained compellingly in terms of the reinforcement of the child's innovative attempts to restore meaningful cognitive mappings of experience.

Piaget's equilibration theory views the child as a primitive scientist impelled, by the tension resulting from sensations of disequilibrium, to make trial and error forays into the environment. Herbert Spencer referred to this as "cognitive disjunction". Dewey spoke of the potential for intellectual growth arising when the actor experiences a contradiction between the expectations aroused by habits built up through past experience of regularities, and the impact of current environmental effects. Modern scholars have used the term "cognitive dissonance" to describe the same sensations. All these can be understood as sources of that *curiosity* which drives animals to restore an internal sense of order by gaining increasing power to control the effects of their actions. Once the existence of this impulsion is accepted, all of Piaget's descriptive constructs that have seemed to lead nowhere can be explained simply and completely by Skinner's theory of reinforcement.

And cognitive neo-associationistresearch can be seen to shed new light on the most complex forms of human thought and action. The two perspectives, thus combined, should prove capable of generating a host of new testable hypotheses and, eventually, of laying the ground for a powerful new integrated paradigm for the study of how people learn. It could herald the breakthrough which many educators would agree has been a long time coming.

BEST LEARNING THEORY FOR INSTRUCTIONAL DESIGN

A solid foundation in learning theory is an essential element in the preparation of Instructional System Design (ISD) professionals because it permeates all dimensions of ISD. Depending on the learners and situation, different learning theories may apply. The instructional designer must understand the strengths and weaknesses of each learning theory to optimize their use in appropriate instructional design strategy. Recipes contained in Instructional Design (ID) theories may have value for novice designers, who lack the experience and expertise of veteran designers. Theories are useful because they open our eyes to other possibilities and ways of seeing the world. Whether we realize it or not, the best design decisions are most certainly based on our knowledge of learning theories. The function of ID is more of an application of theory, rather than a theory itself. Trying to tie Instructional Design to one particular theory is like school vs. the real world. What we learn in a school environment does not always match what is out there in the real world, just as the prescriptions of theory do not always apply in practice. From a pragmatic point of view, instructional designers find what works and use it.

Behaviorism, cognitivism and constructivism - what works where and how do we knit everything together to at least give ourselves some focus in our approach to instructional design? First of all we do not need to abandon the systems approach but we must modify it to accommodate constructivist values. We must allow circumstances surrounding the learning situation to help us decide which approach to learning is most appropriate. It is necessary to realize that some learning problems require highly prescriptive solutions, whereas others are more suited to learner control of the environment.

Jonnassen in *Manifesto for a Constructive Approach to Technology in Higher Education* identified the following types of learning and matched them with what he believes to be appropriate learning theory approaches.

1. *Introductory Learning* - learners have very little directly transferable prior knowledge about a skill or content area. They are at the initial stages of schema assembly and integration. At this stage classical instructional design is most suitable because it is predetermined, constrained, sequential and criterion-referenced.
2. *Advanced Knowledge Acquisition* - follows introductory knowledge and precedes expert knowledge. At this point constructivist approaches may be introduced.
3. *Expertise is the final stage of knowledge acquisition.* In this stage the learner is able to make intelligent decisions within the learning environment. A constructivist approach would work well in this case.

Having pointed out the different levels of learning, Jonassen stresses that it is still important to consider the context before recommending any specific methodology.

Reigeluth's Elaboration Theory which organizes instruction in increasing order of complexity and moves from prerequisite learning to learner control may work in the eclectic approach to instructional design, since the learner can be introduced to the main concepts of a course and then move on to more of a self directed study that is meaningful to them and their particular context. After having compared and contrasted behaviorism, cognitivism and constructivism, Ertmer and Newby feel that the instructional approach used for novice learners may not be efficiently stimulating for a learner who is familiar with the content. They do not advocate one single learning theory, but stress that instructional strategy and content addressed depend on the level of the learners. Similar to Jonassen, they match learning theories with the content to be learned:

> ... a behavioral approach can effectively facilitate mastery of the content of a profession (knowing what); cognitive strategies are useful in teaching problem -solving tactics where defined facts and rules are applied in unfamiliar situations(knowing how); and constructivist strategies are especially suited to dealing with ill-defined problems through reflection-in-action.
>
> *Behavioral*
>
> ... tasks requiring a low degree of processing (e.g., basic paired associations, discriminations, rote memorization) seem to be facilitated by strategies most frequently associated with a behavioral outlook (e.g., stimulus-response, contiguity of feedback/reinforcement).
>
> *Cognitive*
>
> Tasks requiring an increased level of processing (e.g., classifications, rule orprocedural executions) are primarily associated with strategieshaving a stronger cognitive emphasis (e.g., schematic organization, analogical reasoning, algorithmic problem solving).
>
> *Constructive*
>
> Tasks demanding high levels of processing (e.g., heuristic problem solving,personal selection and monitoring of cognitive strategies) are frequently est learned with strategies advanced by the constructivist perspective (e.g., situated learning, cognitive apprenticeships, social negotiation.

Ertmer and Newby believe that the strategies promoted by different learning theories overlap and that learning theory strategies are concentrated along different points of a continuum depending of the focus of the learning theory - the level of cognitive processing required. Ertmer and Newby's suggestion that theoretical strategies can complement the learner's level of task knowledge, allows the designer to make the best use of all available practical applications of the different learning theories. With this approach the designer is able to draw from a large number of strategies to meet a variety of learning situations.

2

CONCEPTS OF TEACHING

Teaching is the purposeful imparting of knowledge or skills to an individual or group. Learning can occur without a teacher, but teaching cannot occur without a student. But does teaching necessarily imply learning? Historically, teaching has been defined in terms of the quantity and quality of the material covered and the method in which it was presented. Learning was the responsibility of the student. Recently, however, more responsibility for student learning has been placed on the teacher. The concept of teaching can be broadened to include verbal instruction, computers, textbooks, and other educational materials such as video. However, the teacher is the person responsible for the instruction — whether a parent, friend, or classroom teacher. A teacher may use various items to aid in instruction, but it is the teacher who makes the decisions regarding the content and techniques used in their instruction.

In teaching, there is the teacher and the students, who work together to educate the students about the particular subject matter. This system of teaching is designed to modify the students' behavior, experience, understanding, and knowledge. Originally, schooling was considered merely a process of learning, memorization, association, and practice. However, the growth of students' intellect coincides with their development through different phases: coordination, symbolization and visual recognition, language, logical thought, and eventually formal structure and explanation. Any attempt at educating a child intellectually must take into account these characteristics. Education must pace development, not ignore it or follow it. A child's educational growth includes physical, emotional, and mental maturation, experience, formal teaching through language, and problem-solving.

The teacher's role involves sharing knowledge and experience with the students at an appropriate time. The teacher leads the students through different learning situations to encourage independent thought, critical analysis, realization, and problem-solving.

The subject matter has an influence on the total teaching environment. Subject matter is traditionally divided into the headings of languages, humanities, sciences, mathematics, and arts. Each group of subjects has something in common with other groups in terms of the demands it makes on the students, but is also unique in its method of development. Languages require verbal learning, primarily based on oral work. The humanities call for an understanding of cause-effect relationships. The sciences require induction from experience, and deduction when scientific laws are formulated into mathematical terms. Mathematics calls for the ability to symbolize and deduce. The arts require creative freedom.

Classroom structure is dynamic in terms of teaching methods, decision-making, the hierarchy of its members, and the existence of cliques. The students conduct themselves under the influence of the group, and each student's achievement and attitude is subject to evaluation by the group. In most classes, the age range of the students is approximately one year. This narrow range allows for uniformity of the subject matter being taught. However, in rural one- and two-teacher schools, students from different age groups and ability levels are mixed together. This changes the teaching method, since it now must cope with smaller subgroups which progress at different rates and need to cover different material. The teacher must find a way to coordinate the work of the smaller groups so that equal attention is given to each group.

CLASSROOM INSTRUCTION METHODS

Typically students are organized into classes and grades according to age. Schools may be comprehensive (containing students pursuing a variety of academic, commercial, and vocational curricula), or be based on the dual-plan (containing only students pursuing a particular curriculum). Some countries have a tripartite system, where there are separate schools for academic study, technical or vocational study, and generalized study. Other countries follow the comprehensive system, but have schools for different grades (elementary schools, junior high or middle schools, and high schools). Both comprehensive and dual-plan schools frequently offer streaming or multitracking, where students are grouped according to age and ability.

Total education is viewed as more than academic achievement, so both comprehensive and dual-plan schools have started introducing non-graded schools. Non-graded schools abolish grade separation, and students are placed individually in "phases" for each subject. This allows students to progress at their own pace, but often means that students end up grouped with students from different age groups - jumping ahead in subjects they are strong in, and falling behind in subjects they find difficult.

General-purpose classrooms are also fairly common. These classes originate from the curriculum being divided into a few general areas of similar intellectual interests, such as humanities, languages, and sciences. The resources made available for teaching each area, including teachers, are then made available in a common teaching space. The typical classroom organization and lessons disappear and are replaced by a flexible system that makes use of the resources available at that particular moment. Concepts similar to the general-purpose classroom have been introduced at the primary school level in the open-plan system.

Team teaching is a method of instruction that attempts to make better use of each teacher's potential within a subject area. It creates a flexible learning environment for both students and teachers, and makes non-streaming more effective. Instead of have several classes each with a different teacher, the students are combined into a single class, with the teachers pooling their efforts. Team teaching allows for a variety of teaching methods, such as large-group lectures by a single teacher, and small-group seminars to allow students to interact with each other and one of the teachers. Team teaching makes better use of each teacher's expertise and interests, and can be more effective than traditional non-streamed classes since the less-able students do not feel segregated, and often get more out of the small-group sessions than a traditional classroom. The flexibility of team teaching is a major advantage, and the variety of teaching methods reaches more students.

Grouping students is also a common technique. The recent trends of "streaming" and "tracking" - dividing students into groups according to age and intellectual ability - have promoted much inquiry. It has attracted both ardent support and extreme condemnation. The uniformity created by putting students with their intellectual peers makes teaching more effective and learning more acceptable. Those opposed to streaming believe that it has a negative effect on the psychological and moral states of children in the lower streams. They also believe that a varied class allows the weaker students to benefit from actively sharing with the stronger students.

TEACHING-LEARNING SITUATIONS

Teaching involves individual lessons which are part of a larger unit. However, each lesson is a self-contained concept within a broader topic and consists of individual teaching-learning-thinking-practice exercises. A single lesson may consist primarily of instruction (a lecture or notes) or hands-on work (experiments/labs), or alternate between these. Although lessons vary depending on the material being taught, resources available, and the teacher, generally a lesson consists of the following sequence of steps:

— *Preparation*: the teacher starts the lesson with the general concept of the lesson, which is associated with something already known by the class.

— *Presentation*: introducing the new material.

— *Association*: the new material is compared with old material and logical connections are made.

— *Generalization*: other examples of the new idea are presented.

— *Application*: the news ideas are applied to further material or investigation (eg. practice problems, a critical thinking exercise, or a lab).

This sequence of steps gives the teacher a clear role and provides the student with the opportunity for active, participatory learning.

The teacher selects and organizes the material that is to be taught in order to guide the students' learning. The students' curiosity, experience, and involvement are also essential to the learning. One problem teachers face is how to maintain the students' interest and curiosity, since those are the main motivators for learning. Sustained interest leads students to set realistic standards for their achievement.

TEACHING OBJECTIVES

The objectives of teaching extend far beyond the subject matter being taught. Essentially, teaching aims at developing well-integrated people who are capable of undertaking a responsible, independent, and active role in society. Teaching objectives extend from intellectual abilities and cognition (social insight) to psychomotor learning (learning practical skills) and affective learning (development of emotions, attitudes, morals, and values).

Cognitive development begins early, with the acquisition of basic language and math skills. Cognition continues to develop throughout a student's schooling, and begins to dominate education at the secondary level. Cognition allows us to generalize, abstract, infer, interpret, explain, and apply information. It makes us critical thinkers capable of making appropriate decisions and judgements, and makes us aware of different viewpoints.

Psychomotor learning encourages the development of physical skills and their appropriate and creative uses. Psychomotor development includes handwriting, art, and games at the elementary level, and practical science and vocational skills later on. Although emotional learning occurs throughout our schooling, it is not always obvious. Teachers may require students to take emotions into account or ask for emotional responses. This helps develop values and attitudes, especially during adolescence.

Theoretical, aesthetic, social, economic, political, and hedonistic values are considered in school curriculums. Art, humanities, and literature are directly involved in emotional learning, while science and mathematics can develop attitudes towards cognitive and theoretical values. When a student learns about a particular type of situation or problem, he will make appropriate emotional responses.

By presenting students with different situations, a wider range of emotional responses can be elicited. During early education, emotions can only be elicited from situations directly affecting the student. However, as the student matures, he becomes increasingly involved with general affairs and learns to associate emotions with circumstances that are removed from his personal life.

INSTRUCTION TECHNIQUES

Direct Instruction

The traditional teacher-centered instruction technique is called direct instruction. The teacher provides the students with much of the information they need, often through lectures, explanations, examples, and problem-solving. Most direct instruction techniques only allow for minimal student-teacher interaction, and need to be supplemented by review, practice, and group discussions. The main strength of direct instruction is that it is efficient, especially in quickly providing information to the students. It is also an effective way to allow students to achieve mastery when learning fundamental facts, rules, formulas, or sequences.

However, direct instruction is not an effective way to teach higher-level thinking, analysis or evaluation. It cannot be used to teach material over a long period of time, or present additional details to students who have already mastered the basic concepts. When direct instruction repeats material that has already been covered, it becomes redundant and boring for the students. However, repetition helps students learn material thoroughly, so the review must become "creative redundancy". Content needs to be repeated in novel ways to keep the students interested. A side effect of direct instruction is competition among the students for grades. This takes the focus off of the learning. Excessive competition leads students to stop caring about what they are learning, and care only about the competition.

Indirect Instruction

The indirect approach to teaching presents students with instructional stimuli in the form of materials, objects, and events, and requires students to go beyond the basic information that they are given to make their own conclusions and generalizations. Indirect instruction allows teachers to engage their students in activities which require the students to learn independently.

Students take an active role in their learning by developing ideas, testing their own conclusions, and discussing their results. This allows students to independently discover patterns and relationships in their learning and knowledge. Students go beyond the basic problems presented to them, allowing them to develop advanced levels of thinking and analysis. Indirect instruction is most effective at teaching a process or method of learning, and allows for a dynamic teaching and learning environment.

Discussion

Discussion involves free, interactive dialogue between teachers and students. It is more than just a question-answer period, and requires the teacher to give control of the classroom to the students. The students guide the discussion, meaning that it may not always progress in the direction the teacher anticipated. A successful discussion requires that all student responses and ideas be accepted and considered, even those that are immature or have not been thought out. Teachers and students need to be open-minded and willing to consider perspectives different from their own.

Cooperative Learning

Cooperative learning is a technique that encourages collaboration, competition, and independence. Teachers encourage independence among the students in terms of achieving their learning goals, and interdependence through interaction. One strength of cooperative learning is its social nature. Students are encouraged to interact and share with one another, which helps reduce the students' desire to talk or gossip with one another about unrelated topics. With interaction constantly occurring, a cooperative learning classroom tends to be somewhat noisy, but classroom management is easier.

Cooperative learning helps students develop conceptual reasoning and problem-solving skills. It also helps creates a warmer relationship among students and a positive attitude towards the subject matter.

Self-Directed Instruction

Students need to be encouraged to actively participate in their own learning process through self-directed instruction. Without taking a role in their own learning, students become too dependent on their teachers and fall behind in independent thought, reasoning, critical-thinking, and problem-solving abilities.

Metacognitive strategies - mental processes students use to understand and remember information - are often used in self-directed instruction. Students often model their strategies after those of a teacher who taught by explaining the reasoning involved and then focused the class on applying that reasoning to a variety problems.

Self-directed instruction teaches students to take learning into their own hands, apply their knowledge to real-world problems, monitor their own achievement, and go beyond the material that is presented to them. Predicting, questioning, summarizing, and clarifying are four important activities that shift the responsibility of the learning to the students.

Teaching Methods

Just like there are many ways people learn, there are many different teaching methods. When deciding which teaching method to use, the teacher needs to consider what learning goal the students are trying to achieve. Not all learning goals can be achieved using the same teaching method. The three most common teaching methods are rote learning, guided problem-solving, and diagnostic teaching.

Rote Learning

Rote learning means memorizing something "by heart", or exactly as it was presented to the student in the textbook or teacher's lecture. Common applications of rote learning are spelling lists, mathematical rules, historical dates, and chemical formulas. After the students have memorized the given material, they are tested by repeating the material exactly as it was originally given to them. Rote learning is well suited for foreign language vocabulary, history, and spelling tests.

Guided Problem-Solving

Guided problem-solving is the method used when teachers try to help students become skilled at solving problems. In the guided approach, the teacher first explains the general concept, and then how to attack that specific type of problem. The teacher demonstrates each step of the solution, and then gives the students similar problems to try on their own. This allows the students to apply the concepts they were initially taught to similar as well as slightly different problems. Guided problem-solving is well suited for the maths and sciences.

Diagnostic Teaching

Diagnostic teaching involves first presenting the students with problems that they are to solve using any method they can. No lecture or explanation is given until after the students have been given adequate time to work on the problems. Once the problems have been solved, the teacher will ask the students to explain how they arrived at their answers. The teacher will then go through the steps required to solve the problem, showing the students which steps they did right and wrong, explaining how to correct any mistakes they may have made.

Teaching Techniques

Teaching techniques are the ways in which the information to be learned is presented. Teaching techniques vary in terms of the medium (textbook, video, computer, etc), structure of the program, how the teacher operates, and how progress is monitored and tested. Several questions should be asked before selecting a teaching technique. Does the technique allow adjustment according to the needs of different students? Does it encourage the students to become actively involved with the learning? Does it adequately cover the material so that it is learned by all the students? Does it adequately monitor the students' progress? Does it permit extra assistance to students who require it? Does it allow an adequate amount of time to practice and integrate the skills?

The teaching technique that is best for the students is often not economically feasible, especially in terms of public schooling. Reducing class size is expensive, and many schools do not have the budget to maintain small classes. Similarly, the teaching resources best suited to the students, such as the latest technology, may not be available to the teacher. Teachers must find the best techniques to teach the students using the resources available to them.

Lecture and Discussion Methods

One of the most common teaching techniques is the lecture method. It is the most economical method of transmitting knowledge, but it does not necessarily hold the student's attention or permit active participation. However, lectures can be effective, if supported by texts and other references. About ninety percent of post-secondary instruction uses the lecture method, but it is significantly less common in primary and secondary schools. At these levels, discussion sessions are more effective in stimulating the students' interests and assessing their understanding of the material.

The discussion method is favored in secondary schools, particularly in the social sciences. Discussion not only helps teach material, but it also develops the thinking process, promotes a positive attitude towards learning, and develops interpersonal skills. Group discussions foster interaction between students whose skills, attitudes, and interests differ, and allow the students to use democratic leadership skills to lead the direction of their discussion and participation. In this manner, discussion sessions help students extend their knowledge through higher-level independent thought.

Grouping

Grouping is a common teaching technique, especially at the elementary level. Organizational arrangements place students together in groups within the classroom to improve the learning conditions. Traditionally, grouping has been the most effective approach to teaching reading and basic math. The teacher follows a detailed program of instruction and examples, and then the groups work together to respond to the questions presented to them.

Grouping allows teachers to place students of the same achievement level together, making it easier for the teacher to work with them. On the other hand, cooperative learning groups place students of different abilities together, so that students within each group can help each other. These groupings are often effective in raising students' achievement while improving interpersonal skills. Grouping has been particularly successful with hard-to-teach and fast-learning students. The recent trends of "streaming" and "tracking" - grouping students according to age and intellectual ability - have promoted much inquiry. It has attracted both ardent support and extreme condemnation. The uniformity created by putting students with their intellectual peers makes teaching more effective and learning more pleasant. Those opposed to streaming believe that it has a negative effect on the psychological and moral states of children in the lower streams. They also believe that a varied class allows the weaker students to benefit from actively sharing with the stronger students.

Tutoring

Tutoring is one-on-one instruction that is usually used to help remedy academic deficiencies. The need for tutoring tends to arise when other teaching methods have failed, or students needs extra instruction about a particular topic or subject with which they are having difficulty. Successful tutoring requires that the tutor has a firm understanding of the material being taught, and is adaptable to the student's learning needs. Tutoring by nonprofessionals, classmates, and older students have shown to be effective in providing extra support to students outside of the traditional classroom setting.

Games and Simulations

Because games and simulations are fun, teachers have sought to use them as an effective way to foster learning. Card and board games are popular to help teach basic reading and arithmetic skills, while simulations teach the principles of complex systems, such as economics, international relations, and power struggles. Simulations tend to focus on current social issues, or historical events. What makes simulations so effective is that they teach problem-solving and decision-making strategies in addition to the facts and principles that define the game.

Simulations are becoming increasingly popular for teaching new types of skills. Simulations can create conditions nearly identical to the actual situation. A common example of this type of simulation is a flight simulator, which introduces pilots to potential situations and problems.

Instructional Media

Instructional media serves as a teaching aid. Teachers spend much time on repetitive tasks such as collecting and assigning books, marking, and preparing worksheets, tests, and lesson plans. Instruction aids help reduce the time spent on these routine tasks, allowing more time to be spent promoting students' understanding and intellectual curiosity, and motivating and providing feedback to them.

Computer Assisted Instruction

In recent years, computer assisted instruction (CAI) has proved to be quite successful, whether inside the classroom or for independent learning. Various computer programs help students learning writing, math, science, and problem-solving, and those which are in the form of games help motivate the students while keeping them interested in what they are learning.

Teaching using a computer has many virtues: it is patient, positive, does not forget, and can keep track of each student's progress. However, the long-term benefits of computer assisted instruction is still unclear. It is not yet known how many students actually learn skills beyond performing the game, or the degree to which teachers need to participate in the process to ensure that the students learn what was intended.

Speaking-Listening Media

For lectures, the teacher can prepare and organize the material in any manner than he thinks will work best, but the students usually respond passively since there is no opportunity for two-way communication or student involvement in the discussion. Furthermore, if the students are occupied with writing notes during the lecture, critical thought about the material is inhibited. Media can help supplement the lecture technique by allowing the students to become actively involved with the material being covered.

Language laboratories are one type of speaking-listening media. Tape recorders allow students to hear model pronunciation of foreign languages and record and playback their own voices as they engage in practice drills. Many language laboratories provide a master control board which allows the teacher to listen to and correct any student individually as they work. Some laboratories are equipped to use filmstrips or videos simultaneously with the tape recorders. This is an effective mode of operant learning, and once basic vocabulary and syntax has been developed the learning can switch to active problem-solving.

Visual and Observational Media

Many students, especially visual learners, benefit from materials such as pictures, diagrams, charts, graphs, cartoons, posters, slides, and videos. Demonstrations and experiments also help reinforce visual learning. Generally, visual media is used to provide concrete examples in order to lead the students to the generalizations, abstract thinking, and explaining that constitutes learning. On its own, visual media can be a hindrance to learning; for examples, interesting pictures in a history textbook do not necessarily help the students' understanding of historical events. However, when combined with careful classroom explanation and discussion, visual aids can help students interpret, infer, and understand the concepts being presented to them.

Reading-Writing Media

Reading and writing form the basis of traditional education, requiring a sophisticated understanding of language. Textbooks are often essential in the classroom, providing extensive coverage of material at an appropriate level for the student. However, textbooks provide no feedback to or interaction with the student, and the teacher needs to fill this gap.

Programmed learning is a new form of reading and writing. Linear Programming - the most basic form of programmed learning - divides a subject into its components and arranges the parts into a sequential order. At each step in the reading, the student must respond and is immediately given feedback on his response. The program is structured so that most students' responses will be correct, encouraging them to continue. Another form of programmed learning is Branching Programming, which gives the student pieces of information and provides several possible answers to questions. The program progresses or detours the student according to his responses. This type of program reinforces the learning by backtracking over problem areas. These types of reading-writing media allow students to progress at their own rate and work independently; however, it can quickly become dull and tedious for the student.

Motivating Students

There is a distinctive relationship between a teacher's conduct and the students' learning ability. Teachers need to encourage and foster their students' success. Often teaching strategies alone are not enough to motivate students to succeed. Teachers need to encourage success by praising and encouraging students for high achievement, showing students respect, holding high expectations for all students, avoiding negative comments and sarcasm, offering extra help whenever needed, and taking an interest in the students' lives. This informal motivation helps establish a warm and caring classroom environment in which the students feel as though they can succeed.

By knowing a student's outside motivation, interests, and strengths, the teacher can more effectively encourage and support the student's learning inside the classroom. Knowing this information about a student helps the teacher relate to the student, while creating a more favorable teacher-student relationship. The better a teacher knows a student, the easier it is to understand their difficulties, needs, and motivators. Often by participating with or seeing students in their extra-curricular activities, teachers come to learn about their different sides. Students appreciate this extra effort and interest, and teachers can use their new insights to help the student succeed academically.

Motivating students to learn and succeed often means directly involving them in the learning process. Students need to have input into the types of instructional material used, teaching methods, and scheduling. Active and participatory learning activities, such as games, simulations, media, computer-based learning, and group work, can also motivate students.

Tests and grades can help motivate students as well as discourage them. They are only motivation when the topic or difficulty level allows that particular student a high rate of success. When students repeatedly do poorly, especially when they are trying their hardest, they quickly become demotivated. When students cannot rise to the challenges being presented to them, most will become frustrated and stop trying.

TASKS OF TEACHING

The instructional process involves five primary tasks:

1. Choosing objectives (content and performances)
2. Understanding student characteristics
3. Understanding and using ideas about the nature of learning and motivation
4. Selecting and using ways of teaching
5. Evaluating student learning

It is helpful to think of each task as a set of problems for both teachers and their students. Educational psychology can help teachers make wiser decisions as they formulate solutions. Although we present the tasks as a chronological list, the instructional process is actually a cycle, which goes back and forth between these tasks.

The Tasks in the Cycle

1. The teacher begins with some idea of objectives concerning the content that students should be helped to learn and the performances they should be helped to acquire for that content.
2. In choosing objectives, the teacher uses information about the important characteristics of the students. Tasks 1 and

2 occur simultaneously, and interact. You need to understand your students' stage of development and their abilities, strengths, and weaknesses. In the students' words, "The teacher should know us and then treat us appropriately. For example, she should realize how much we do (and don't) know."

3. Next the teacher must understand learning and motivation so as to understand and choose teaching methods and practices that fit what is known about students' learning and motivation. Teachers can apply knowledge about learning and motivation both before and during instruction.

4. After all the preinstructional decisions, the teacher selects and uses teaching methods and practices, such as lecturing, explaining, discussing, showing movies or videotapes, tutoring, providing computer-assisted instruction, leaving students alone, or some combination of these activities.

5. Both throughout the process and usually at the end of a cycle the teacher assesses students' achievement of educational objectives. Students need to be told when they are (or are not) doing a good job. They need guidance on how to improve, for example, by being told to check their comprehension by putting an idea into their own words. Students demand fairness in how they are assessed and graded.

If assessment shows that students have achieved the objectives, the teacher can go on to new objectives. But if assessment reveals that some or all of the students have not learned the content and performances that were taught, the teacher will need to reflect on why and adjust instruction accordingly. Remember that the process is a cycle; "recycling" is expected.

TEACHING STANDARDS AND OBJECTIVES

People involved in all kinds of educational tasks — not only teaching but also curriculum designing and achievement testing — insist that statements of standards and objectives are helpful, even essential. Unless they think about objectives, teachers tend to focus primarily on the content of instruction classroom activities and ignore how students should learn to perform with that content.

Think about your own experiences as a student. Have you ever wished a teacher had told you more clearly what you should have been learning and why? Without the teacher's focus on students' performance goals, students often assume that they need only to remember content. A history teacher, for example, may want students to be able to see connections between historical and present-day events. But if the teacher does not explain this intention to the students, they may assume that they should simply remember what they read rather than trying to look at contemporary problems in historical perspective.

Objectives can apply to education as a whole or only to teaching. Many educational objectives — self-fulfillment, appreciation of the nature of a good life, love of knowledge — are broader than any single teacher can hope to achieve.

In recent years critics of American education have argued that the achievement of U.S. students falls below that of students in other countries with which the nation must compete economically. These critics place much of the blame for these shortcomings on what they consider to be the inadequate standards of achievement set by American educators.

So a new focus on educational standards has motivated educators to reexamine the ways in which objectives are formed and used. This focus has led to the standards-based reform movement and the development of new curriculum standards in various subject-matter fields. The standards emerging from educators and professional organizations in art, social studies, mathematics, and other professions, which are intended to guide our states, districts, and teachers, set forth the contents and performances considered most important. For example, for mathematics, science, and social studies, respectively, the National Council of Teachers of Mathematics, the National

Research Council and the National Center for History in the Schools have each issued content standards.

We provide this information about the use of standards in educational reform because it is receiving considerable attention. The question is whether these statements of standards and objectives will improve education across the country. However, we must add an important caution. Not everyone in education believes that all the criticisms of American schooling are justified; Berliner and Biddle, among others, have challenged the validity of many of the test results and assumptions on which the criticisms are based.

The same educators point to the importance of opportunity-to-learn standards as well as content and performance standards. Opportunity-to-learn standards have to do with the quality of educational resources provided — the teachers available, the amount of time available for learning, the availability of computers for learning, and all the other characteristics of schooling that provide students with the opportunity to meet the standards and achieve the objectives. If those opportunities to learn are not equal for all of America's children, then school improvement through standards-based reform may occur only in the schools that can afford to implement the opportunity-to-learn standards. Children attending schools in poorer districts may have trouble meeting the new national content and performance standards.

Teacher's Role in Determining Content

At the same time, the teacher's decisions about and choices of content will often be guided by the concerns of educational psychology. Some psychological guidelines are as follows:

1. *Appropriateness in difficulty.* The content's difficulty should be appropriate to the students' ability, maturity, and level of background knowledge, so that the teacher does not demand more (or less) than they are capable of learning at their level.

Teachers too often expect too little of their students, particularly poor and minority students, and underestimate what they are capable of learning. And much research demonstrates that teachers' expectations, both positive and negative, affect students' achievement.

2. *Appropriateness to learning processes.* What we know about the various ways in which learning can take place should be used to choose and shape the content. Such knowledge helps a teacher to avoid content that conflicts with natural learning processes, and can be used to help students use those processes to foster achievement.

3. *Appropriateness to students' motivations.* Content should be chosen in the light of students' motivations. Motivations include interests, appreciations, aspirations, and ambitions, and all of them affect learning. So understandings about motivation should provide bases for the decisions teachers must make in choosing content (and methods of teaching) that will engage their students.

4. *Appropriateness to teaching methods.* Choices of content depend in part on what teaching methods and practices are feasible. Some kinds of content are better taught to some students, in some situations, by one kind of teaching — a lecture, cooperative learning, or a hands-on exercise — rather than another. In turn, some kinds of teaching are more feasible than others.

5. *Appropriateness to assessment.* Finally, choices of content may be influenced by what educational psychology says about ways of assessing student achievement. Achievement can be measured in many different ways, ranging from multiple-choice tests to portfolios containing products of student work. Good assessment practices are themselves determined by psychologically sound ideas about the nature of desirable achievement, so they are tied closely to the teacher's content decisions.

All five factors will help you as a classroom teacher to determine what content to teach. The best thinking and experience of those who focus primarily on what should be taught — curriculum specialists, textbook authors, committees of teachers, and many others — do not exempt you, the individual teacher, from thinking about content choice.

Standards, Objectives, and Goals in Terms of Student Performance

Statements of objectives act as maps guiding teacher and students. To find a city, we do not need a road map that specifies every village and creek; in fact, such specificity could get in the way. But to find a house, we need a street map. Similarly, in teaching we may need general or specific objectives, or both.

General Objectives

No teacher should be required to base instruction on the hundreds of objectives and subobjectives that could be specified for a unit of instruction. General objectives can describe the broad outlines of what students should achieve in a given content area.

Objectives in any content area can be visualized as forming a pyramid. At the apex is a single term (reading, algebra, world history). Just below that are various divisions of that area (in reading: decoding skills, word identification, etc.; in algebra: understanding the equation principle, etc.; in world history: political, cultural). Below that level, still more specific subdivisions can be identified (in decoding skills: pronouncing vowels; in equations: linear and quadratic equations; in cultural history: a day in the life of ancient Rome, etc.). The specification can go on indefinitely.

But where to draw the line? The teacher, using objectives as a road map, must decide. It depends on how well the teacher knows the "territory." When teaching content for the first time, the teacher may need much specificity, just as the newcomer to a state needs both a state road map and a town's street map. But the teacher (traveler) who has taught the content before (knows the state) may need only specific objectives (a street map) to find his or her way. And the veteran needs neither objectives nor maps. For most teachers, as they gain experience the amount of specificity they need diminishes. But beginners may need specific reminders.

Specific Objectives

Within each of the general objectives, teachers may have to develop more specific objectives. When doing so, they find the advice of Mageruseful.

1. *State objectives in terms of performances* — what teachers can see or hear students do once they have learned. Performances include mental processes — ways of thinking and feeling, and evidence of these ways in the form of products such as what students have done, said, written, enacted, drawn, or built. For instance, a general objective for students reading this book might be "understanding educational psychology." To state part of the objective in terms of performances, we could state that students should "be able to grasp the significance of empirical methods in education." Or that students should "know and appreciate the concepts and principles of educational psychology." But we must then spell out how students should be able to perform when they "understand," "grasp significance," "know," or "appreciate."

   Think of the objective as stating the terminal performance — what the student will be able to do at the end of instruction. We specify performances more when we say that students should be able to:

   — differentiate among the correlational, experimental, and interpretive methods in educational psychology.

   — give original examples of situations calling for general only and for both general and specific objectives.

— make up a 10-item multiple-choice test.

Each of these objectives is more precise than general objectives that merely use words like *understand* or *appreciate*. Differentiating, describing, and making up original examples tell us what performance to look for and describe terminal performances clearly and explicitly.

2. *State conditions of performance* — the situation or setting in which the student should be able to perform. That is, simple statements of wanted performance may not be enough. Often we should also specify the important conditions under which the performance is expected to occur. For example, suppose our objective is, "Students should be able to contrast the correlational and experimental methods of research." We might want to add to it such conditions as "using provided (or student-identified) examples of actual research articles"; "with or without class notes (or the text)"; "at home (or in class)"; "orally (or in writing)."

3. *State acceptable levels of performance* — what will be considered adequate achievement. Should you refer to a necessary rate of speed? Should students be able to solve only one type of problem? or three? or four out of six? questions in only one form? in several forms? That is, how can you make clear to the student what you will consider to be the standard for judging the learning to be a success?

   For example, it may not be enough to say, "Students should recognize the writing style of Ernest Hemingway." It might be better to say, "Given ten pairs of short prose passages, each pair having one selection by Ernest Hemingway and one by a different author, students should be able to choose at least nine of the ten selections written by Hemingway." Look again at the examples in Table 2.2 and see if you can find the part of each objective statement that expresses the level of performance expected.

To apply and illustrate what we have just said: we could state our objective as, "Given this introduction and one hour's time, you will be able to construct ten objectives in a subject-matter area of your choice, at least eight of which meet the criteria listed above."

Classifying Objectives

What kinds of objectives are there? Educators and psychologists have developed taxonomies of objectives. These are classi_cation schemes for making distinctions to help teachers organize their thinking about objectives. They also help in teaching students and evaluating their achievement.

Identifying Three Domains

One major set of distinctions draws upon the differences among cognitive, affective, and psychomotor performances.

1. *Cognitive objectives* deal with intellectual processes such as knowing, perceiving, recognizing, thinking, conceiving, judging, and reasoning. When a teacher is concerned about Josh's inability to spell words correctly, she is referring to an objective in the cognitive domain.
2. *Affective objectives* deal with feelings — likes and dislikes, emotions, attitudes, appreciations, interests, values, and the like. When the teacher worries about Josh's boredom with reading, she is dealing with the affective domain.
3. *Psychomotor objectives* deal with skilled ways of moving, such as handwriting, typewriting, dancing, and blowing glass for a chemistry experiment.

These three kinds of performance are never completely isolated from one another. But it often is useful to focus on one at a time.

MOTIVATION—AN IMPORTANT ASPECT OF TEACHING

Motivation is typically defined as the forces that account for the arousal, selection, direction, and continuation of behavior.

Nevertheless, many teachers have at least two major misconceptions about motivation that prevent them from using this concept with maximum effectiveness. One misconception is that some students are unmotivated. Strictly speaking, that is not an accurate statement. As long as a student chooses goals and expends a certain amount of effort to achieve them, he is, by definition, motivated. What teachers really mean is that students are not motivated to behave in the way teachers would like them to behave. The second misconception is that one person can directly motivate another. This view is inaccurate because motivation comes from within a person.

Many factors determine whether the students in your classes will be motivated or not motivated to learn. You should not be surprised to discover that no single theoretical interpretation of motivation explains all aspects of student interest or lack of it. Different theoretical interpretations do, however, shed light on why some students in a given learning situation are more likely to want to learn than others. Furthermore, each theoretical interpretation can serve as the basis for the development of techniques for motivating students in the classroom. Several theoretical interpretations of motivation — some of which are derived from discussions of learning presented earlier — will now be summarized.

Behavioral Views of Motivation

Operant Conditioning and Social Learning Theory

The Effect of Reinforcement:

Skinner developed the technique of programmed instruction to make it possible for students to be reinforced for every correct response. According to Skinner, supplying the correct answer—and being informed by the program that it is the correct answer—motivates the student to go on to the next frame; and as the student works through the program, the desired terminal behavior is progressively shaped.

Following Skinner's lead, many behavioral learning theorists devised techniques of behavior modification on the assumption that students are motivated to complete a task by being promised a reward of some kind. Many times the reward takes the form of praise or a grade. Sometimes it is a token that can be traded in for some desired object; and at other times the reward may be the privilege of engaging in a self-selected activity.

Operant conditioning interpretations of learning may help reveal why some students react favorably to particular subjects and dislike others. For instance, some students may enter a required math class with a feeling of delight, while others may feel that they have been sentenced to prison. Skinner suggests that such differences can be traced to past experiences. He would argue that the student who loves math has been shaped to respond that way by a series of positive experiences with math. The math hater, in contrast, may have suffered a series of negative experiences.

The Power of Persuasive:

Models Social learning theorists, such as Albert Bandura, call attention to the importance of observation, imitation, and vicarious reinforcement (expecting to receive the same reinforcer that we see someone else get for exhibiting a particular behavior). A student who identifies with and admires a teacher of a particular subject may work hard partly to please the admired individual and partly to try becoming like that individual. A student who observes an older brother or sister reaping benefits from earning high grades may strive to do the same with the expectation of experiencing the same or similar benefits. A student who notices that a classmate receives praise from the teacher after acting in a certain way may decide to imitate such behavior to win similar rewards. Both vicarious reinforcement and direct reinforcement can raise an individual's sense of self-efficacy for a particular task, which, in turn, leads to higher levels of motivation.

Cognitive Views of Motivation

Cognitive views stress that human behavior is influenced by the way people think about themselves and their environment. The direction that behavior takes can be explained by four influences: the inherent need to construct an organized and logically consistent knowledge base, one's expectations for successfully completing a task, the factors that one believes account for success and failure, and one's beliefs about the nature of cognitive ability.

The Impact of Cognitive Development

This view is based on Jean Piaget's principles of equilibration, assimilation, accommodation, and schema formation. Piaget proposes that children possess an inherent desire to maintain a sense of organization and balance in their conception of the world. A sense of equilibration may be experienced if a child assimilates a new experience by relating it to an existing scheme, or the child may accommodate by modifying an existing scheme if the new experience is too different.

In addition, individuals will repeatedly use new schemes because of an inherent desire to master their environment. This explains why young children can, with no loss of enthusiasm, sing the same song, tell the same story, and play the same game over and over and why they repeatedly open and shut doors to rooms and cupboards with no seeming purpose. It also explains why older children take great delight in collecting and organizing almost everything they can get their hands on and why adolescents who have begun to attain formal operational thinking will argue incessantly about all the unfairness in the world and how it can be eliminated.

The Need for Achievement

Have you ever decided to take on a moderately difficult task (like take a course on astronomy even though you are a history major and have only a limited background in science) and then found that you had somewhat conflicting feelings about it? On the one hand, you felt eager to start the course, confident that you would be pleased with your performance. But on the other hand, you also felt a bit of anxiety because of the small possibility of failure. Now try to imagine the opposite situation. In reaction to a suggestion to take a course outside your major, you flat out refuse because the probability of failure seems great, while the probability of success seems quite small.

In the early 1960s John Atkinson proposed that such differences in achievement behavior are due to differences in something called the need for achievement. Atkinson described this need as a global, generalized desire to attain goals that require some degree of competence. He saw this need as being partly innate and partly the result of experience. Individuals with a high need for achievement have a stronger expectation of success than they do a fear of failure for most tasks and therefore anticipate a feeling of pride in accomplishment.

When given a choice, high-need achievers seek out moderately challenging tasks because they offer an optimal balance between challenge and expected success. By contrast, individuals with a low need for achievement avoid such tasks because their fear of failure greatly outweighs their expectation of success, and they therefore anticipate feelings of shame. When faced with a choice, they typically opt either for relatively easy tasks because the probability of success is high or rather difficult tasks because there is no shame in failing to achieve a lofty goal.

Atkinson's point about taking fear of failure into account in arranging learning experiences has been made more recently by William Glasser in Control Theory in the Classroom and The Quality School. Glasser argues that for people to succeed at life in general, they must first experience success in one important aspect of their lives. For most children, that one important part should be school. But the traditional approach to evaluating learning, which emphasizes comparative grading (commonly called "grading on the curve"), allows only a minority of students to achieve A's and B's and feel successful. The self-worth of the remaining students (who may be quite capable) suffers, which depresses their motivation to achieve on subsequent classroom tasks.

The Humanistic View of Motivation

Abraham Maslow earned his Ph.D. in a psychology department that supported the behaviorist position. After he graduated, however, he came into contact with Gestalt psychologists (a group of German psychologists whose work during the 1920s and 1930s laid the foundation for the cognitive theories of the 1960s and 1970s), prepared for a career as a psychoanalyst, and became interested in anthropology. As a result of these various influences, he came to the conclusion that American psychologists who endorsed the behaviorist position had become so preoccupied with overt behavior and objectivity that they were ignoring other important aspects of human existence (hence the term humanistic to describe his views). When Maslow observed the behavior of especially well-adjusted persons—or self-actualizers, as he called them—he concluded that healthy individuals are motivated to seek fulfilling experiences.

Maslow's Theory of Growth Motivation

Maslow describes seventeen propositions that he believes would have to be incorporated into any sound theory of growth motivation (or need gratification) to meet them. Referring to need gratification as the most important single principle underlying all development, he adds that "the single, holistic principle that binds together the multiplicity of human motives is the tendency for a new and higher need to emerge as the lower need fulfills itself by being sufficiently gratified". He elaborates on this basic principle by proposing a five-level hierarchy of needs. Physiological needs are at the bottom of the hierarchy, followed in ascending order by safety, belongingness and love, esteem, and self-actualization needs. This order reflects differences in the relative strength of each need. The lower a need is in the hierarchy, the greater is its strength because when a lower-level need is activated (as in the case of extreme hunger or fear for one's physical safety), people will stop trying to satisfy a higher-level need (such as esteem or self-actualization) and focus on satisfying the currently active lower-level need.

The first four needs (physiological, safety, belongingness and love, and esteem) are often referred to as deficiency needs because they motivate people to act only when they are unmet to some degree. Self-actualization, by contrast, is often called a growth need because people constantly strive to satisfy it. Basically, self-actualization refers to the need for self-fulfillment — the need to develop all of one's potential talents and capabilities. For example, an individual who felt she had the capability to write novels, teach, practice medicine, and raise children would not feel self-actualized until all of these goals had been accomplished to some minimal degree. Because it is at the top of the hierarchy and addresses the potential of the whole person, self-actualization is discussed more frequently than the other needs.

Maslow originally felt that self-actualization needs would automatically be activated as soon as esteem needs were met, but he changed his mind when he encountered individuals whose behavior did not fit this pattern. He concluded that individuals whose self-actualization needs became activated held in high regard such values as truth, goodness, beauty, justice, autonomy, and humor.

In addition to the five basic needs that compose the hierarchy, Maslow describes cognitive needs (such as the needs to know and to understand) and aesthetic needs (such as the needs for order, symmetry, or harmony). While not part of the basic hierarchy, these two classes of needs play a critical role in the satisfaction of basic needs. Maslow maintains that such conditions as the freedom to investigate and learn, fairness, honesty, and orderliness in interpersonal relationships are critical because their absence makes satisfaction of the five basic needs impossible.

The Impact of Cooperative Learning on Motivation

Classroom tasks can be structured so that students are forced to compete with one another, work individually, or cooperate with one another to obtain the rewards that teachers make available for successfully completing these tasks. Traditionally, competitive arrangements have been assumed to be superior to the other two in increasing motivation and learning. But reviews of the research literature by David Johnson and Roger Johnson found cooperative arrangements to be far superior in producing these benefits. In this section we will describe cooperative-, competitive, and individual learning arrangements (sometimes called goal structures or reward structures), identify the elements that make up the major approaches to cooperative learning, and examine the effect of cooperative learning on motivation, achievement, and interpersonal relationships.

Types of Classroom Reward Structures

Competitive goal structures are typically norm referenced. This traditional practice of grading on the curve predetermines the percentage of A, B, C, D, and F grades regardless of the actual distribution of test scores. Because only a small percentage of students in any group can achieve the highest rewards and because this accomplishment must come at some other students' expense, competitive goal structures are characterized by negative interdependence. Students try to outdo one another, view classmates' failures as an advantage, and come to believe that the winners deserve their rewards because they are inherently better.

Some researchers have argued that competitive reward structures lead students to focus on ability as the primary basis for motivation. This orientation is reflected in the question "Am I smart enough to accomplish this task?" When ability is the basis for motivation, competing successfully in the classroom may be seen as relevant to self-esteem (since nobody loves a loser), difficult to accomplish, and uncertain (success depends on how everyone else does). These perceptions may cause some students to avoid challenging subjects or tasks, to give up in the face of difficulty, to reward themselves only if they win a competition, and to believe that their own successes are due to ability, whereas the successes of others are due to luck.

Individualistic goal structures are characterized by students working alone and earning rewards solely on the quality of their own efforts. The success or failure of other students is irrelevant. All that matters is whether the student meets the standards for a particular task. Thirty students working by themselves at computer terminals are functioning in an individual reward structure. According to Carole Ames and Russell Ames, individual structures lead students to focus on task effort as the primary basis for motivation. Whether a student perceives a task as difficult depends on how successful she has been with that type of task in the past.

Cooperative goal structures are characterized by students working together to accomplish shared goals. What is beneficial for the other students in the group is beneficial for the individual and vice versa. Because students in coöperative groups can obtain a desired reward only if the other students in the group also obtain the same reward, cooperative goal structures are characterized by positive interdependence. Also, all groups may receive the same rewards, provided they meet the teacher's criteria for mastery. For example, a teacher might present a lesson on map reading, then give each group its own map and a question-answering exercise. Students then work with each other to ensure that all know how to interpret maps. Each student then takes a quiz on map reading. All teams whose average quiz scores meet a preset standard receive special recognition.

Cooperative structures lead students to focus on effort and cooperation as the primary basis of motivation. This orientation is reflected in the statement "We can do this if we try hard and work together." In a cooperative atmosphere, students are motivated out of a sense of obligation: one ought to try, contribute, and help satisfy group norms. William Glasser is a fan of cooperative learning. He points out that student motivation and performance tend to be highest for such activities as band, drama club, athletics, the school newspaper, and the yearbook, all of which require a team effort.

Suggestions for Motivating Students to Learn

1. Use behavioral techniques to help students exert themselves and work toward remote goals.
2. Make sure that students know what they are to do, how to proceed, and how to determine when they have achieved goals.
3. Do everything possible to satisfy deficiency needs — physiological, safety, belongingness, and esteem.
    a. Accommodate the instructional program to the physiological needs of your students.
    b. Make your room physically and psychologically safe.
    c. Show your students that you take an interest in them and that they belong in your classroom.
    d. Arrange learning experiences so that all students can gain at least a degree of esteem.
4. Enhance the attractions and minimize the dangers of growth choices.
5. Direct learning experiences toward feelings of success in an effort to encourage an orientation toward achievement, a positive self-concept, and a strong sense of self-efficacy.

a. Make use of objectives that are challenging but attainable and, when appropriate, that involve student input.

b. Provide knowledge of results by emphasizing the positive.

6. Try to encourage the development of need achievement, self-confidence, and self-direction in students who need these qualities.

   a. Use achievement-motivation training techniques.

   b. Use cooperative-learning methods.

7. Try to make learning interesting by emphasizing activity, investigation, adventure, social interaction, and usefulness.

ROLE OF ASSESSMENT IN TEACHING

Assessing student learning is something that every teacher has to do, usually quite frequently. Written tests, book reports, research papers, homework exercises, oral presentations, question-and-answer sessions, science projects, and artwork of various sorts are just some of the ways in which teachers measure student learning, with written tests accounting for about 45 percent of a typical student's course grade. It is no surprise, then, that the typical teacher can spend between one-third and one-half of her class time engaged in one or another type of measurement activity. Yet despite the amount of time teachers spend assessing student learning, it is a task that most of them dislike and that few do well. One reason is that many teachers have little or no in-depth knowledge of assessment principles. Another reason is that the role of assessor is seen as being inconsistent with the role of teacher.

Broadly conceived, classroom assessment involves two major types of activities: collecting information about how much knowledge and skill students have learned (measurement) and making judgments about the adequacy or acceptability of each student's level of learning (evaluation). Both the measurement and evaluation aspects of classroom assessment can be accomplished in a number of ways. To determine how much learning has occurred, teachers can, for example, have students take exams, respond to oral questions, do homework exercises, write papers, solve problems, and make oral presentations. Teachers can then evaluate the scores from those activities by comparing them either to one another or to an absolute standard.

Measurement

Measurement is the assignment of numbers to certain attributes of objects, events, or people according to a rule-governed system. For example, we can measure someone's level of typing proficiency by counting the number of words the person accurately types per minute or someone's level of mathematical reasoning by counting the number of problems correctly solved. In a classroom or other group situation, the rules that are used to assign the numbers will ordinarily create a ranking that reflects how much of the attribute different people possess.

Evaluation

Evaluation involves using a rule-governed system to make judgments about the value or worth of a set of measures. What does it mean, for example, to say that a student answered eighty out of one hundred earth science questions correctly? Depending on the rules that are used, it could mean that the student has learned that body of knowledge exceedingly well and is ready to progress to the next unit of instruction or, conversely, that the student has significant knowledge gaps and requires additional instruction.

Need of Assessing Students' Learning

We will use this section to address four of the most common reasons for assessment: to provide summaries of learning, to provide information on learning progress, to diagnose specific strengths and weaknesses in an individual's learning, and to motivate further learning.

Summative Evaluation

The first, and probably most obvious, reason for assessment is to provide to all interested parties a clear, meaningful, and useful summary or accounting of how well a student has met the teacher's objectives. When testing is done for the purpose of assigning a letter or numerical grade, it is often called *summative evaluation* since its primary purpose is to sum up how well a student has performed over time and at a variety of tasks.

Formative Evaluation

A second reason for assessing students is to monitor their progress. The main things that teachers want to know from time to time is whether students are keeping up with the pace of instruction and are understanding all of the material that has been covered so far. For students whose pace of learning is either slower or faster than average or whose understanding of certain ideas is faulty, you can introduce supplementary instruction (a workbook or a computer-based tutorial program), remedial instruction (which may also be computer based), or in-class ability grouping. Because the purpose of such assessment is to facilitate or form learning and not to assign a grade, it is usually called *formative evaluation*.

Diagnosis

A third reason follows from the second. If you discover a student who is having difficulty keeping up with the rest of the class, you will probably want to know why in order to determine the most appropriate course of action. This purpose may lead you to construct an assessment that will provide you with specific diagnostic information.

Effects on Learning

A fourth reason for assessment of student performance is that it has potentially positive effects on various aspects of learning and instruction. As Terence Crooks points out, classroom assessment guides students' "judgment of what is important to learn, affects their motivation and self-perceptions of competence, structures their approaches to and timing of personal study, consolidates learning, and affects the development of enduring learning strategies and skills. It appears to be one of the most potent forces influencing education".

Ways to Measure Student Learning

Just as measurement can play several roles in the classroom, teachers have several ways to measure what students have learned. Which type of measure you choose will depend, of course, on the objectives you have stated. For the purposes of this discussion, objectives can be classified in terms of two broad categories: knowing about something and knowing how to do something.

Measures that attempt to assess the range and accuracy of someone's knowledge are usually called written tests. And measures that attempt to assess how well somebody can do something are often referred to as performance tests. Again, keep in mind that both types have a legitimate place in a teacher's assessment arsenal. Which type is used, and to what extent, will depend on the purpose or purposes you have for assessing students.

Written Tests

Teachers spend a substantial part of each day assessing student learning, and much of this assessment activity involves giving and scoring some type of written test. Most written tests are composed of one or more of the following item types: selected response (multiple choice, true-false, and matching, for example), short answer, and essay. They are designed to measure how much people know about a particular subject. In all likelihood, you have taken hundreds of these types of tests in your school career thus far.

Selected-Response Tests

Selected-response tests are so named because the student reads a relatively brief opening statement (called a *stem*) and selects one of the provided alternatives as the correct answer. Selected-response tests are typically made up of multiple-choice, true-false, or matching items. Quite often all three item types are used in a single test. Selected-response tests are sometimes called "objective" tests because they have a simple and set scoring system. If alternative (b) of a multiple-choice item is keyed as the correct response and the student chose alternative (d), the student is marked wrong, regardless of how much the teacher wanted the student to be right. But that doesn't mean selected-response items are totally free of subjective influences.

After all, whoever created the test had to make subjective judgments about which areas to emphasize, how to word items, and which items to include in the final version. Finally, selected-response tests are typically used when the primary goal is to assess what might be called foundational knowledge. This is the basic factual information and cognitive skills that students need in order to do such high-level tasks as solve problems and create products.

A major advantage of selected-response tests is efficiency — a teacher can ask many questions in a short period of time. Another advantage is ease and reliability of scoring. With the aid of a scoring template (such as a multiple-choice answer sheet that has holes punched out where the correct answer is located), many tests can be quickly and uniformly scored.

Because items that reflect the lowest level of Bloom's Taxonomy (verbatim knowledge) are the easiest to write, most teacher-made tests are composed almost entirely of knowledge-level items. As a result, students focus on verbatim memorization rather than on meaningful learning. Another disadvantage is that, while we get some indication of what students know, such tests tell us nothing about what students can do with that knowledge.

Short-Answer Tests

Instead of selecting from one or more alternatives, the student is asked to supply a brief answer consisting of a name, word, phrase, or symbol. Like selected-response tests, short-answer tests can be scored quickly, accurately, and consistently, thereby giving them an aura of objectivity. They are primarily used for measuring foundational knowledge.

Short-answer items are relatively easy to write, so a test, or part of one, can be constructed fairly quickly. They allow for either broad or in-depth assessment of foundational knowledge since students can respond to many items within a short space of time. Since students have to supply an answer, they have to recall, rather than recognize, information.

This item type has the same basic disadvantages as the selected-response items. Because these items ask only for short verbatim answers, students are likely to limit their processing to that level, and these items provide no information about how well students can use what they have learned. In addition, unexpected but plausible answers may be difficult to score.

Essay Tests

The student is given a somewhat general directive to discuss one or more related ideas according to certain criteria. One example of an essay question is "Compare operant conditioning theory and information-processing theory in terms of basic assumptions, typical research findings, and classroom applications."

Essay tests reveal how well students can recall, organize, and clearly communicate previously learned information. When well written, essays tests call on such higher-level abilities as analysis, synthesis, and evaluation. Because of these demands, students are more likely to try to meaningfully learn the material over which they are tested.

Consistency of grading is likely to be a problem. Two students may have essentially similar responses, yet receive different letter or numerical grades. These test items are also very time consuming to grade. And because it takes time for students to formulate and write responses, only a few questions at most can be given.

Performance Tests

In recent years many teachers and measurement experts have argued that the typical written test should be used far less often because it reveals little or nothing of the depth of students' knowledge and how students use their knowledge to work through questions, problems, and tasks. The solution that these experts have proposed is to use one or more of what are called performance tests.

Performance tests attempt to assess how well students use foundational knowledge to perform complex tasks under more or less realistic conditions. At the low end of the realism spectrum, students may be asked to construct a map, interpret a graph, or write an essay under highly standardized conditions. That is, everyone completes the same task in the same amount of time and under the same conditions. At the high end of the spectrum, students may be asked to conduct a science experiment, produce a painting, or write an essay under conditions that are similar to those of real life. For example, students may be told to produce a compare-and-contrast essay on a particular topic by a certain date, but the resources students choose to use, the number of revisions they make, and when they work on the essay are left unspecified. Another term that is often used to encompass both performance testing and authentic assessment, and to distinguish them from traditional written tests, is *alternative assessment*.

Currently, there are four ways in which the performance capabilities of students are typically assessed: direct writing assessments, portfolios, exhibitions, and demonstrations.

— *Direct Writing Assessments:* These tests ask students to write about a specific topic ("Describe the person whom you admire the most, and explain why you admire that person.") under a standard set of conditions. Each essay is then scored by two or more people according to a set of defined criteria.

— *Portfolios*: A portfolio may contain one or more pieces of a student's work, some of which demonstrate different stages of completion. For example, a student's writing portfolio may contain business letters; pieces of fiction; poetry; and an outline, rough draft, and final draft of a research paper. Through the inclusion of various stages of a research paper, both the process and the end product can be assessed. Portfolios can also be constructed for math and science as well as for projects that combine two or more subject areas. Often the student is involved in the selection of what is included in his portfolio. The portfolio is sometimes used as a showcase to illustrate exemplary pieces, but it also works well as a collection of pieces that represent a student's typical performances. In its best and truest sense, the portfolio functions not just as a housing for these performances but also as a means of self-expression, self-reflection, and self-analysis for an individual student.

— *Exhibitions*: Exhibitions involve just what the label suggests — a showing of such products as paintings, drawings, photographs, sculptures, videotapes, and models. As with direct writing assessments and portfolios, the products a student chooses to exhibit are evaluated according to a predetermined set of criteria.

— *Demonstrations*: In this type of performance testing, students are required to show how well they can use previously learned knowledge or skills to solve a somewhat unique problem (such as conducting a scientific inquiry to answer a question or diagnosing the cause of a malfunctioning engine and describing the best procedure for fixing it) or perform a task (such as reciting a poem, performing a dance, or playing a piece of music).

Once you have collected all the measures you intend to collect — for example, test scores, quiz scores, homework assignments, special projects, and laboratory experiments — you will have to give the numbers some sort of value (the essence of evaluation). As you probably know, this is most often done by using an A to F grading scale. Typically, a grade of A indicates superior performance; a B, above-average performance; a C, average performance; a D, below-average performance; and an F, failure. There are two general ways to approach this task. One approach involves comparisons among students. Such forms of evaluation are called *norm-referenced* since students are identified as average (or normal), above average, or below average. An alternative approach is called *criterion-referenced* because performance is interpreted in terms of defined criteria. Although both approaches can be used, we favor criterion-referenced grading for reasons we will mention shortly.

Norm-Referenced Grading

A norm-referenced grading system assumes that classroom achievement will naturally vary among a group of heterogeneous students because of differences in such characteristics as prior knowledge, learning skills, motivation, and aptitude. Under ideal circumstances, this variation produces a bell-shaped, or "normal," distribution of scores that ranges from low to high, has few tied scores, and has only a very few low scores and only a very few high scores. For this reason, norm-referenced grading procedures are also referred to as "grading on the curve."

Criterion-Referenced Grading

A criterion-referenced grading system permits students to benefit from mistakes and to improve their level of understanding and performance. Furthermore, it establishes an individual reward structure, which fosters motivation to learn to a greater extent than other systems.

Under a criterion-referenced system, grades are determined through comparison of the extent to which each student has attained a defined standard (or criterion) of achievement or performance. Whether the rest of the students in the class are successful or unsuccessful in meeting that criterion is irrelevant. Thus, any distribution of grades is possible. Every student may get an A or an F, or no student may receive these grades. For reasons we will discuss shortly, very low or failing grades tend to occur less frequently under a criterion-referenced system.

A common version of criterion-referenced grading assigns letter grades on the basis of the percentage of test items answered correctly. For example, you may decide to award an A to anyone who correctly answers at least 85 percent of a set of test questions, a B to anyone who correctly answers 75 to 84 percent, and so on down to the lowest grade. To use this type of grading system fairly, which means specifying realistic criterion levels, you would need to have some prior knowledge of the levels at which students typically perform. You would thus be using normative information to establish absolute or fixed standards of performance. However, although norm-referenced and criterion-referenced grading systems both spring from a normative database (that is, from comparisons among students), only the former system uses those comparisons to directly determine grades.

Criterion-referenced grading systems (and criterion-referenced tests) have become increasingly popular in recent years primarily because of three factors. First, educators and parents complained that norm-referenced tests and grading systems provided too little specific information about student strengths and weaknesses. Second, educators have come to believe that clearly stated, specific objectives constitute performance standards, or criteria, that are best assessed with criterion-referenced measures. Third, and perhaps most important, contemporary theories of school learning claim that most, if not all, students can master most school objectives under the right circumstances. If this assertion is even close to being true, then norm-referenced testing and grading procedures, which depend on variability in performance, will lose much of their appeal.

Suggestions for Effective Assessment

1. As early as possible in a report period, decide when and how often to give tests and other assignments that will count toward a grade, and announce tests and assignments well in advance.
2. Prepare a content outline and/or a table of specifications of the objectives to be covered on each exam, or otherwise take care to obtain a systematic sample of the knowledge and skill acquired by your students.
3. Consider the purpose of each test or measurement exercise in light of the developmental characteristics of the students in your classes and the nature of the curriculum for your grade level.
4. Decide whether a written test or a performance test is most appropriate.
5. Make up and use a detailed answer key.
    a. Evaluate each answer by comparing it to the key.
    b. Be willing and prepared to defend the evaluations you make.
6. During and after the grading process, analyze questions and answers in order to improve future exams.

3

Teaching and Learning Process

The increased complexity of today's world present new challenges and put new demands on our education system. There has been generally a growing awareness of the necessity to change and improve the preparation of students for productive functioning in the continually changing and highly demanding environment. In confronting this challenge it is necessary to consider the complexity of the education system itself and the multitude of problems that must be addressed. Clearly, no simple, single uniform approach can be applied with the expectation that significant improvements of the system will occur.

Any strategy for change must contend with the diverse factors affecting the education system, the interactions of its parts, and the intricate interdependencies within it and with its environment. As we consider these problems, we become increasingly cognizant of the various possibilities of using concepts and methods of the study of complex systems for providing direction and strategies to facilitate the introduction of viable and successful changes. A key insight from complex systems is that simple solutions are not likely to be effective in cases such as the education system, and that providing a balance or coexistence of what seem to be opposites may provide the greatest opportunities for successful courses of action.

EDUCATIONAL GOALS

The approaches to teaching can be categorized according to major educational goals that affect teaching strategies. On one hand the goal of education is viewed as the transmission of knowledge by the teachers to the students. On the other hand the goal of education is viewed as facilitating students' autonomous learning and self expression. The former approach which converges toward the teaching of specified subject matter, may be termed 'convergent' teaching and the latter approach which stresses open ended self-directed learning may be termed 'divergent' teaching.

The convergent approach is highly structured and teacher-centered; the students are passive recipients of knowledge transmitted to them and learning achievements are measured by standardized tests. The divergent approach is flexible, student-centered, where the students are active participants in the learning process and learning achievements are assessed by a variety of evaluation tools such as self-evaluation in parallel to teacher evaluation; documentation portfolios; and special projects.

In the highly complex education system there may be various combinations of the different approaches to teaching and probably no 'pure' convergent or divergent teaching. Still, the tendency in the education system of today is toward the convergent approach. In fact, among the current suggestions for implementing educational reforms to deal with the considerable problems of the education system, there has been a strong emphasis on setting convergent goals, an aspect of which is the use of across-the-board standardized testing.

Testing has been commonly viewed as a prudent way to determine the success or failure of the teaching and learning process. There has been a relatively limited use of other means of evaluation which are more complicated and more demanding in terms of application and interpretation.

As educators seek ways to meet the demands put upon the education system in today's world of rapid changes and ever increasing complexity, it may be helpful to recognize that there is a need for both convergent and divergent approaches to teaching and learning. Educators who stress the importance of the acquisition of specific knowledge as a useful way to prepare the students for productive future functioning, must come to realize that even for the purpose of this goal alone, a divergent approach is needed today.

With the great proliferation of knowledge and rapid changes in most fields as well as the appearance of many new fields, it is critical to develop students' capacity for self-directed learning and self growth. On the other hand, those who emphasize the importance of autonomous growth and creative self-expression, must realize that the students need academic skills (such as reading, writing, calculating, etc.) as prerequisites for productive self expression. Since the creative process involves new ways of using existing knowledge, it is important to provide opportunities for students to acquire such knowledge (which can be acquired by convergent teaching).

Hence, convergent and divergent teaching strategies are both needed and the challenging question is how to find the balance between them within the complexity of the process of teaching and learning. It is likely that the two approaches may increasingly become not mutually exclusive but interrelated and interdependent. An important development is the growing awareness that academic achievement could improve by adapting teaching to students individual differences. This awareness is finding its most distinct expression in the education system's attempts to deal with the issues of students with special needs. However, other aspects of adaptation to students' individual differences get far less attention.

In general, adaptation to individual differences under convergent teaching tends to be limited. The students are all expected to strive toward one goal of learning specified required knowledge; some may attain it and others may fall by the wayside or be given some remediation with limited results. Nevertheless, there are various possibilities of effective adaptation to individual differences under convergent teaching. In addition to adaptation in the rate of learning, where each student can be allowed to work at his/her own pace, there are many possibilities of adaptation through the use of diverse methods of teaching. Even when all the students are taught the same material, teachers can use different methods, different techniques or different media, to cater to individual differences in abilities and personality characteristics. Such a 'multi-convergent' approach can be more effective in giving the students opportunities to use their aptitudes and inclinations for learning and attaining higher achievements.

As the students experience success and consequently a sense of competence, their motivation is enhanced to pursue further learning. Such an approach has a better potential for success than the common reality of students with learning difficulties, who often struggle through remediation with a sense of inadequacy and discouraging experiences of failure.

Adaptation to individual differences under divergent teaching may be expected to be productive because of its emphasis on student autonomous, active, self-reliant learning. Yet, there are students who may not function well under divergent conditions because of their strong need for guidance, direction, and structure. Divergent teaching can cater to such needs by individual guidance, along with ongoing assessment and subsequent modifications. This is a 'guided-divergent' approach which is more structured and less flexible than the open divergent teaching but less narrow and limiting than convergent teaching.

TEACHING STRATEGIES AND STUDENTS CHARACTERISTICS

Among the most difficult problems faced by the education system are those associated with teaching effectiveness. The current preparation of teachers for specific age levels, specific subject matter, specific academic skills, etc., does not take into consideration sufficiently the complexity of factors such as students' various characteristics. There is a strong need to train teachers to adapt instruction to the diverse student abilities, learning styles, personality traits and needs by using more differentiated teaching strategies.

In addition to the preparation of teachers to more differentiated teaching, there could be more divergent use of teaching resources. Worthwhile teaching can be done with advantageous results by persons other than the traditional classroom teachers. For example, valuable teaching can be done by peers of different ages and abilities. Also, parents, grandparents, and relatives could participate in and contribute productively to the teaching process. Furthermore, teaching can be enhanced by volunteers, retirees, people with various areas of expertise from the worlds of science, business, engineering, medicine, public service, entertainment, and others. Also, high-tech resources such as multimedia technology, computer programs, telecommunication, the Internet, audio-visual techniques, and others can provide beneficial options.

Student learning can be greatly enriched further by traveling - near and far; interaction with people of different cultures; different geographical areas; different occupations, different ways of life; different outlooks. Undoubtedly, many possibilities exist that are not often implemented even though they could make the teaching and learning process more effective and more beneficial by providing a variety of experiences and alternative strategies for adaptation to students' characteristics.

Ability levels and patterns of different abilities. Presently, the practice in some schools is to adapt teaching to different ability levels by forming classes or groups of students of similar levels (usually based on achievement tests or psychological tests) taught by teachers who tend to treat the students as if they were in homogeneous groups. Obviously, once a group of two students is formed, it cannot be considered homogeneous. Even if the two have an identical IQ, for instance, the profile of different abilities can be quite dissimilar and many other personality characteristics add to the dissimilarity of the students' attributes that affect their learning.

The over-simplification of today's ways of adaptation to students' differences in abilities and other characteristics has resulted in many difficulties in the academic performance of many students. In some cases this has led to phenomena such as, "learning disabilities", "conduct problems", "attitude problems", "anxiety and school phobias". The complexity of this issue is apparent as one considers results of research studies or surveys measuring students' performance under conditions aimed at "slow" versus "fast" learners.

The differences evident in rate of learning are only one aspect of the diverse effects of students with different abilities studying under different conditions. For instance, the type and manner of teaching has differential effects: students with higher ability tend to perform better under non-directive teaching methods while those with lower ability tend to do better under directive methods.

Furthermore, the multiplicity and differentiality of mental abilities must be taken into consideration when teaching at any level of the education system. There has been a growing acknowledgement of the importance of adapting teaching to a variety of intelligences, as well as providing for special learning needs. The diversity of patterns of mental abilities is well recognized today, yet little has been done to develop adequate conditions aimed at adapting teaching to this diversity. It is possible to design instructional strategies and learning materials that provide options and flexibility for matching students' particular patterns of abilities.

Thus, teaching strategies can be differentially facilitating various ability patterns. The interaction between specific aptitudes and specific teaching styles can be important in considering the various options of implementing changes in the teaching and learning process. Also, matching teachers' styles with students' ability patterns can have significant effects on students' attitudes, motivation, and achievements.

Learning styles and preferences affect the way students approach any task and the way they function under different conditions and different learning environments. Learning styles such as reflectivity/impulsivity, field-dependence/field-independence, and mental self-government, as well as preferences for interactive visual or auditory presentations, or other ways of representing information have effects on students' academic performance.

Some educators have begun to acknowledge the importance of adapting teaching strategies to students different learning styles, but no earnest efforts have been devoted to this promising endeavor. The adaptation of teaching to learning styles may include not only more appropriately differentiated teaching strategies but also may add to the dependability of the evaluation measures of what students have learned. Thus, the effectiveness of teaching and the pertinence of the assessment of learning achievements can be enhanced by teachers' adaptation of instructional strategies to students learning styles.

Personality Characteristics. To some extent there is recognition among educators that personality characteristics such as self-reliance, attitudes, anxiety, independence, emotional stability have differential effects on students learning achievements. There is some acknowledgement that attention should be paid to students personality needs and to particular aspects of students different cultural backgrounds.

Nevertheless, while the effect of personality characteristics on learning is significant, very little has been done or even suggested regarding the adaptation of teaching to students different personality traits and needs. Among the reasons for that is the very large number of traits with a wide variety of tests to measure them and the problem of their lower validation than the ability tests. Also, the complexity of the interactions of personality characteristics with various other factors affecting learning seems too difficult to tackle. Many educators and educational administrators are convinced that it is very difficult to implement multi-dimensional teaching strategies in the classroom.

However, it is possible to analyze the interactions between students' and teachers' characteristics and closely examine the resulting different learning outcomes. For example, students of higher ability levels who are also self-reliant, independent, with lower anxiety tend to do better under divergent teaching and self-directed learning conditions, while students of lower ability levels who are also dependent, and anxious, tend to do better under convergent teaching with clear structure and much direction. Such interactions need to be explored further to find more about the various factors affecting the teaching learning process. The outcomes of such exploration can be very helpful in the search for enhancing teaching effectiveness and students achievements.

In sum, the attempts to match teaching strategies with students characteristics may become critical steps toward dealing with some of the particularly difficult problems of the teaching and learning process. Admittedly, many difficulties are faced not only by teachers but also by administrators and policy makers in the endeavor to adapt instructional strategies to students characteristics, but the methods and concepts of the field of complex systems can provide ways of implementing such changes in the attempts to introduce reforms to the education system.

Inter-Disciplinary Curriculum

One of the most exciting developments in the world of science today is the growing involvement of researchers in interdisciplinary collaborations, and the increase in cross-fertilization of ideas and research endeavors of people in different fields of science.. The benefits for cross-disciplinary scientific work are invaluable and the various application possibilities are promising not only for science but for many aspects of daily living.

These developments have direct implications for the education system. The tendency in our schools is to teach bits and pieces of information related to particular disciplines. In view of the cross-disciplinary trends, the curriculum can be integrated around topics that reflect the patterns, interactions, and interdependencies of the different fields. This can provide students with ways to study and attempt to comprehend the world around them through concepts and ideas that are less disparate or disconnected.

The growing inter-disciplinary collaborations and cooperative sharing of information from different fields and the efforts to find pragmatic solutions to global problems have further implications for education. There are important implications for the preparation of students to function and be productive in a world with diverse populations, different economic conditions, multitudes of cultural, religious and ethnic groups, and many other different factors. Furthermore, it is highly beneficial to begin early in the educational process to organize learning around problem solving, critical thinking, and dealing with issues arising from different fields of study and different aspects of real life conditions.

An integrated, inter-disciplinary curriculum links a variety of learning subjects as they are related to the topics of integrated curriculum units. The emphasis on connecting and synthesizing information around topics of interest to the students provides favorable conditions for the acquisition of knowledge from different disciplines through congruous concepts and ideas. Integrated curriculum units are chosen by the students with the teacher and involve teams of students working cooperatively toward common goals. Small groups, pairs, or individuals can work on relevant tasks and materials that can be shared with the other students and yield peer-to-peer learning. Experiencing the benefits of contributing to the goals of the unit by members of the team is empowering and gratifying and is also a beneficial way of preparing them for future functioning in the world. Moreover, the opportunity given to each student to capitalize on his/her strengths can become a strong motivating factor in pursuing further learning and further giving to others.

In terms of teaching strategies, an integrated curriculum encourages a multi-dimensional approach to the educational process and tends to combine regularly multi-convergent and divergent strategies of teaching. There are also various options in the way teachers are assigned to classroom teaching. Individual teachers may find it difficult to implement multi-dimensional strategies in teaching any class, even when small in size. but teachers can work in teams using different teaching strategies compatible with individual teachers' particular capabilities, cognitive styles and personality characteristics.. They can also organize various teaching experiences with the assistance of volunteers, specialists, peers and others who could contribute to the teaching process. In terms of the structure and settings adapted to different teaching and learning conditions, there can be alternative places for learning, e.g. learning centers, laboratories, libraries, outdoors, community institutions and businesses, museums, and various organizations.

The structure and organization of the student body can be in the form of small and large groups; study pairs; and individualized study arrangements. Social alternatives are possible in heterogeneous groups with a great deal of interchange within them and between them and other groups. Clearly, student groups may vary in age, cultural and socioeconomic background, special interests and special needs.

There are various alternatives in the types of learning that an integrated curriculum can include:

— Required subjects and basic academic skills some of which are taught in a convergent way, using, in addition to teachers' didactic presentations, programmed instruction, multi-media technologies, computer programs, videos, and other techniques involving technological innovations.

— A number of required subjects and academic skills can be taught in a multi-convergent way where methods of teaching are adapted to students' different abilities, needs and interests. For example, different intelligences may be emphasized such as, linguistic intelligence, logical-mathematical intelligence, spatial intelligence, musical intelligence, bodily-kinesthetic intelligence, and others.

— A major part of the program can be devoted to integrated inter-disciplinary curriculum units chosen by teachers and students together. These units enable students to acquire knowledge and skills associated with different disciplines through congruous meaningful learning revolving around a topic of interest to the students. The work on the units is undertaken by groups of students who are encouraged to take active part in the decision-making process and focus on aspects of the units in which they can best develop their capabilities, satisfy their interests, and fulfill their needs. Each student is given the opportunity to use their strengths (academic or non-academic) to contribute to the common goals of the group. In working on these integrated units, guided divergent teaching is used as needed.

At the end of a period of work on the unit, the group can celebrate with other students, parents, administrators and others involved in the school, the conclusion and accomplishments of the work on the unit. Each student in the group is encouraged to contribute whatever they can to such celebrations by presenting their work through various performances, presentations, exhibits, videos and other contributions to the festive activities. Such celebrations can become useful ways of evaluating the students' learning achievements

— Individually chosen projects where the students can work on topics they have chosen and where they could apply their strong skills and competencies, wherever they lie. Students can be encouraged to present their work on their project to the group in any way compatible with their tendencies. The students can present their work to their peers and teachers as an exhibit, as an oral presentation, as written material, as a play, a video, or any other means of communicating and disseminating information. Divergent teaching is the approach used for those individually selected, and often independently pursued, projects.

MODELS OF TEACHING-LEARNING PROCESS

Many researchers have tried to put together classroom- or school-based models that describe the teaching-learning process. A model is a visual aid or picture which highlights the main ideas and variables in a process or a system. The models discussed and compared here are Carrol's Model, Proctors Model, Cruickshanks Model, Gage and Berliner's Model and Huitt's Model.

John Carroll's Model

Most current models that categorize the variables or explanations of the many influences on educational processes today stem from Carroll's seminal article defining the major variables related to school learning. Carroll specialized in language and learning, relating words and their meanings to the cognitive concepts and constructs which they create. In his model, Carroll states that time is the most important variable to school learning. A simple equation for Carroll's model is:

School Learning = f (time spent/time needed).

Carroll explains that time spent is the result of opportunity and perseverance. Opportunity in Carroll's model is determined by the classroom teacher; the specific measure is called allotted or allocated time (i.e., time allocated for learning by classroom teachers.) Perseverance is the student's involvement with academic content during that allocated time. Carroll proposed that perseverance be measured as the percentage of the allocated time that students are actually involved in the learning process and was labeled engagement rate. Allocated time multiplied by engagement rate produced the variable Carroll proposed as a measure of time spent, which came to be called engaged time or time-on-task.

Carroll proposed that the time needed by students to learn academic content is contingent upon aptitude (the most often used measure is IQ), ability to understand the instruction presented (the extent to which they possessed prerequisite knowledge), and the quality of instruction students receive in the process of learning. Carroll proposed that these specific teacher and student behaviors and student characteristics where the only variables needed to predict school learning.

The principles of this model can be seen in Bloom's Mastery Learning model. Bloom, a colleague of Carroll's, observed that in traditional schooling a student's aptitude for learning academic material (IQ) is one of the best predictor's of school achievement. His research demonstrated that if time is not held constant for all learners (as it is in traditional schooling) then a student's mastery of the prerequisite skills, rather than aptitude, is a better predictor of school learning. Mastery Learning's basic principle is that almost all students can earn A's if

1) students are given enough time to learn normal information taught in school, and
2) students are provided quality instruction.

By quality instruction Bloom meant that teachers should:

(1) organize subject matter into manageable learning units,

(2) develop specific learning objectives for each unit,

(3) develop appropriate formative and summative assessment measures, and

(4) plan and implement group teaching strategies, with sufficient time allocations, practice opportunities, and corrective reinstruction for all students to reach the desired level of mastery.

Proctor's Model

Prior to the sixties the research on important school- and classroom-related variables was directed toward the best traits or characteristics of teachers in an attempt to identify good teaching and the important characteristics of schools and communities that support good teaching. Proctor provides a model that updates this view by including important teacher and student behaviors as predictors of student achievement. It is derived from other teacher- and classroom-based models but is redesigned to emphasize teacher expectations.

Proctor states that it is possible for a self-fulfilling prophesy to be an institutional phenomenon and the climate of a school can have an effect on the achievement of its learners. The attitudes, the norms, and the values of an educational faculty and staff can make a difference in achievement test scores. The paradigm most influencing Proctor's model is that of a social nature and not of a teacher/student one-on-one relationship. The other models include the variables that provide the focus for this model, but show these variables in a more subordinate manner.

Proctor's model begins with the factor of the School's Social Climate. Some of the variables included in this would be attitudes, norms, beliefs, and prejudices. This school climate is influenced by a number of factors, including such student characteristics as race, gender, economic level, and past academic performance.

The student characteristics also influence teacher attitudes and teacher efficacy. More recent studies support Proctor's position that student self-image and behavior are affected by teacher efficacy.

The next category of variables is the interaction among the individuals involved in the schooling process. This includes the input of administrators as well as that of teachers and students. If expectations of learning are high (i.e., the school has good, qualified teachers and students who can learn) and there is high quality instructional input, corrective feedback, and good communication among students, parents, and educators, then the intermediate outcomes of student learning and student self-expectation goes up. On the other hand, adverse or negative attitudes on the part of instructors and administrators will cause student self-esteem, and consequently, student achievement to spiral downwards.

The interactions in Proctor's model include the school's overall policy on allowing time for children to learn or promoting other forms of student-based help when needed. This could include quality of instruction or teacher classroom behaviors. These behaviors have an effect on student classroom performance (especially academic learning time and curriculum coverage) and self-expectations .

Finally, the student's achievement level in Proctor's model is an outcome of all previous factors and variables. It is hypothesized that there is a cyclical relationship among the variables. In Proctor's model, the main concept is that achievement in a specific classroom during a particular school year is not an end in itself. It is refiltered into the social climate of the school image and the entire process begins all over again. Proctor's model implies that change can be made at any point along the way. These changes will affect school achievement, which will continue to affect the social climate of the school.

Cruickshank's Model

The model by Cruickshank is more classroom- and teacher-based; he was heavily influenced by models created by Mitzel, Biddle, and Flanders. Mitzel contributed the concept of classifying variables as "product, process, or presage". Product is learning on the part of the student (change in behavior or behavior potential) while process involves interaction between student and teacher. Presage is the teacher's intelligence, level of experience, success and other teacher characteristics. Presage is supposed to affect process and then, of course, process will affect the product.

Biddle showed a relationship between specific learning activities and teacher effects. In his model, Biddle offers seven categories of variables related to schooling and student achievement: school and community contents, formative experiences, classroom situations, teacher properties, teacher behaviors, intermediate effects, and long-term consequences. This provides the foundation for Cruickshank's model.

Biddle also contributed a model of the transactional process of the classroom by analyzing the structure and function of the communication process. This is reflected in Cruickshank's model through the use of arrows depicting the interaction between teacher and pupil classroom behavior.

Biddle constructed his models to help answer questions he thought parents might ask, such as: "How often does my child get individual attention from the teacher?" Or, "Does the teacher really understand Junior's special problem?". Biddle also helped define non-cognitive variables which contribute to the affective domain (i.e., self-concept and self-esteem of the students). An example of these variables would be teacher genuineness, "teacher-offered conditions of respect...and modification of low self-concept".

Flanders offered the variables of teacher- and student-classroom-talk and devised an instrument which focused on this behavior. "His was the most frequently used instrument. It permitted observation of teachers' use of 'verbal influence,' defined as 'teacher talk' and 'pupil talk,' in a variety of classroom situations". Cruickshank put them all together and added additional presage variables such as pupil characteristics, properties (abilities and attitudes) and school, community and classroom climate.

Gage and Berliner's Model

Gage and Berliner developed a model of the instructional process that focuses on those variables that must be considered by the classroom teacher as she designs and delivers instruction to students. This model attempts to define more precisely what is meant by "quality instruction" and presents five tasks associated with the instruction/learning process. The model is classroom- and teacher-based and centers around the question, "What does a teacher do?"

A teacher begins with objectives and ends with an evaluation. Instruction connects objectives and evaluations and is based on the teacher's knowledge of the students' characteristics and how best to motivate them. If the evaluations do not demonstrate that the desired results have been achieved, the teacher re-teaches the material and starts the process all over again. Classroom management is subsumed under the rubric of motivating students. Gage and Berliner suggest that the teacher should use research and principles from educational psychology to develop proper teaching procedures to obtain optimal results.

Huitt's Model

The most recently developed model to be discussed identifies the major categories of variables that have been related to school achievement. The model is not only school-, classroom-, teacher-, and student-based, but includes additional contextual influences as well. Huitt's model attempts to categorize and organize all the variables that might be used to answer the question, "Why do some students learn more than other students?" This is a revision of a model by Squires, Huitt and Segars which focused only on those variables thought to be under the control of educators.

This earlier model focused on school- and classroom-level processes that predicted school learning as measured on standardized tests of basic skills. One important addition in this model is the redefinition of Academic Learning Time. It had long been recognized that Carroll's conceptualization of time spent measured the quantity of time engaged in academics, but was lacking in terms of the quality of that time.

As discussed in Proctor's model, Fisher and his colleagues had added the concept of success as an important component of quality of time spent and coined the term Academic Learning Time (ALT) which they defined as "engaged in academic learning at a high success rate." Brady, Clinton, Sweeney, Peterson, & Poynor added another quality component—the extent to which content covered in the classroom overlaps to content tested—which they called content overlap. Squires et al. used the more inclusive definition of ALT proposed by Caldwell, Huitt & Graeber—"the amount of time students are successfully engaged on content that will be tested."

Huitt's model adds variables related to context and student and teacher characteristics, some of which were the focus of the models by Proctor and Cruickshank. It is an interactive model along the lines of Biddle and Ellena, Cruickshank, and Laosa.

Huitt advocates that important context variables must be considered because our society is rapidly changing from an agricultural/industrial base to an information base. From this perspective, children are members of a multi-faceted society, which influences and modifies the way they process learning as well as defines the important knowledge and skills that must be acquired to be successful in that society. Huitt's model shows a relationship among the categories of Context (family, home, school, and community environments), Input (what students and teachers bring to the classroom process), Classroom Processes (what is going on in the classroom),and Output (measures of learning done outside of the classroom). These categories appear superimposed in the model since it is proposed they are essentially intertwined in the learning process.

This model shows Input and Output as the beginning and end of the teaching/learning process. Huitt believes that educators must first identify or propose an end result because how you identify and measure the end product (Output) will influence the selection of important predictor variables. Until the outcome objectives are known, nothing else can be considered. Once outcome measures are selected, educators can begin to focus on those variables that can explain fluctuation or variability in those measures. Considering or changing specific goals or objectives may change the predictor variables from each of the other three categories. Thus, the Output or Outcome category is the most important and the focus of Huitt's model.

In the United States, the most often cited Output measures are scores on standardized tests of basic skills such as reading, language arts, and mathematics as well as science and social studies. Since the United States is ranked 14th out of 15 countries in mathematics knowledge and 13th in science, we need to take a very close look at how we can improve achievement on these measures.

However, student achievement in basic skills is not the only desired outcome of American education. The Secretary of Labor presented additional requirements in the report by the Secretary's Commission on Achieving Necessary Skills (SCANS). The SCANS report focuses on the skills necessary for students to find work in the information economy. It addresses two categories of skills: foundations (basic skills, thinking skills and personal qualities) that provide the platform on which the other skills will be built and competencies (handling resources, interpersonal skills, informational skills, system skills, and technology utilization skills) that more closely describe what workers will actually be doing.

The most direct impact on important measures of school learning are those variables related to Classroom Processes. This category includes two major subcategories (Teacher Behavior and Student Behavior), and an Other (or miscellaneous) subcategory that includes such variables as classroom climate and student leadership roles..

The category of Teacher Behavior includes the subcategories of planning (getting ready for classroom interaction), management (getting the class under control), and instruction (guiding the learning process). In general, planning activities have little predictable relationship to student achievement. Both management and instructional variables are moderately related to achievement, but the lack of a strong relationship may be due to be a factor of teacher inconsistency. That is, teachers often change their management and instructional practices based on the time of day or the characteristics of a particular group of students.

Three single variables, teachers providing corrective feedback (e.g., give an explanation of what is correct or incorrect and why), teachers' use of reinforcement, and level of student-teacher interaction seem to be the best single classroom predictors of student success. Direct or explicit instruction appears to be the best model of instruction when scores on standardized tests of basic skills is used as the outcome measure.

Huitt supports Proctor's position that intermediate outcomes, or more specifically Academic Learning Time (ALT) is one of the best Classroom Process predictors of student achievement. As stated above ALT is defined as "the amount of time students are successfully involved in the learning of content that will be tested." There are three components to ALT and each is as important as the other. The first is Content

Overlap, defined as "the extent to which the content objectives covered on the standardized test overlaps with the content objectives covered in the classroom." This variable has also been labeled as "time-on-target." The idea is simple: if an objective or topic is not taught, it is not likely to be learned, and therefore we cannot expect students to do well on measures of that content. In fact, to the extent the content is not specifically taught, the test becomes an intelligence test rather than an achievement test. The fact that many educators do not connect instructional objectives to specific objectives that will be tested, is one reason that academic aptitude or IQ is such a good predictor of scores on standardized tests. Both tests measure the same construct: the amount of general knowledge an individual has obtained that is not necessarily taught in a structured learning setting.

The second component of ALT is Student Involvement, defined the same way that Carroll defined engaged time or time-on-task (allocated time X engagement rate). If the students are not provided enough time to learn material or are not actively involved while teachers are teaching they are not as likely to do well on measures of school achievement at the end of the year. The last element is that of Success, defined as "the percentage of classwork that students complete with a high degree of accuracy." If a student is not successful throughout the year on classroom academic tasks, that student will likely not demonstrate success on the achievement measure at the end of the year.

Huitt proposes that these three components of Academic Learning Time should be considered as the "vital signs" of a classroom. Just as a physician looks at data regarding temperature, weight, and blood pressure before asking any further questions or gathering any other data, supervisors need to look at the content overlap, involvement, and success before collecting any other data or making suggestions about classroom modifications. Classrooms where students are involved and making adequate progress on important content are reasonably healthy and quite different from those classrooms where students are not.

In addition to the teacher's classroom behavior, other time components such as the number of days available for going to school (the school year), the number of days the student actually attends school (attendance year), and the number of hours the student has available to go to school each day (school day) can influence ALT. None of these additional time variables were included in Carroll's model.

What teachers and students do in the classroom will depend to some extent on the characteristics or qualities they bring to the teaching/learning process. In Huitt's (1995) model these are labeled Input variables. The subcategory of Teacher Characteristics includes such variables as values and beliefs; knowledge of students and the teaching/learning process; thinking, communication and performance skills; and personality. While each of these is important to the classroom environment, teacher efficacy is one of the best predictors of student success from this subcategory. If a teacher believes that, in general, students can learn the knowledge or skills, and that, specifically, he can teach them, then that teacher is more likely to use the knowledge and skills he has and the students are more likely to learn.

A second subcategory of Input is Student Characteristics. This includes all of the descriptions of students that might have an influence on the teaching/learning process and student outcome. Study Habits; Learning Style; Age; Sex/Gender; Race/Ethnicity; Motivation; and Moral, Socioemotional, Cognitive, and Character Development all become important in the relationship of classroom processes/behavior and school achievement. However, student aptitude and/or prerequisite skills are probably the best student characteristic predictors. If time is held constant, then intelligence or ability to learn academic content will be a better predictor than prior knowledge because the amount of content learned in the classroom is allowed to vary. That is, if everyone has the same amount of time in which to learn, then the speed at which one learns (aptitude) will be the best predictor of achievement. However, if we vary the time students have to learn and keep the content to be learned constant (such as in Mastery Learning), then prior knowledge is more salient. Though we do not initially modify the student characteristics that each student brings to the classroom, as Proctor pointed out the teacher can arrange the teaching/learning process and modify each student's experience. This results in different Outcomes, which in turn becomes the Input for the next learning cycle.

Finally, Huitt includes the category of Context that includes such subcategories as School Processes and Characteristics, Family, Community, State and Federal Government, TV/Movies, and the Global Environment. For example, research shows that student achievement is impacted by class size and school size. While all of the variables in these subcategories are important and influence variables in the other three major categories, probably the two most important are Family and the Global Environment.

Mother's education and family expectations for student achievement have been shown to be excellent predictors of student achievement as well as the amount of technology in the home. Perhaps even more significant is the movement from the industrial age to the information age. This is because it is redefining the outcomes that ought to be the focus of schooling and is providing new technologies that can radically alter the teaching/learning process.

An simple example of how some of these variables might interact is shown in the following model. The size and region of the community combine with family characteristics and processes to impact teacher and student characteristics. School and state policies combine with teacher and student characteristics to impact teacher behavior, while student characteristics and teacher behavior influence student behavior.

Student classroom behavior then influences teacher classroom behavior in an interactive pattern that eventually results in student achievement as measured by instruments influenced by state policies. Student achievement at the end of one school year then becomes a student characteristic at the beginning of the next.

BEHAVIOURISM, CONSTRUCTIVISM AND TEACHING-LEARNING PROCESS

The continued expansion of education clearly indicates that teachers are in a position to exert an ever-increasing amount of influence on everyone's life. It is reasonable to say that the kind of future we and our children will experience would be influenced more by teachers than any other professional group. The world of tomorrow will be shaped not only by what today's students learn but by the way they learn it, for it is the way knowledge is presented that determines how students will learn to solve problems.

Teachers need a rich understanding of facts and theories about learning which will help us view learning realistically, increase our awareness of the different ways we can teach that will most benefit our students and enable us to understand why teachers succeed or fail.

Contributors of Behaviourism

The behaviourist approach to studying learning focuses on environmental conditions that stimulate learning. Behaviour-oriented researchers attempt to discover the rules that govern the formation of relationships between stimuli and responses. Thus, behaviourist theories are often referred to as stimulus-response (S-R) theories.

One of the earliest contributions to understanding learning in terms of S-R connections was made by Ivan P. Pavlov. Pavlov discovered 'Classical Conditioning', a process wherein a neutral stimulus (such as a bell) that produces an orienting response when presented by itself, is capable of eliciting a conditioned response (such as salivation), after being paired with an unconditioned stimulus (such as meat).

Pavlov's work was employed by John B. Watson, to demonstrate that emotional reactions of humans could be modified by classical conditioning procedures. He coined the term 'behaviourism'. Later, E.L.Thorndike enumerated the various laws of learning that have important implications for educational practise including the value of reinforcement, repetition and readiness to learn.

Another behaviourist explanation of learning was offered by B.F.Skinner, who did much work on Operant Conditioning. To produce operant conditioning, a stimulus is introduced after an organism makes a particular response (or an operant). When this operant is followed by reinforcement the probability of its reoccurrence increases. Skinner observed that a great deal of human behaviour is modified by reinforcement.

Contributors of Constructivism

Constructivism refers to a philosophy of teaching and learning that stands diametrically opposed to behaviourism. Several of the concepts underlying the constructivist approach to learning have been reflected in the work of Dewey, Piaget, Vygotsky, Bruner and other educational theorists and researchers.

Learning, according to the constructivists, is a process whereby new meanings are created by the learner within the context of his/her current knowledge. Constructivists view children as inherently active, self-regulating learners who construct knowledge in developmentally appropriate ways within their social context. Constructivists believe that only full participation of children in their own learning will lead to deep, real and rich understanding and use of knowledge which in turn will lead to the ability to apply what is learned.

Behavioural Models in Schools Today

Contemporary schooling and much of the work we do with children with learning disabilities is largely influenced by the behaviouristic principles we have just reviewed. Some of the instructional outgrowths of this theory are:

Quantification

A fundamental principle of curriculum design, lesson planning and classroom management is that education must be quantifiable in terms of amount or time. Thus, we count everything - the number of school days, the number of periods, the number of hours spent on a subject etc.

Task Analysis

Most learning that is useful for students is complex and can be difficult for an individual to learn all at once. This difficulty is compounded by the learning problems of children with learning disability. Instructions need to be systematic, constantly building on previous learning. To this end, task analysis can be an effective procedure for developing a progressive series of linked steps.

Reinforcement Strategies and Behaviour Modification

Thorndike's laws of readiness and effect and Skinnerian reinforcement principles, are mainstays of the motivation and control tactics that today's teachers routinely employ. In a well-managed classroom or resource room today, the teacher will choose instructional materials that are interesting and age-suitable to the students. She will have a clear system of positive reinforcement, negative reinforcement or rarely even punishment, or will employ a system of differential reinforcement etc.

Direct Instruction

The Skinnerian influence is particularly clear in methods that can be grouped under the term direct instruction or explicit teaching. One of the most acknowledged principles to be applied in the remedial treatment of children with learning disability is direct instruction. Haring & Bateman make the point that children with learning disabilities do not learn by osmosis, as other children seem to. Rather, they need direct, intensive, and systematic inputs from, and interaction with the teacher.

Strategy Instruction

Individuals with learning disabilities need to learn the same things that other students learn. To do this successfully, they have a particular need to learn how to efficiently and effectively engage in the process of learning. One way students can increase the efficiency and effectiveness of their learning is to become more strategic

Role of the Teacher

An appraisal of these instructional outgrowths of the behaviourist's school of thought gives us a clear view of the teacher's role according to this view of learning. The teacher's primary responsibility is to arrange the instructional environment to provide opportunities for supervised practise, feedback, and application.

Constructivism in Schools Today

Constructivism represents a philosophy about teaching and learning rather than one specific approach or instruction practise. Generally adherents of this philosophy believe that children will learn all they need to learn and will develop their skills through social interaction and immersion in authentic learning experiences within meaningful contexts. Some outgrowths of this approach are:

Interdisciplinary Curriculum

Over the past few years, interest in and need for curriculum integration has intensified. Curriculum becomes more relevant when there are connections between subjects and when knowledge is presented in a unified manner.

An important aspect of this curriculum design is the use of long-term integrated projects. Knowledge is not a stack of separate lessons but is rather a network of inter-related ideas. For students with learning disabilities finding active linkages, various areas of knowledge may be the best way to learn.

Open Classrooms

The constructivist view that the learning of young people will be facilitated if the learning environment offers a wide variety of materials that can be touched and handled or provides contact with objects and events outside the school. Horwitz who studied the psychological effects of open classrooms found that the choice of activities by students, richness and variety of materials, integration of curricular areas and preference for individual or small-group activities had a positive impact on the attainment of cognitive goals.

Cooperative Learning

Constructivism views learning as a socially situated activity. A number of researchers have concluded that the cognitive processes most necessary for a deep level understanding occur only through interaction with other people. This is supported by the work of Vygotsky, who believes that the internal development processes that are necessary for learning, are only able to develop when children are interacting with people in their environment and in cooperation with their peers.

Cooperative learning groups are heterogeneous groups of children created to facilitate social interaction, communication, collective problem solving, brainstorming, and construction of meaning and ownership of learning.

To give you a general sense of what cooperative learning is like and to avoid limiting you to any one individual's approach, the following discussion is a synthesis of the main features of each approach.

— *Group Heterogeneity:* The size of cooperative-learning groups is relatively small and as heterogeneous as circumstances allow. The recommended size is usually four to five students. At the very least, groups should contain both males and females and students of different ability levels. If possible, different ethnic backgrounds and social classes should be represented as well.

— *Group Goals/Positive Interdependence:* A specific goal, such as a grade or a certificate of recognition, is identified for the group to attain. Students are told that they will have to support one another because the group goal can be achieved only if each member learns the material being taught (in the case of a task that culminates in an exam) or makes a specific contribution to the group's effort (in the case of a task that culminates in a presentation or a project).

— *Promotive Interaction:* This element is made necessary by the existence of positive interdependence. Students are shown how to help each other overcome problems and complete whatever task has been assigned. This may involve episodes of peer tutoring, temporary assistance, exchanges of information and material, challenging of each other's reasoning, feedback, and encouragement to keep one another highly motivated.

— *Individual Accountability:* This feature stipulates that each member of a group has to make a significant contribution to achieving the group's goal. This may be satisfied by achieving a minimal score on a test, having the group's test score be the sum or average of each student's quiz scores, or having each member be responsible for a particular part of a project (such as doing the research and writing for a particular part of a history report).

— *Interpersonal Skills:* Positive interdependence and promotive interaction are not likely to occur if students do not know how to make the most of their face-to-face interactions. And you can safely assume that the interpersonal skills most students possess are probably not highly developed. As a result, they have to be taught such basic skills as leadership, decision making, trust building, clear communication, and conflict management. The conflict that arises over differences of opinion, for example, can be constructive if it is used as a stimulus to search for more information or to rethink one's conclusions. But it can destroy group cohesion and productivity if it results in students stubbornly clinging to a position or referring to each other as "stubborn," "dumb," or "nerdy."

Equal Opportunities for Success: Because cooperative groups are heterogeneous with respect to ability and their success depends on positive interdependence, promotive interaction, and individual accountability, it is important that steps be taken to ensure that all students have an opportunity to contribute to their team. You can do this by awarding points for degree of improvement over previous test scores, having students compete against comparable members of other teams in a game- or tournament-like atmosphere, or giving students learning assignments (such as math problems) that are geared to their current level of skill.

Team Competition: This may seem to be an odd entry in a list of cooperative-learning components, especially in light of the comments we made earlier about the ineffectiveness of competition as a spur to motivation. But we're not being contradictory. The main problem with competition is that it is rarely used appropriately. When competition occurs between well-matched competitors, is done in the absence of a norm-referenced grading system, and is not used too frequently, it can be an effective way to motivate students to cooperate with each other.

Effects of cooperative learning: In the vast majority of studies, forms of cooperative learning have been shown to be more effective than noncooperative reward structures in raising the levels of variables that contribute to motivation, in raising achievement, and in producing positive social outcomes.

— *Effect on Motivation:* Because a student's sense of self-esteem can have a strong effect on motivation, this variable has been examined in several cooperative-learning studies. The results are encouraging, yet confusing. Slavin found that in eleven of fifteen studies, cooperative learning produced bigger increases in some aspect of self-esteem (general self-esteem, academic self-esteem, social self-esteem) than the noncooperative method with which it was compared. But these effects were not consistent across studies. Some researchers would report increases in academic self-esteem or social self-esteem, but others would find no effect.

  Adding to the confusion is the conclusion drawn by Johnson and Johnson that cooperative learning consistently produced higher self-efficacy scores than did competitive or individualistic conditions. Such inconsistencies may reflect weaknesses in the self-esteem instruments that were used, weaknesses in the designs of the studies (many cooperative-learning studies last anywhere from a few days to a few weeks, yet changes in self-esteem happen slowly), or differences in specific cooperative-learning programs. Perhaps future research will clarify this issue.

  Another way in which cooperative learning contributes to high levels of motivation is in the proacademic attitudes that it fosters among group members. Slavin cites several studies in which students in cooperative-learning groups felt more strongly than did other students that their groupmates wanted them to come to school every day and work hard in class.

Probably because of such features as promotive interaction and equal opportunities for success, cooperative learning has been shown to have a positive effect on motivation inducing attributions. Students in cooperative-learning groups were more likely to attribute success to hard work and ability than to luck.

A strong indicator of motivation is the actual amount of time students spend working on a task. Most studies have found that cooperative-learning students spend significantly more time on-task than do control students.

— *Effect on Achievement:* Slavin examined several dozen studies that lasted four or more weeks and that used a variety of cooperative-learning methods. Overall, students in cooperative-learning groups scored about one-fourth of a standard deviation higher on achievement tests than did students taught conventionally. This translates to an advantage of 10 percentile ranks (60th percentile for the average cooperative-learning student versus 50th percentile for the average conventionally taught student). But the beneficial effect of cooperative learning varied widely as a function of the particular method used. The best performances occurred with two techniques called Student Teams-Achievement Divisions and Teams-Games-Tournaments. The cooperative-learning features that seem to be most responsible for learning gains are group goals and individual accountability.

David Johnson, Roger Johnson, and Karl Smith also reviewed much of the cooperative-learning literature but drew a somewhat different conclusion. They found that the test scores of students in the cooperative-learning groups were about two-thirds of a standard deviation higher than the test scores of students in competitive or individualistic situations. This translates to an advantage of 25 percentile ranks (75th versus 50th). It's not clear why Slavin's analysis produced a somewhat lower estimate of the size of the advantage produced by cooperative learning. It may be due in part to differences in the studies cited by each;

Slavin focused on studies lasting at least four weeks. It may also be due to differences in the cooperative techniques used by various researchers.

In addition to achievement outcomes, researchers have also assessed the impact of cooperative learning on problem solving. Given the complex nature of problem solving and the multiple resources that a cooperative group has at its disposal, one would logically expect cooperative learning to have a positive effect on this outcome as well. This hypothesis was confirmed by Zhining Qin, David Johnson, and Roger Johnson. After reviewing forty-six studies, they concluded that students of all age levels (elementary, secondary, college, adult) who worked cooperatively outscored students who worked competitively. The average student in a cooperative group solved more problems correctly than 71 percent of the students who worked competitively.

— *Effect on Social Relationships:* In most studies students exposed to cooperative learning were more likely than students who learned under competitive or individualistic conditions to name a classmate from a different race, ethnic group, or social class as a friend or to label such individuals as "nice" or "smart." In some studies the friendships that were formed were deemed to be quite strong. A similar positive effect was found for students with mental disabilities who were mainstreamed. Finally, the cooperation skills that students learn apparently transfer. Cooperative-learning students were more likely than other students to use the cooperative behaviors they were taught when they worked with new classmates.

Students who learn cooperatively tend to be more highly motivated to learn because of increased self-esteem, the proacademic attitudes of groupmates, appropriate attributions for success and failure, and greater on-task behavior. They also score higher on tests of achievement and problem solving and tend to get along better with classmates of different racial, ethnic, and social class backgrounds. This last outcome should be of particular interest to those of you who expect to teach in areas marked by cultural diversity.

Why Does Cooperative Learning Work?: When researchers attempt to explain the widespread positive effects that are typically found among studies of cooperative learning, they usually cite one or more of the following explanations.

— *Motivational Effect:* The various features of cooperative learning, particularly positive interdependence, are highly motivating because they encourage such achievement-oriented behaviors as trying hard, attending class regularly, praising the efforts of others, and receiving help from one's groupmates. Learning is seen as an obligation and a valued activity because the group's success is based on it and one's groupmates will reward it.

— *Cognitive Development Effect*: According to Lev Vygotsky, collaboration promotes cognitive growth because students model for each other more advanced ways of thinking than any would demonstrate individually. According to Jean Piaget, collaboration among peers hastens the decline of egocentrism and allows the development of more advanced ways of understanding and dealing with the world.

— *Cognitive Elaboration Effect*: New information that is elaborated (restructured and related to existing knowledge) is more easily retrieved from memory than is information that is not elaborated. A particularly effective means of elaboration is explaining something to someone else. Now that you are familiar with interpretations of motivation, it is time to consider in the Suggestions for Teaching that follow how the information and speculations you've learned can be converted into classroom practice.

Cooperative Learning in Multicultural Education Programs: The general idea behind cooperative learning is that by working in small heterogeneous groups (of four or five students total) and by helping one another master the various aspects of a particular task, students will be more motivated to learn, will learn more than if they had to work independently, and will forge stronger interpersonal relationships than they would by working alone.

There are several forms of cooperative learning, one of which is Student Team Learning. Student Team Learning techniques are built on the concepts of team reward, individual accountability, and equal opportunities for success. Team reward means that teams are not in competition with one another for limited rewards. All of the teams, some of them, or none of them may earn whatever rewards are made available depending on how well the team's performance matches a predetermined standard. Individual accountability means that each member of the team must perform at a certain level for the team's effort to be judged successful. It is not permissible for one team member's above-average performance to compensate for another team member's below-average performance. Finally, equal opportunities for success allow students of all ability levels to contribute to their team's success by improving on their own past performances.

Robert Slavin, a leading exponent of cooperative learning, reports that cooperative learning produced significantly higher levels of achievement than did noncooperative arrangements in sixty-three of ninety-nine studies (64 percent). The results for the Student Team Learning programs have been the most consistently positive. Although cooperative learning is a generally effective instructional tactic, it is likely to be particularly useful with Hispanic-American and Native American students. Children from both cultures often come from extended families that emphasize cooperation and sharing. Thus, these students may be more prepared than other individuals to work productively as part of a group by carrying out their own responsibilities as well as helping others do the same.

Discovery Learning

From the work of Piaget, Bruner, Dewey and several others grew our understanding that minds acquire knowledge through an active quest for it. This leads to the idea that the teacher must engage the mind in that quest - to challenge, puzzle, encourage exploration, and guide exploration. This general collection of teaching ideas grew into what is known as discovery learning.

Instructional Strategies

A teacher adhering to the constructivist theory has a wide array of instructional techniques to choose from. A few of them are listed below:

— *Scaffolding*-This is a procedure by which the teacher provides supports that students cannot yet provide. Generally, the student presents ideas, the teacher raises issues that the student has not considered or clarifies certain ideas and together they work out solutions .

— *Exploration and Reflection* - In this procedure the teacher pushes the students into new domains of application requiring them to manipulate, interact, talk and figure out a situation. Reflection is a process that the teacher encourages the students to engage in while exploring or subsequent to exploration when students mentally or verbally go over their experiences to gain insight.

— *Brainstorming* - This is one of a number of techniques in which a problem is posed and students are encouraged to find as many solutions and answers as possible. The student is encouraged to use the problem as the starting point and seek many different solutions instead of the right one. It is claimed that groups that brainstormed could produce solutions that were superior to solutions that would have been attained if each of their members had worked alone.

— *The Teachable Moment and Mini lessons* - Constructivist teachers teach through the provision of authentic and meaningful experiences and oppose decontextualised direct teaching. Teaching of specific skills or specific information happens while the children are engaged in meaningful activity and when the children indicate readiness to learn in what is termed the teachable moment.

Peterson & Eeds state that teachers "act as a guide, naming elements in the context of the conversation as they arise, and "shoot arrows" of literary insight at appropriate moments for the children's consideration."

A Balanced and Integrated Approach

To this future teacher of students with learning disabilities who neither belongs to the constructivist camp nor the behaviourist camp, with an interest in how best children learn, the loud rhetoric from both sides seems pointless. Reviewing the considerable literature on behaviourist and constructivist theories and instructional practises one is struck by the immense potential each carries if only used appropriately. Constructivist approaches to learning with their rich social interaction authentic learning experiences, focus on problem solving, discussion and inquiry, discovery learning and capitalisation of student interests undoubtedly has positive outcomes for children with learning disabilities.

While encouraging this approach, there seems to be no need to reject explicit skill instruction which is vital to the growth and success of children with learning disabilities who have greater difficulty than their peers in attaining fluency and automaticity with skills and strategies. Student needs should guide our teaching. This skill instruction can be integrated into the larger constructivist-learning context.

LEARNING STRATEGIES

Learning strategies refer to methods that students use to learn and range from techniques for improved memory to better studying or test-taking strategies. For example, the *loci method* is a classic memory improvement technique; it involves making associations between facts to be remembered and particular locations (usually familiar ones). To remember something, you simply visualise places and the associated facts. Such systematic procedures or strategies for improving memory are called *mnemonics* and include keyword mnemonics, pegword mnemonics, chainword or linking mnemonics.

Some learning strategies involve specific changes to the how instruction should be designed. For example, the use of questions before, during or after instruction, has been shown to increase the degree of learning. Methods that attempt to increase the degree of learning that occurs have been called 'mathemagenic'. A typical study skill program is SQ3R which suggests 5 steps:

— *Survey* the material to be learned;

— Develop *Questions* about the material;

— *Read* the material;

— *Recall* the key ideas; and,

— *Review* the material.

A number of learning theories emphasise the importance of using learning strategies—for example, lateral thinking.

Locus of control

Perhaps one of the most talked about concepts in CAL is the locus of control in learning activities—specifically, whether the locus of control is centred on the learner(s), the computer or perhaps, the teacher. In terms of classifying CAL, it is possible to offer views on the nature of control in learning activities. For example, in the classification by educational paradigm, there is a continuum that represents learner control, with least control being offered to the learner by software of the instructional paradigm, and most control offered by software of the conjectural and emancipatory paradigms.

Similarly, there is a continuum within the classification by software type. Here, least learner control is provided by using the computer as a tuter; and most control is offered by using the computer as a tool.

Mastery

In an individualistic goal structure (rather than cooperative goal structure), students work independently and are evaluated only on their own achievements, regardless of how others do in the learning task. One popular teaching method consistent with individualistic goal structures is *mastery learning*, a concept that is based on the assumption that given enough time and appropriate instruction, most students can master the learning objectives.

John B. Carroll first argued for the concept of mastery learning in 1963, suggesting that the focus of instruction should be the time required for different students to learn the same material—this contrasted with the then-classic model, in which all students are given the same amount of time to learn and the instructional focus is on student differences in ability.

The idea of mastery learning amounts to a radical shift in responsibility for teachers: the blame for a student's failure rests with the instruction not a lack of ability on the part of the student. In a mastery learning environment, the challenge becomes providing enough time and employing instructional strategies so that all students can achieve the same level of learning

The key elements in mastery learning are:

— Clearly specifying what is to be learned and how it will be evaluated;

— Allowing students to learn at their own pace;

— Assessing student progress and providing appropriate feedback or remediation; and,

— Testing that final learning critierion has been achieved.

Mastery learning has been widely applied in schools and training settings, and research shows that it can improve instructional effectiveness. On the other hand, there are some theoretical and practical weaknesses including the fact that people do differ in ability and tend to reach different levels of achievement. Furthermore, mastery learning programmes tend to require considerable amounts of time and effort to implement which most teachers and schools are not prepared to expend. The mastery learning model is closely aligned with the use of instructional objectives and the systematic design of instructional programs. The framework provided by Skinner with its emphasis on individualised learning and the importance of feedback (i.e. reinforcement) is also relevant to mastery learning.

The concept and elements of mastery learning are reflected in much of CAL, since educational programs, whatever type of software they belong to, usually facilitate individual students to learn at their own pace and provide some feedback and reinforcement; in some cases, particularly for drill and practice software, remediation is also given.

Memory

Memory is one of the most important concepts in learning - if things are not remembered, learning cannot take place. Futhermore, memory serves as a battleground for opposing theories and paradigms of learning. According to some behaviourist theories (e.g. Thorndike; Skinner), remembering is a function of Stimulus-Response pairings which acquire strength due to contiguity or reinforcement. On the other hand, cognitive theories of learning (e.g. Miller) insist that *meaning* plays an important role in remembering.

In particular, Miller suggests that information is organised in memory into meaningful 'chunks'. For working memory, this is important, since working memory is limited to the *number* of bits of information it can hold, rather than the size of each bit—and so by deliberately 'chunking' information commited to memory (remembering six digits in chunks of two digits each, thereby reducing the amount of information to be remembered from six to three) it is possible to manipulate more information in working memory. The limitations of working memory have been shown, of late, to have important consequences for designing instructional software.

The idea that memory is always an active reconstruction of existing knowledge is championed by Bruner and is also found in the theories of Ausubel and Schank . Some theories of memory have concerned themselves with the nature of the processing. For example, Paivio suggests a dual coding scheme for verbal and visual information, specifying how information should be organised for optimal learning.

Mental models

Mental models are representations of reality that people use to understand specific phenomena. Norman describes them as follows:

> In interacting with the environment, with others, and with the artifacts of technology, people form internal, mental models of themselves and of the things with which they are interacting. These models provide predictive and explanatory power for understanding the interaction.

Mental models are consistent with theories that postulate internal representations in thinking processes. Johnson-Laird proposes mental models as the basic structure of cognition: 'It is now plausible to suppose that mental models play a central and unifying role in representing objects, states of affairs, sequences of events, the way the world is, and the social and psychological actions of daily life.' . Holland, et al., suggest that mental models are the basis for all reasoning processes.

Some of the characteristics of mental models are:

— They are incomplete and constantly evolving.

- They are usually not accurate representations of a pheneomena; they typically contain errors and contradictions.
- They are parsimonous and provide simplified explanations of complex phenomena.
- They often contain measures of uncertainty about their validity that allow them to used even if incorrect.
- They can be represented by sets of condition-action rules.

Mental models can be closely aligned with computer.

Nature of Learning Tactics

A learning strategy is a general plan that a learner formulates for achieving a somewhat distant academic goal (like getting an A on your next exam). Like all strategies, it specifies what will be done to achieve the goal, where it will be done, and when it will be done.

A learning tactic is a specific technique (like a memory aid or a form of notetaking) that a learner uses to accomplish an immediate objective.

As you can see, tactics have an integral connection to strategies. They are the learning tools that move you closer to your goal. Thus, they have to be chosen so as to be consistent with the goals of a strategy.

If you had to recall verbatim the preamble to the U.S. Constitution, for example, would you use a learning tactic that would help you understand the gist of each stanza or one that would allow for accurate and complete recall? It is surprising how often students fail to consider this point.

Because understanding the different types and roles of tactics will help you better understand the process of strategy formulation, we will discuss tactics first.

Types of Tactics

Most learning tactics can be placed in one of two categories based on each tactic's intended primary purpose. One category, called memory-directed tactics, contains techniques that help produce accurate storage and retrieval of information. The second category, called comprehension-directed tactics, contains techniques that aid in understanding the meaning of ideas and their interrelationships. Within each category there are specific tactics from which one can choose. Because of space limitations, we cannot discuss them all. Instead, we have chosen to briefly discuss a few that are either very popular with students or have been shown to be reasonably effective. The first two, rehearsal and mnemonic devices, are memory-directed tactics. Both can take several forms and are used by students of almost every age. The last two, notetaking and self-questioning, are comprehension-directed tactics and are used frequently by students from the upper elementary grades through college.

— *Rehearsal:* The simplest form of rehearsal, rote rehearsal, is one of the earliest tactics to appear during childhood and is used by most everyone on occasion. It is not a particularly effective tactic for long-term storage and recall because it does not produce distinct encoding or good retrieval cues (although, as discussed earlier, it is a useful tactic for purposes of short-term memory).

  According to research reviewed by Kail, most five- and six-year-olds do not rehearse at all. Seven-year-olds sometimes use the simplest form of rehearsal. By eight years of age, instead of rehearsing single pieces of information one at a time, youngsters start to rehearse several items together as a set.

  A slightly more advanced version, called cumulative rehearsal, involves rehearsing a small set of items for several repetitions, dropping the item at the top of the list and adding a new one, giving the set several repetitions, dropping the item at the head of the set and adding a new one, rehearsing the set, and so on.

By early adolescence rehearsal reflects the learner's growing awareness of the organizational properties of information. When given a list of randomly arranged words from familiar categories, thirteen-year-olds will group items by category to form rehearsal sets.

— *Mnemonic Devices:* A mnemonic device is a memory-directed tactic that helps a learner transform or organize information to enhance its retrievability. Such devices can be used to learn and remember individual items of information (a name, a fact, a date), sets of information (a list of names, a list of vocabulary definitions, a sequence of events), and ideas expressed in text.

These devices range from simple, easy-to-learn techniques to somewhat complex systems that require a fair amount of practice. Since they incorporate visual and verbal forms of elaborative encoding, their effectiveness is due to the same factors that make imagery and category clustering successful—organization and meaningfulness.

— *Self-Questioning*: Since students are expected to demonstrate much of what they know by answering written test questions, self-questioning can be a valuable learning tactic.The key to using questions profitably is to recognize that different types of questions make different cognitive demands. Some questions require little more than verbatim recall or recognition of simple facts and details. If an exam is to stress factual recall, then it may be helpful for a student to generate such questions while studying. Other questions, however, assess comprehension, application, or synthesis of main ideas or other high&endash;level information.

Since many teachers favor higher-level test questions, we will focus on self&endash;questioning as an aid to comprehension. Much of the research on self-questioning addresses two basic questions:

1. Can students as young as those in fourth grade be trained to write comprehension questions about the content of a reading passage?

2. And does writing such questions lead to better comprehension of the passage in comparison to students who do not write questions?

The answer to both questions is yes if certain conditions are present. Research on teaching students how to generate questions as they read suggests that the following conditions play a major role in self-questioning's effectiveness as a comprehension-directed learning tactic:

1. The amount of prior knowledge the questioner has about the topic of the passage.
2. The amount of metacognitive knowledge the questioner has compiled.
3. The clarity of instructions.
4. The instructional format.
5. The amount of practice allowed the student.
6. The length of each practice session.

— *Notetaking:* As a learning tactic, notetaking comes with good news and bad. The good news is that notetaking can benefit a student in two ways. First, the process of taking notes while listening to a lecture or reading a text leads to better retention and comprehension of the noted information than just listening or reading does.

Second, the process of reviewing notes produces additional chances to recall and comprehend the noted material. The bad news is that we know very little at the present time about the specific conditions that make notetaking an effective tactic.

Using Learning Strategies Effectively

The Components of a Learning Strategy

As noted, a learning strategy is a plan for accomplishing a learning goal. It consists of six components: metacognition, analysis, planning, implementation of the plan, monitoring of progress, and modification. To give you a better idea of how to formulate a learning strategy of your own, here is a detailed description of each of these components.

1. *Metacognition*. In the absence of some minimal awareness of how we think and how our thought processes affect our academic performance, a strategic approach to learning is simply not possible.

   We need to know, at the very least, that effective learning requires an analysis of the learning situation, formulation of a learning plan, skillful implementation of appropriate tactics, periodic monitoring of our progress, and modification of things that go wrong.

   In addition, we need to know why each of these steps is necessary, when each step should be carried out, and how well prepared we are to perform each step.

   Without this knowledge, students who are taught one or more of the learning tactics mentioned earlier do not keep up their use for very long, nor do they apply the tactics to relevant tasks.

2. *Analysis*. Any workable plan must be based on relevant information. By thinking about the type of task that one must confront, the type of material that one has to learn, the personal characteristics that one possesses, and the way in which one's competence will be tested, the strategic learner can generate this information by playing the role of an investigative journalist and asking questions that pertain to what, when, where, why, who, and how.

   In this way the learner can identify important aspects of the material to be learned (what, when, where), understand the nature of the test that will be given (why), recognize relevant personal learner characteristics (who), and identify potentially useful learning activities or tactics (how).

3. *Planning*. Once satisfactory answers have been gained from the analysis phase, the strategic learner then

formulates a learning plan by hypothesizing something like this:

> "I know something about the material to be learned (I have to read and comprehend five chapters of my music appreciation text within the next three weeks), the nature of the criterion (I will have to compare and contrast the musical structure of symphonies that were written by Beethoven, Schubert, and Brahms), my strengths and weaknesses as a learner (I am good at tasks that involve the identification of similarities and differences, but I have difficulty concentrating for long periods of time), and the nature of various learning activities (skimming is a good way to get a general sense of the structure of a chapter; mnemonic devices make memorizing important details easier and more reliable; notetaking and self-questioning are more effective ways to enhance comprehension than simple rereading).
>
> "Based on this knowledge, I should divide each chapter into several smaller units that will take no longer than thirty minutes to read, take notes as I read, answer self-generated compare-and-contrast questions, use the loci mnemonic to memorize details, and repeat this sequence several times over the course of each week."

4. *Implementation.* of the plan. Once the learner has formulated a plan, each of its elements must be implemented skillfully.

   A careful analysis and a well-conceived plan will not work if tactics are carried out badly. Of course, a poorly executed plan may not be entirely attributable to a learner's tactical skill deficiencies.

   Part of the problem may be a general lack of knowledge about what conditions make for effective use of tactics (as is the case with notetaking).

5. *Monitoring of progress.* Once the learning process is under way, the strategic learner assesses how well the chosen tactics are working.

Possible monitoring techniques include writing out a summary, giving an oral presentation, working practice problems, and answering questions.

6. *Modification.* If the monitoring assessment is positive, the learner may decide that no changes are needed.

If, however, attempts to memorize or understand the learning material seem to be producing unsatisfactory results, the learner will need to reevaluate and modify the analysis. This, in turn, will cause changes in both the plan and the implementation.

There are two points we would like to emphasize about the nature of a learning strategy.

The first is that learning conditions constantly change. Subject matters have different types of information and structures, teachers use different instructional methods and have different styles, exams differ in the kinds of demands they make, and the interests, motives, and capabilities of students change over time.

Accordingly, strategies must be formulated or constructed anew as one moves from task to task rather than selected from a bank of previously formulated strategies. The true strategist, in other words, is very mentally active.

The second point is that the concept of a learning strategy is obviously complex and requires a certain level of intellectual maturity.

Thus, you may be tempted to conclude that, although you could do it, learning to be strategic is beyond the reach of most elementary and high school students. Research evidence suggests otherwise, however. A study of high school students in Scotland, for example, found that some students are sensitive to contextual differences among school tasks and vary their approach to studying accordingly.

Furthermore, research in the United States suggests that elementary grade youngsters can be trained to use many of the strategy components just mentioned.

Research on Learning Strategy Training: Reciprocal Teaching

A study of strategy training aimed at improving reading comprehension is the reciprocal teaching (RT) program of Annemarie Palincsar and Ann Brown.

As the title of this program indicates, students learn certain comprehension skills by demonstrating them to each other. Palincsar and Brown trained a small group of seventh graders whose reading comprehension scores were at least two years below grade level to use the techniques of summarizing, self-questioning, clarifying, and predicting to improve their reading comprehension. These four methods were chosen because they can be used by students to improve and monitor comprehension.

During the early training sessions, the teacher explained and demonstrated the four methods while reading various passages. The students were then given gradually increasing responsibility for demonstrating these techniques to their peers, with the teacher supplying prompts and corrective feedback as needed.

Eventually, each student was expected to offer a good summary of a passage, pose questions about important ideas, clarify ambiguous words or phrases, and predict upcoming events, all to be done with little or no intervention by the teacher.

Palincsar and Brown found that the RT program produced two general beneficial effects.

First, the quality of students' summaries, questions, clarifications, and predictions improved. Early in the program students produced overly detailed summaries and many unclear questions. But in later sessions concise summaries and questions dealing explicitly with main ideas were the rule.

For example, questions on main ideas increased from 54 percent to 70 percent. In addition, the questions were increasingly stated in paraphrase form rather than as verbatim statements from the passage.

Second. RT-trained students scored as well as a group of average readers on tests of comprehension (about 75 percent correct for both groups) and much better than a group taught how to locate information that might show up in a test question (75 percent correct versus 45 percent correct).

Most impressively. these levels of performance held up for at least eight weeks after the study ended (no measures were taken after that point) and generalized to tests of social studies and science (20 percent correct prior to training versus 60 percent correct after training).

Subsequent research on the effectiveness of RT has continued to produce positive findings across a broad age spectrum (fourth grade through college). On the average, RT students have scored at the 62nd percentile on standardized reading comprehension tests (compared to the 50th percentile for the average control student) and at the 81st percentile rank on reading comprehension tests that were created by the experimenters.

SUGGESTIONS FOR TEACHERS TO PERFOM EFFECTIVELY IN THE CLASSROOM

1. Demonstrate a variety of learning tactics. and allow students to practice them.

   a. Teach students how to use various forms of rehearsal and mnemonic devices.

      At least two reasons recommend the teaching of rehearsal. One is that maintenance rehearsal is a useful tactic for keeping a relatively small amount of information active in short-term memory.

      The other is that maintenance rehearsal is one of a few tactics that young children can learn to use. If you do decide to teach rehearsal, we have two suggestions:

First, remind young children that rehearsal is something that learners consciously decide to do when they want to remember things.

Second, remind students to rehearse no more than seven items (or chunks) at a time.

Upper elementary grade students (fourth, fifth, and sixth graders) can be taught advanced forms of maintenance rehearsal, such as cumulative rehearsal, and forms of elaborative rehearsal, such as rehearsing sets of items that form homogeneous categories. As with younger students, provide several opportunities each week to practice these skills.

As you prepare class presentations or encounter bits of information that students seem to have difficulty learning, ask yourself if a mnemonic device would be useful. You might write up a list of the devices discussed earlier and refer to it often.

Part of the value of mnemonic devices is that they make learning easier. They are also fun to make up and use. Moreover, rhymes, acronyms, and acrostics can be constructed rather quickly.

You might consider setting aside about thirty minutes two or three times a week to teach mnemonics. First, explain how rhyme, acronym, and acrostic mnemonics work, and then provide examples of each. For younger children use short, simple rhymes like "Columbus crossed the ocean blue in fourteen hundred ninety-two." For older students, the rhymes can be longer and more complex.

Acrostics can be used to remember particularly difficult spelling words. The word *arithmetic* can be spelled by taking the first letter from each word of the following sentence: *a rat in the house may eat the ice cream*. Once students understand how the mnemonic is supposed to work, have them construct mnemonics to learn various facts and concepts. You might offer a prize for the most ingenious mnemonic.

b. *Teach students how to formulate comprehension questions.*

We concluded earlier that self-questioning could be an effective comprehension tactic if students were trained to write good comprehension questions and given opportunities to practice the technique. We suggest you try the following instructional sequence:

— Discuss the purpose of student-generated questions.

— Point out the differences between knowledge&endash:level questions and comprehension-level questions. An excellent discussion of this distinction can be found in the Taxonomy of Educational Objectives. Handbook I: Cognitive Domain

— Provide students with a sample paragraph and several comprehension questions. Again, good examples of comprehension questions and guidelines for writing your own can be found in the Taxonomy.

— Hand out paragraphs from which students can practice constructing questions.

— Provide corrective feedback.

— Give students short passages from which to practice.

— Provide corrective feedback.

c. *Teach students how to take notes.*

— Despite the limitations of research on notetaking. mentioned earlier, three suggestions should lead to more effective notetaking.

First, provide students with clear, detailed objectives for every reading assignment. The objectives should indicate what parts of the assignment to focus on and how that material should be processed (whether memorized verbatim, reorganized and paraphrased, or integrated with earlier reading assignments).

Second, inform students that notetaking is an effective comprehension tactic when used appropriately. Think, for example, about a reading passage that is long and for which test items will demand analysis and synthesis of broad concepts. Tell students to concentrate on identifying main ideas and supporting details, paraphrase this information, and record similarities and differences.

Third, provide students with practice and corrective feedback in answering questions that are similar to those on the criterion test.

— Encourage students to think about the various conditions that affect *how* they learn and remember.

The very youngest students (through third grade) should be told periodically that such cognitive behaviors as describing, recalling, guessing, and understanding mean different things, produce different results, and vary in how well they fit a task's demands.

For older elementary school and middle school students, explain the learning process more simply, focusing on the circumstances in which different learning tactics are likely to be useful. Then, have students keep a diary or log in which they note when they use learning tactics, which ones, and with what success.

Look for cases where good performance corresponds to frequent reported use of tactics, and positively reinforce those individuals. Encourage greater use of tactics among students whose performance and reported use of them are below average.

While this same technique can be used with high school and college students, they should also be made aware of the other elements that make up strategic learning.

Discuss the meaning of and necessity for analyzing a learning task, developing a learning plan, using appropriate tactics, monitoring the effectiveness of the plan, and implementing whatever corrective measures might be called for.

— Each time you prepare an assignment, think about learning strategies that you and your students might use.

As noted in our earlier discussion of age trends in metacognition, virtually all elementary school students and many high school students will not be able to devise and use their own coordinated set of learning strategies.

Accordingly, you should devise such strategies for them, explain how the strategies work, and urge them to use these techniques on their own.

With high school students, you might consider giving a how to study lecture at the beginning of a report period to provide your students with general information about learning strategies. Even if you do give such an orientation, however, it would still be wise to give specific instructions as each assignment is made.

CONCEPT MAPPING OF THINKING AND LEARNING

Concept mapping is a diagrammatic mode of expression. It constitutes a powerful tool for use in teaching, learning and research at all levels, and we encourage you to give it a try. Explaining to students why you are using the technique and setting aside a little time for its use will rapidly move both student and teacher up the learning curve. Although concept mapping can be applied to any discipline, here we draw examples from the sciences.

Concept mapping was developed by Joseph Novak, an educational psychologist. Novak and Gowin describe the logic of concept mapping through the definition of three key terms: concept, proposition and learning.

A concept is "a perceived regularity, designated by a label." Some examples from science would be force, methylation, recombination and cosine. The concept can be one or more words, and can be simple or complex.

A proposition (statement, assertion) is "a link between concepts." In an example from biology, "crossing over gives rise to recombination", the proposition "gives rise" links two concepts, crossing over and recombination. In an example from physics, "force = mass x acceleration," the propositions "=" and "x" link three concepts: force, mass and acceleration.

The rules for propositions are that they must be concise yet as complete as possible, and understandable to another reader. When several concepts are arranged on a page linked by propositions, they constitute a concept map. Most propositions are directional, shown on the map by an arrow.

Learning is "the active construction of new propositions." Thus, concept mapping closely mirrors the processes of thinking and learning. Because of this, it is a skill that is transferable to any situation where the creative processing of ideas is required.

We distinguish at least three types of concept maps:

— *Trees (hierarchical maps).* These are arrangements of concepts in terms of some type of classification, starting at the top of the page with the broadest, and subdividing progressively down the page.

— *Webs.* These are non-hierarchical arrangements in which as many interconnecting propositions as possible are shown.

— *Wheels.* These maps have a central "hub" concept with propositions radiating out like spokes. Secondary rings of spokes are also possible.

Rafferty discusses the construction of concept maps, and their use in three types of learning - concept learning, representational learning and propositional learning.

Broadly speaking, concept maps can be used to organize existing knowledge, or to create new knowledge. You might use concept maps to:

— help your students with personal study

— assess student performance through assignments

— assist in curriculum or course design

— organize research ideas in lab meetings, designing grant applications or outlining publications.

Stoddart et al. developed a method to assess student learning using concept maps in combination with a rubric to extract quantitative information about the quality of understanding from each map.

According to Kinchin, concept maps have been said to provide a "window into students' minds." That's quite a claim, but we hope you will try out this valuable tool in communicating the structure of complex ideas as part of your teaching, learning and research activities at UBC.

IMPACTS OF TECHNOLOGICAL REVOLUTION IN LEARNING

We have all experienced a learning moment when we were so focussed or engulfed in the learning, that everything else did not matter. Candidly, the raison d'être or motivation for our focus may have been that we had a boss or teacher breathing down our neck or an impending exam was to quantify our level of knowledge or intelligence or a particular moment necessitated that a skill be learned very quickly. Regardless of the motivating factors for this moment of focussed learning, the experience is what psychologists Mihaly Czikszentmihalyi and Ellen Langer label in their respective theories, as moments of "optimum flow" or "mindfulness". According to psychologist Mihaly Czikszentmihalyi, optimum flow occurs when:

> Alientation gives way to involvement, enjoyment replaces boredom, helplessness turns into a feeling of control, and psychic energy works to reinforce the sense of self, instead of being lost in the service of external goals.

Replicating such moments of optimum flow is the job of educators regardless of the domain, whether it be school, the workplace in job training, or the military, etc. Moreover, certain learning theorists are advocating the greater use of technology, namely computers, in learning situations because they see enormous potential of computer technology to replicate these optimum moments of flow.

Learning is a personal act. We each place our own personal stamp on how we learn, what we learn and when we learn. We in effect have our own learning style. Howard Gardner's theory of multiple intelligences which acknowledges learning as an holistic experience is, at present, one of the most well known descriptors of human cognitive profiles.

The act of learning is paradoxical in nature. It can at times appear to be a very simple act. So simple, that we do not question its presence in how we go about our daily activities, for it is natural to our existence as learning organisms. Yet, when we encounter difficulties in learning something, we no longer take the learning process for granted. It is only then that our metacognition or awareness of how we learn is heightened.

Learning is taken for granted as a natural process. As simple a process it may seem, the root of understanding how we learn is not as straight forward. The existence of numerous definitions and theories of learning attest to the complexity of this process. A random sampling of any educational psychology text will illustrate the variance in views to what exactly is learning and how we do learn. In Educational Psychology: An Introduction, for example, the authors write, "Learning implies a change in the individual as a result of some intervention. It may be viewed as an outcome or as a process." While this definition reflects a behaviorist view of learning, for it equates learning as an outcome, it is a starting point for the authors to expand their description of learning into many other realms, namely the different theories of learning.

While it may seem somewhat premature to evaluate the aforementioned definition of learning and to equate it with a specific theory, it is important to recognize that "intervention" in the learning process can imply many different things. The degree of intervention, by who or what and how, are the defining factors of a learning theory. These factors help distinguish the many different theories. As you will see these theories are not stagnant. They are evolving and changing as we discover new ways of viewing human cognition. "The mechanistic model of the mind of the behavior era has given way to the logical-computational model favored by artificial intelligence and cognitive science theorists".

Don Tapscott, in his book *Growing Up Digital: The Rise of the Net Generation*, argues that we are now in a digital era of learning. According to Tapscott, a transformation in learning is taking place from what he labels "broadcast" learning to "interactive" learning. No longer are today's generation of learners satisfied in being the passive recipients of the traditional teaching process, rather, they want to discover it for themselves by becoming interactive with the learning. The net generation children using web sites are beginning to process information and learn differently than the boomers before them. New media tools offer great promise for a new model of learning - one based on discovery and participation.

4

BEHAVIOURISTIC APPROACH TO LEARNING

THE BASICS OF BEHAVIOURISM

Behaviourism, as a learning theory, can be traced back to Aristotle, whose essay "Memory" focused on associations being made between events such as lightning and thunder. Other philosophers that followed Aristotle's thoughts are Hobbs, Hume, Brown, Bain and Ebbinghause.

The theory of behaviourism concentrates on the study of overt behaviours that can be observed and measured. It views the mind as a "black box" in the sense that response to stimulus can be observed quantitatively, totally ignoring the possibility of thought processes occurring in the mind.

Behaviourism labelled as a teaching approach is often referred to as directed instruction. As you compare this theory with the Constructivist view of learning, this label will become self-evident. Also in contrast to Constructivism, it has been labelled an objectivist theory of learning.

Behaviourism is dominated by the constraints of its (naïve) attempts to emulate the physical sciences, which involves a refusal to speculate about what happens inside the organism. Anything which relaxes this requirement slips into the cognitive realm. Much behaviourist experimentation is undertaken with animals and generalised. In educational settings, behaviourism implies the dominance of the teacher, as in behaviour modification programmes. It can, however, be applied to an understanding of unintended learning.

THEORISTS ASSOCIATED WITH BEHAVIOURISM

Theorists associated with behaviourism are:

— J.B Watson

— E. L Thorndike

— B.F Skinner

The concern or emphasis of Behaviourism is observable indicators that learning is taking place. Contrasting this view of learning is the emphasis of cognitive psychologists who equate learning with the mental processes of the mind. Behaviourists do not deny the existence of these mental processes. In fact, they acknowledge their existence as an unobservable indication of learning.

The focus of Behaviourism is on the conditioning of observable human behaviour. J. B Watson, the father of Behaviourism, defined learning as a sequence of stimulus and response actions in observable cause and effect relationships. The behaviourists' example of classical conditioning demonstrates the process whereby a human learns to respond to a neutral stimulus in such a manner that would normally be associated with an unconditioned stimulus. The supporting example often cited with classical conditioning is the case of Pavlov's dog.

The focus of Pavlov's experiment was the digestive process in animals. In conducting the experiment, Pavlov noticed that the dog would salivate (response), upon hearing the ringing of a bell. This occurred because the dog had learned to associate its unconditional stimuli (normally feeding), with the neutral stimuli of the bell ringing simultaneously with the feeding process. Watson, believed that the stimuli that humans receive may be generated internally (for example hunger), or externally (for example, a loud noise).

B.F. Skinner expanded on the foundation of Behaviourism, established by Watson, and on the work of Edward Thorndike, by focussing on operant conditioning. According to Skinner, voluntary or automatic behaviour is either strengthened or weakened by the immediate presence of a reward or a punishment. "The learning principle behind operant conditioning is that new learning occurs as a result of positive reinforcement, and old patterns are abandoned as a result of negative reinforcement." In his book entitled, The Technology of Teaching, Skinner wrote:

> The application of operant conditioning to education is simple and direct. Teaching is the arrangement of contingencies of reinforcement under which students learn. They learn without teaching in their natural environments, but teachers arrange special contingencies which expedite learning, hastening the appearance of behaviour which would otherwise be acquired slowly or making sure of the appearance of behaviour which otherwise never occur.

Skinner believed that more complex learning could be achieved by this process of contingencies and reinforcement "... through successive stages in the shaping process, the contingencies of reinforcement being changed progressively in the direction of the required behaviour."

Applying the theoretical principles of Behaviourism to learning environments, it is easy to recognize that we have many "behaviourist artifacts" in our learning world. A dissection of the traditional teaching approaches used for years would reveal the powerful influence that Behaviourists have had on learning. The concept of directed instruction, whereby a teacher is providing the knowledge to the students either directly or through the set up of "contingencies", is an excellent example of the Behaviourist model of learning. The use of exams to measure observable behaviour of learning, the use of rewards and punishments in our school systems, and the breaking down of the instruction process into "conditions of learning" (as developed by Robert Gagne), are all further examples of the Behaviourist influence.

With the advent of the computer in school, C.A.I., or computer-assisted instruction has become a prominent tool for teaching, because from a Behaviourist perspective, it is an effective way of learning. CAI uses the drill and practice approach to learning new concepts or skills. The question acting as the stimulus, elicits a response from the user. Based on the response a reward may be provided. The "contingencies" of learning are translated into different levels of the program. Rewarding the user to a different level for correct responses follows exactly the approach of operant conditioning. Educators have espoused CAI as an effective teaching approach because it allows for self-paced instruction and it liberates them from the direct instruction of all their students so as to focus on those students with particular needs.

Pavlov (1849 - 1936)

For most people, the name "Pavlov" rings a bell (pun intended). The Russian physiologist is best known for his work in classical conditioning or stimulus substitution. Pavlov's most famous experiment involved food, a dog and a bell.

Pavlov's Experiment

— Before conditioning, ringing the bell caused no response from the dog. Placing food in front of the dog initiated salivation.

— During conditioning, the bell was rung a few seconds before the dog was presented with food.

— After conditioning, the ringing of the bell alone produced salivation

Stimulus and Response Items of Pavlov's Experiment

Food	Unconditioned Stimulus
Salivation	Unconditioned Response (natural, not learned)
Bell	Conditioned Stimulus
Salivation	Conditioned Response (to bell)

Other Observations Made by Pavlov

— *Stimulus Generalization*: Once the dog has learned to salivate at the sound of the bell, it will salivate at other similar sounds.

— *Extinction*: If you stop pairing the bell with the food, salivation will eventually cease in response to the bell.

— *Spontaneous Recovery*: Extinguished responses can be "recovered" after an elapsed time, but will soon extinguish again if the dog is not presented with food.

— *Discrimination*: The dog could learn to discriminate between similar bells (stimuli) and discern which bell would result in the presentation of food and which would not.

— *Higher-Order Conditioning*: Once the dog has been conditioned to associate the bell with food, another unconditioned stimulus, such as a light may be flashed at the same time that the bell is rung. Eventually the dog will salivate at the flash of the light without the sound of the bell.

Thorndike (1874 - 1949)

Edward Thorndike did research in animal behaviour before becoming interested in human psychology. He set out to apply "the methods of exact science" to educational problems by emphasizing "accurate quantitative treatment of information". "Anything that exists, exists in a certain quantity and can be measured". His theory, Connectionism, stated that learning was the formation of a connection between stimulus and response.

— The "law of effect" stated that when a connection between a stimulus and response is positively rewarded it will be strengthened and when it is negatively rewarded it will be weakened. Thorndike later revised this "law" when he found that negative reward, (punishment) did not necessarily weaken bonds, and that some seemingly pleasurable consequences do not necessarily motivate performance.

— The "law of exercise" held that the more an S-R (stimulus response) bond is practiced the stronger it will become. As with the law of effect, the law of exercise also had to be updated when Thorndike found that practice without feedback does not necessarily enhance performance.

— The "law of readiness" : because of the structure of the nervous system, certain conduction units, in a given situation, are more predisposed to conduct than others.

Thorndike's laws were based on the stimulus-response hypothesis. He believed that a neural bond would be established between the stimulus and response when the response was positive. Learning takes place when the bonds are formed into patterns of behaviour.

Watson (1878 - 1958)

John B. Watson was the first American psychologist to use Pavlov's ideas. Like Thorndike, he was originally involved in animal research, but later became involved in the study of human behaviour.

Watson believed that humans are born with a few reflexes and the emotional reactions of love and rage. All other behaviour is established through stimulus-response associations through conditioning.

Watson's Experiment

Watson demonstrated classical conditioning in an experiment involving a young child (Albert) and a white rat. Originally, Albert was unafraid of the rat; but Watson created a sudden loud noise whenever Albert touched the rat. Because Albert was frightened by the loud noise, he soon became conditioned to fear and avoid the rat. The fear was generalized to other small animals. Watson then "extinguished" the fear by presenting the rat without the loud noise. Some accounts of the study suggest that the conditioned fear was more powerful and permanent than it really was. Certainly Watson's research methods would be questioned today; however, his work did demonstrate the role of conditioning in the development of emotional responses to certain stimuli. This may explain certain fears, phobias and prejudices that people develop.

Skinner (1904 - 1990)

Like Pavlov, Watson and Thorndike, Skinner believed in the stimulus-response pattern of conditioned behaviour. His theory dealt with changes in observable behaviour, ignoring the possibility of any processes occurring in the mind. Skinner's 1948 book, *Walden Two* , is about a utopian society based on operant conditioning. He also wrote,*Science and Human Behaviour*, in which he pointed out how the principles of operant conditioning function in social institutions such as government, law, religion, economics and education. Skinner's work differs from that of his predecessors (classical conditioning), in that he studied operant behaviour (voluntary behaviours used in operating on the environment).

Skinner's Operant Conditioning Mechanisms

— *Positive Reinforcement or reward*: Responses that are rewarded are likely to be repeated. (Good grades reinforce careful study.)

— *Negative Reinforcement*: Responses that allow escape from painful or undesirable situations are likely to be repeated. (Being excused from writing a final because of good term work.)

— *Extinction or Non-Reinforcement* : Responses that are not reinforced are not likely to be repeated. (Ignoring student misbehaviour should extinguish that behaviour.)

— *Punishment*: Responses that bring painful or undesirable consequences will be suppressed, but may reappear if reinforcement contingencies change. (Penalizing late students by withdrawing privileges should stop their lateness.)

Skinner and Behavioural Shaping

If placed in a cage an animal may take a very long time to figure out that pressing a lever will produce food. To accomplish such behaviour successive approximations of the behaviour are rewarded until the animal learns the association between the lever and the food reward. To begin shaping, the animal may be rewarded for simply turning in the direction of the lever, then for moving toward the lever, for brushing against the lever, and finally for pawing the lever.

Behavioural chaining occurs when a succession of steps need to be learned. The animal would master each step in sequence until the entire sequence is learned.

Reinforcement Schedules

Once the desired behavioural response is accomplished, reinforcement does not have to be 100%; in fact it can be maintained more successfully through what Skinner referred to as partial reinforcement schedules. Partial reinforcement schedules include interval schedules and ratio schedules.

— *Fixed Interval Schedules:* the target response is reinforced after a fixed amount of time has passed since the last reinforcement.

— *Variable Interval Schedules:* similar to fixed interval schedules, but the amount of time that must pass between reinforcement varies.

— *Fixed Ratio Schedules:* a fixed number of correct responses must occur before reinforcement may recur.

— *Variable Ratio Schedules:* the number of correct repetitions of the correct response for reinforcement varies.

Variable interval and especially, variable ratio schedules produce steadier and more persistent rates of response because the learners cannot predict when the reinforcement will come although they know that they will eventually succeed.

BEHAVIOURISM AND INSTRUCTIONAL DESIGN

In Paul Saettler's book *The History of American Educational Technology*, he states that behaviourism did not have an impact on educational technology until the 1960s, which was the time that behaviourism actually began to decrease in popularity in American psychology. Saettler identified six areas that demonstrate the impact of behaviourism on Educational Technology in America: the behavioural objectives movement; the teaching machine phase; the programmed instruction movement; individualized instructional approaches, computer-assisted learning and the systems approach to instruction.

Behavioural Objectives Movement

A behavioural objective states learning objectives in "specified, quantifiable, terminal behaviours". Behavioural objectives can be summed up using the mnemonic device ABCD.

Example: After having completed the unit the student will be able to answer correctly 90% of the questions on the posttest.

A - Audience - the student

B - Behaviour - answer correctly

C - Condition - after having completed the unit, on a post test

D - Degree - 90% correct

To develop behavioural objectives a learning task must be broken down through analysis into specific measurable tasks. The learning success may be measured by tests developed to measure each objective.

The advent of behavioural objectives can be traced back to the Elder Sophists of ancient Greece, Cicero, Herbart and Spencer, but Franklin Bobbitt developed the modern concept of behavioural objectives in the early 1900s.

Taxonomic Analysis of Learning Behaviours

Bloom's Taxonomy of Learning

In 1956 Bloom and his colleagues began development of a taxonomy in the cognitive, attitudinal (affective) and psychomotor domains. Many people are familiar with *Bloom's Cognitive taxonomy*:

— knowledge

— comprehension

— application

— analysis

— synthesis

— evaluation

Gagne's Taxonomy of Learning

Robert Gagne developed his taxonomy of learning in 1972. Gagne's taxonomy was comprised of five categories:

— verbal information
— intellectual skill
— cognitive strategy
— attitude
— motor skill

Mastery Learning

Mastery learning was originally developed by Morrison in the 1930s. His formula for mastery was "Pretest, teach, test the result, adapt procedure, teach and test again to the point of actual learning.". Mastery learning assumes that all students can master the materials presented in the lesson. Bloom further developed Morrison's plan, but mastery learning is more effective for the lower levels of learning on Bloom's taxonomy, and not appropriate for higher level learning.

Military and Industrial Approach

For military and industrial training, "behavioural objectives were written descriptions of specific, terminal behaviours that were manifested in terms of observable, measurable behaviour." Robert Mager wrote *Preparing Instructional Objectives,* in 1962 which prompted interest and use of behavioural objectives among educators. Gagne and Briggs who also had backgrounds in military and industrial psychology developed a set of instructions for writing objectives that is based on Mager's work. By the late 1960's most teachers were writing and using behavioural objectives. There were, of course, people who questioned the breaking down of subject material into small parts, believing that it would lead away from an understanding of the "whole".

Accountability Movement

A movement known as scientific management of industry arose in the early 1900s in response to political and economic factors of that time. Franklin Bobbitt proposed utilization of this system in education stressing that the standards and direction of education should stem from the consumer - society. Bobbitt's ideas exemplified the idea of accountability, competency-based education and performance-based education, which because of similar economic and political factors, experienced a revival in America during the late 1960s and 1970s.

Teaching Machines and Programmed Instruction Movement

Although the elder Sophists, Comenius, Herbart and Montessori used the concept of programmed instruction in their repertoire, B.F. Skinner is the most current and probably best known advocate of teaching machines and programmed learning. Contributors to this movement include the following:

— *Pressey* - introduced a multiple-choice machine at the 1925 American Psychological Association meeting.

— *Peterson* - a former student of Pressey's who developed "chemosheets" in which the learner checked their answers with a chemical-dipped swab.

— *W.W.II* - devises called "phase checks", constructed in the 1940s and 1950s, taught and tested such skills and dissassembly-assembly of equipment.

— *Crowder* - designed a branched style of programming for the US Air force in the 1950s to train troubleshooters to find malfunctions in electronic equipment.

— *Skinner* - based on operant conditioning Skinner's teaching machine required the learner to complete or answer a question and then receive feedback on the correctness of the response. Skinner demonstrated his machine in 1954.

Early Use of Programmed Instruction

After experimental use of programmed instruction in the 1920s and 1930s, B. F. Skinner and J.G. Holland first used programmed instruction in behavioural psychology courses at Harvard in the late 1950s. Use of programmed instruction appeared in elementary and secondary schools around the same time. Much of the programmed instruction in American schools was used with individuals or small groups of students and was more often used in junior high schools than senior or elementary schools.

Early use of programmed instruction tended to concentrate on the development of hardware rather than course content. Concerned developers moved away from hardware development to programs based on analysis of learning and instruction based on learning theory. Despite these changes, programmed learning died out in the later part of the 1960s because it did not appear to live up to its original claims .

Individualized Approaches to Instruction

Similar to programmed learning and teaching machines individualized instruction began in the early 1900s, and was revived in the 1960s. The Keller Plan, Individually Prescribed Instruction, Program for Learning in Accordance with Needs, and Individually Guided Education are all examples of individualized instruction in the U.S.

Keller Plan (1963)

Developed by F.S. Keller, a colleague of Skinner, the Keller plan was used for university college classes.

Main features of Keller Plan:

— individually paced.

— mastery learning.

— lectures and demonstrations motivational rather than critical information.

— use of proctors which permitted testing, immediate scoring, tutoring, personal-social aspect of educational process.

Individually Prescribed Instruction (IPI)

Individually Prescribed Instruction (IPI) Methoda was Developed by Learning Research and Development Center of the University of Pitsburgh.Lasted into the 1970s when it lost funding and its use dwindled. Main features of IPI are:

— prepared units.

— behavioural objectives.

— planned instructional sequences.

— used for reading, math and science.

— included pretest and posttest for each unit.

— materials continually evaluated and upgraded to meet behavioural objectives.

Program for Learning in Accordance with Needs (PLAN)

Headed by Jon C. Flanagan, PLAN was developed under sponsorship of American Institutes for Research (AIR), Westinghouse Learning Corporation and fourteen U.S. School districts.

Abandoned in late 1970s because of upgrading costs.

Main features of PLAN :

— schools selected items from about 6,000 behavioural objectives.

— each instructional module took about two weeks instruction and were made up of approximately. five objectives.

— mastery learning.

— remedial learning plus retesting.

Computer-Assisted Instruction (CAI)

Computer-assisted instruction was first used in education and training during the 1950s. Early work was done by IBM and such people as Gordon Pask, and O.M. Moore, but CAI grew rapidly in the 1960s when federal funding for research and development in education and industrial laboratories was implemented. The U.S. government wanted to determine the possible effectiveness of computer-assisted instruction, so they developed two competing companies, (Control Data Corporation and Mitre Corporation) who came up with the PLATO and TICCIT projects. Despite money and research, by the mid seventies it was apparent that CAI was not going to be the success that people had believed. Some of the reasons are:

— CAI had been oversold and could not deliver.

— lack of support from certain sectors.

— technical problems in implementation.

— lack of quality software.

— high cost.

Computer-assisted instruction was very much drill-and-practice - controlled by the program developer rather than the learner. Little branching of instruction was implemented although TICCIT did allow the learner to determine the sequence of instruction or to skip certain topics.

Systems Approach to Instruction

The systems approach developed out of the 1950s and 1960s focus on language laboratories, teaching machines, programmed instruction, multimedia presentations and the use of the computer in instruction. Most systems approaches are similar to computer flow charts with steps that the designer moves through during the development of instruction. Rooted in the military and business world, the systems approach involved setting goals and objectives, analyzing resources, devising a plan of action and continuous evaluation/modification of the program.

TYPES OF HUMAN BEHAVIOURAL LEARNING (CONDITIONING)

Conditioning is the term used to designate the types of human behavioural learning. Since the 1920s, conditioning has been the primary focus of behaviour research in humans as well as animals. There are four main types of conditioning:

Classical Conditioning

Classical conditioning, also called associative learning, is based on stimulus-response relationships. A stimulus is an object or situation that elicits a response by one of our sense organs, like how a bright light makes us blink. Associative learning allows us to associate two or more stimuli and change our response to one or more of them as a result of simultaneous experience.

According to classical conditioning, learning occurs when a new stimulus begins to elicit behaviour similar to the behaviour produced by an old stimulus. Studies into classical condition began in the early 1900s by the Russian physiologist Ivan P. Pavlov. Pavlov trained dogs to salivate in response to two stimuli: noise or light, and food or a sour solution. The dogs' salivation is automatically elicited by the food and sour solution, so these were called the unconditional stimulus. However, when the noise or light (conditional stimulus) was repeatedly paired with the food or sour solution over an extended period of time, the dogs would eventually salivate at the noise or light alone. This is a prime example of a conditioned response.

Unconditional stimuli, such as the food and sour solution, allow the learning to occur, while also serving to reinforce the learning. Without an unconditional stimulus in his experiment, Pavlov could not have taught the dogs to salivate at the presence of the noise or light.

Classical conditioning is particularly important in understanding how people learn emotional behaviour. For example, when we develop a new fear, we have learned to fear a particular stimulus which has been combined with another frightening stimulus.

Operant Conditioning

Operant conditioning is goal-directed behaviour. We learn to perform a particular response as a result of what we know will happen after we respond. For example, a child may learn to beg for sweets if the begging is usually successful. There is no single stimulus that elicits the begging behaviour, but instead it occurs because the child knows that this action may result in receiving treats. Every time the child receives sweets after begging, the behaviour is reinforced and the tendency of the child to beg will increase.

During the 1930s, American psychologist and behaviourist Burrhus F. Skinner performed several important experiments into operant conditioning. Using what is now termed a Skinner Box, he trained rats to press levers to receive food. A hungry rat would be placed in a box containing a special lever attached to concealed food. At first the hungry rat would wander around the box, investigating its surroundings. Eventually it would accidentally press the lever thereby releasing a food pellet into the box.

At first the rat would not show any signs of associating the two events, but over time its exploring behaviour becomes less random as it begins to press the lever more often. The food pellet reinforced the rat's response of pressing the lever, so eventually the rat would spend most of its time just sitting and pressing the lever. This type of learning is based on the idea that if a behaviour is rewarded, the behaviour will occur more frequently. There are four main types of operant learning:

— *Positive Reinforcement:* The more often the subject performs the action, the more the stimulus is reinforced (for example, pressing a lever for food)

— *Negative Reinforcement:* Performing an action removes an undesirable stimulus (for example, studying for an exam removes anxiety)

— *Punishment*: Performing an action elicits an undesirable stimulus (for example, receiving a shock by pressing a lever)

— *Omission Training:* Performing an action prevents the delivery of a pleasant stimulus (for example, disciplining a child by sending him to his room)

Multiple-Response Learning

When we learn skills, we must first learn a sequence of simple movement-patterns. We combine these movement-patterns to form new, more complicated behavioural patterns with stimuli guiding the process. For example, efficient typing requires us to put together many finger movements, which are guided by the letters or words that we want to type. We must first learn to type each letter, and then learn to put the movements together to type words and then phrases.

To investigate this type of learning, psychologists have observed animals learning to run through mazes. An animal first wanders aimlessly through the maze, periodically coming to a choice-point, where it must turn either left or right. Only one choice is correct, but the correct direction cannot be determined until the animal has reached the end of the maze. By running through the maze numerous times, the animal can learn the correct sequence of turns to reach the end. It has been found that the sequences of turns near the two ends of the maze are learned more easily than the parts near the middle. Similarly, when we try to learn a list of items, we usually find the beginning and the end easier than the middle.

An extension of multiple-response learning is latent learning, where learning occurs in the absence of an immediate reward. If rats are allowed to repeatedly run a maze without a reward at the end, they will learn the maze quite slowly.

However if they have first been allowed to run the maze without reward, and then food is placed at the end, these rats will learn the maze very quickly. This shows that learning had been occurring the entire time, but did not become evident until it was activated by a reward.

Insight Learning

Insight refers to learning to solve a problem by understanding the relationships of various parts of the problem. Often insight occurs suddenly, such as when a person struggles with a problem for a period of time and then suddenly understands its solution. Therefore insight learning is solving problems without experience. Instead of learning by trial-and-error (such as in maze running), insight learning involves trials occurring mentally.

In the early 1900s, Wolfgang Kohler performed insight experiments on chimpanzees. Kohler showed that the chimpanzees sometimes used insight instead of trial-and-error responses to solve problems. When a banana was placed high out of reach, the animals discovered that they could stack boxes on top of each other to reach it. They also realized that they could use sticks to knock the banana down. In another experiment, a chimp balanced a stick on end under a bunch of bananas suspended from the ceiling, then quickly climbed the stick to obtain the entire bunch intact and unbruised. Kohler's experiments showed that primates can both see and use the relationships involved to reach their goals.

MISCONCEPTIONS ABOUT BEHAVIOURISM AND HUMAN LEARNING

Two points are often misunderstood in relation to behaviourism and human learning:

— *The scale:* Although later modifications of behaviourism are known as S-O-R theories (Stimulus-Organism-Response), recognising that the organism's (in this case, person's) abilities and motivations need to be taken into account, undiluted behaviourism is concerned with conditioning and mainly with reflex behaviour. This operates on a very short time-scale — from second to second, or at most minute to minute — on very specific micro-behaviour. To say that a course is behaviourally-based because there is the reward of a qualification at the end is stretching the idea too far.

— *Its descriptive intention:* Perhaps because behaviourists describe experiments in which they structure learning for their subjects, attention tends to fall on ideas such as — behaviour modification and the technology of behaviourism. However, behaviourism itself is more about a description of how [some forms of] learning occur in the wild, as it were, than about how to make it happen, and it is when it is approached from this perspective that it gets most interesting. It accounts elegantly, for example, for ways in which attempts to discipline unruly students actually make the situation worse rather than better.

NEW APPROCH TO BEHAVIOURISM

The idea of behaviourism is abroad. In the most diverse quarters its lingo, if not its substance, is spreading like wildfire. In the first place, it is to be observed that ever since the days of Ebbinghaus's experiments on memory the inadequacy of the merely introspective method as such has been becoming more and more obvious. And the recent work in mental tests and animal psychology has strengthened this conviction.

In the second place, there has always been a formal logical difficulty about the introspective method which has troubled certain minds. That is, the definition of psychology as the examination and analysis of private conscious contents has been something of a logical sticker. For how *can* one build up a science upon elements which by very definition are said to be private and non-communicable? And, thirdly, the introspective method is practically arduous and seemingly barren of results. It is these three features, then, which seem to have been primarily responsible for the spread and catching of behaviouristic categories.

What, now, does the behaviourist offer as a substitute? We turn to the arch-behaviourist, Watson. Behaviourism, he says, will be the study of stimulus and response such that given the stimulus we can predict the response, and given the response we can predict the stimulus. But how does he define stimulus and response? He defines them, he says, in the terms in which physiology defines them; that is, stimuli are such things as "rays of light of different wave lengths, sound waves differing in amplitude, length, phase and combination, gaseous particles given off in such small diameters that they affect the membrane of the nose," etc., and responses are such things as "muscle contractions and gland secretions."

The possibility of a behaviourism which shall be not a mere physiology but something different has apparently already occurred to a number of writers. Thus, for example, Holt says that "the phenomena evinced by the integrated organism are no longer merely the excitation of nerve or the twitching of muscle, nor yet the play merely of reflexes touched off by stimuli. These are all present and essential to the phenomena in question, but they are merely the components — now the biological sciences have long recognized this *new and further thing and called it 'behaviour'*." Mrs. de Laguna also explicitly states that what we want is a behaviourism which is not mere physiology. "In order to understand behaviour we must resolve it into a system of interrelated *functions*, just as in order to understand the physiological workings of the human body we must envisage the complex of chemical and mechanical processes as falling into such fundamental groups as digestion, circulation, etc., constitutive of the physiological economy. Now just as there is a physiological economy, so there is a larger vital economy in closest union with, yet distinguishable from it. This is the system of behaviour, by means of which the being, animal or human, maintains his relations with the environment and forms a factor in its transformation. The science of behaviour has the task of tracing the lineaments of this larger economy."

A.P. Weiss also seems, to some slight extent at any rate, to lean towards this same view of the desirability of a non-physiological behaviourism. For example, the following: "The investigation of the internal neural conditions form part of the behaviouristic programme, of course, but the inability to trace the ramification of any given nervous excitation through the nervous system is no more a restriction on the study of effective stimuli and reactions in the educational, industrial or social phases of life than is the physicist's inability to determine just what is going on in the electrolyte of a battery while a current is passing, a limitation that makes research in electricity impossible."

The two essential theses which we wish to maintain in this section are, first, that such a true non-psychological behaviourism is really possible; and, second, that when it is worked out this new behaviourism will be found capable of covering not merely the results of mental tests, objective measurements of memory, and animal psychology as such, but also all that was valid in the results of the older introspective psychology. And this new formula for behaviourism which we would propose is intended as a formula for *all* of psychology — a formula to bring formal peace, not merely to the animal worker, but also to the addict of imagery and feeling tone.

But how can this be done? By what single common set of concepts can we possibly take care both of the facts of gross behaviour and of those of consciousness and imagery?

Before attempting to suggest such a set of concepts, let us indulge in a preliminary epistomological skirmish. Let us start from the usual dualistic hypothesis implicit in traditional psychological thinking. Suppose, that is, we assume that consciousness is (for the purposes of psychology at any rate if not for those of an ultimate metaphysics) a new kind of something or other which is added to certain behaviour situations but not to others. Introspective psychology claims the study and analysis of this new something or other as its own peculiar field. Consciousness is assumed by it to be something private to each individual which he alone can analyze and report upon. And the introspective account purports to be such an analysis and report. What now can our behaviourism answer to this? Our behaviourism will reply that whether or not there is such a private something or other present in the conscious behaviour situation and lacking in the unconscious one, this private something or other never 'gets across,' as such, from one individual to another. All the things that do 'get across' are merely *behaviour* phenomena or the objective possibilities of such phenomena.

Let us now turn to some of the actual concepts which seem to be required by such a point of view. We will confine ourselves to four: *stimulating agency*, *behaviour-cue*, *behaviour-object*, and *behaviour-act*. They may be thought of as very loosely analogous to the physiologist's concepts of external stimulus, receptor-process, conductor-process, and effector-process.

The *stimulating agency* may be defined in any standardized terms, those of physics, of physiology, or of common sense, and it constitutes the independent, initiating cause of the whole behaviour phenomenon. Thus on different occasions it may consists variously in, and be describable as, as sense-organ stimulation (in the case of perceptual behaviour), as the administering of a particular drug, *e.g.*, hasheesh (in the case of hallucinatory behaviour), or as the neurological end-result of a preceding activity (in the case of a behaviour based upon memory or recall).

The nature of the *behaviour-cue* will be understood most readily from a consideration of the dialectic which underlies the experimental work on sensory discrimination in animals. In such work the results, when strictly interpreted, are found to tell us nothing but the possibility of differences of behaviour as a result of different stimulating agencies. If, for example, we find that a mouse can learn to behave differently as result of blue and yellow stimuli but not as a result of a red and green stimuli, we do not conclude anything as regards the animal's consciousness of these colors, as such, but merely something as regards the behaviour-cues which these colors are capable of evoking in him. That is, blue and yellow wave-lengths are capable of producing in him two different behaviour-cues, whereas red and green wave-lengths are capable of producing in him only one. In other words, where the older psychology talked about sense-qualities our new behaviourism will talk about behaviour-cues.

The new concept is identifiable with the older one in so far, but only in so far, as the latter explained the possibility or lack of possibility of differences of *behaviour*. The new concept departs utterly from the old in so far as the latter implied something concerning 'immediate feels' as such. By applying different stimulating agencies to our organism we discover the number and range of his possible behaviour-cues. We learn which stimulating agencies he can use as a basis for differences of behaviour and which he can not use as cues for different behaviours. And we learn something concerning the degrees of difference between these different behaviour-cues. For example, we learn that, in a human of normal color vision, although the stimulating-agencies designated as orange and red wave-lengths produce behaviour-cues which are different from one another, still these behaviour-cues are more similar to one another (in that, on occasion, they are more likely to lead to an identical behaviour) than are the two behaviour-cues produced by the stimulating agencies known as red and green wave-lengths-and so on.

In other words the sum of the behaviour-cues possible for any given organism constitutes a total system which is to be defined not merely in terms of its relation to the stimulating agencies which evoke its members, but also in terms of the interrelations of similarity and difference between those members. We do not learn, however, anything about sensation-qualities, as such, neither when we observe the gross behaviour of another organism nor when we ask the latter to *introspect*. We learn the nature of his behaviour-cues. We do not learn the nature of his 'immediate feels'.

Let us turn now to a consideration of the next of our four concepts, that of the *behaviour-object*. Just as the concept of the behaviour-cue was found to bear a certain relation to a concept of the older psychology (viz., that of sense quality) so the concept of the behaviour-object bears an analogous relation to another concept of the older psychology; viz., that of the perceived or apperceived *meaning*. A behaviour-object results from a behaviour-cue or a group of behaviour-cues which , because of a particular behaviour situation, possesses for the organization in question a specific behaviour-meaning.

For example, we present an ordinary western European with a chair, it produces in him, because of the structure of his sense-organs and as a result of its color, shape, etc., certain specific behaviour-cues. In addition, however, because of his particular training and past experience and state of behaviour-readiness at the moment such behaviour-cues resulting from these shapes, colors, etc., arouse in him a very specific group of behaviour-tendencies; *e.g.*, those of sitting upon, getting up from, kneeling on, moving up to the table, etc. This group of aroused tendencies defines his behaviour-object. That is, they constitute on that particular occasion the behaviour-meaning of the colors, shapes, etc.

To use the terminology of the older psychology we would say that the behaviour-cues in question are here apperceived as the behaviour-object chair. On another occasion, however, this same group of behaviour-cues might be apperceived not as a chair, but as a very different sort of behaviour-object. If we were drunk, it might be apperceived, not as a thing to sit on, to kneel on, but as a thing to run away from, to scream at, etc. Thus, the behaviour-object is to be defined in the last analysis simply in terms of the group of behaviours to which it may lead. And it is to be emphasized that it, no more than the behaviour-cue, can be defined in terms of 'immediate conscious feels.' For no one of us ever knows for certain what another organism's 'conscious feels' may be. We know only the behaviour implications of those conscious feels.

We turn now to the last of our four concepts — that of the *behaviour-act*. The behaviour-act is simply the name to be given to the final bits of behaviour as such. The behaviour-act together with the stimulating agencies constitute the fundamentals upon which the rest of the system is based. They are such entities as to 'sniff,' to 'sit,' to 'scratch,' to 'walk,' to 'gallop,' to 'talk.' They are directly correlated with the action system of the given organism. They vary and increase in number with the growth and development of the organism. But it is they alone which, at any given stage in this growth and development, tell us all that we know of such an organism's 'mentality'. Used as a means of comparing different stimulating agencies on the basis simply of the relative discriminability and non-discriminability of the latter, the behaviour-acts provide us with our definition of behaviour-cues (*i.e.*, sensation and image qualities). And used to discover the totality of different alternative behaviour which may result from a given collection of behaviour-cues, the behaviour acts provide us with our definition of behaviour-objects (*i.e.*, perceptions and ideations).

If, now, we sum up the situation it will appear that the problems for our behaviouristic science must fall into three groups: those of (1), given the stimulating agency, determining the behaviour-cues, (2), given the behaviour-cues, determining the behaviour-object, and (3), given the behaviour-object, determining the behaviour-act. The first of these problems is the well known one of the older physiological psychology of determining the relations between sensory and image qualities and their underlying physiological conditions. The second problem, that of the relation of behaviour-object to behaviour-cue, is the old one of perception and apperception.

Our re-wording of it will not make it any the less easy of final solution. Finally, the problem of the relation of behaviour-act to behaviour-object is the extremely important problem of *motive*. It is the problem of desire, emotion, instinct, habit, determining set. It is a problem which the older analytical formulation tended to obscure and make almost impossible. If our behaviouristic formulation has any practical value at all-if, that is, it has any value in addition to that of unifying under a single rubric all the different types of method which psychology employs, then that practical value will be in the more successful treatment which it will allow and suggest for this matter of motive, determining set, and the like.

Images and ideas would be simply a particular case where behaviour-object and behaviour-cue have different space and time implications from those holding in the case of presented objects and qualities. And feelings and emotions would be treated as combining both behaviour-objects and behaviour-cues in that they involve both discriminable qualities and specific unvarying types of behaviour (for example, approach, avoidance, and the like). Finally, language in general and introspection in particular are simply themselves behaviour-acts which in the last analysis indicate to the observer the very same behaviour-cues and behaviour-objects which might be indicated by the mere gross forms of behaviour for which they are substitutes.

PRESENT FORMS OF BEHAVIOURISM

Behaviourism, beginning as a laboratory technique and a critique of method in concrete experiment, has advanced rapidly to a place as an accredited system of psychology, stressing the importance of objective methods and of physiological interpretations. The history of the movement is still reflected in the tendency of its exponents to stress experimental method rather than interpretation, in the lack of any systematic formulation of the relations of the science to the specific problems of the older subjective psychology, and in a certain shifting of ground in behaviouristic discussions which indicates that the behaviourists themselves are not yet quite certain of the philosophic implications of their system. Too often a statement of an extreme position is followed by a partial retraction or qualification which leaves the reader in doubt as to the degree of heterodoxy expressed. This hesitation before the plunge is not discreditable to the behaviourist: so great a departure from tradition in psychology demands caution. Moreover, the behaviourist is primarily an experimentalist and believes that many of the supposed problems of philosophy will, with increasing knowledge, resolve themselves into concrete laboratory problems. Why then dispute fruitlessly and at length about them before data are at hand for their solution?

Nevertheless, preoccupation with experimental problems will not excuse behaviourism for certain apparent inconsistencies in its doctrines. In various discussions of the scope of behaviourism three distinct and incompatible formulations are discernible. All involve the conviction that a complete description and explanation of behaviour can be given in terms of the physicochemistry of bodily activity. They differ, however, in the place assigned to 'mind' in the system. The formulations are as follow.

1. Facts of conscious experience exist and are capable of treatment, as distinct from behaviour. The behaviourist is not interested in them, since they are irrelevant to his problems, and leaves them to the tender mercies of the introspective psychologists or philosophers. This is merely psychophysical parallelism with emphasis on the physical. It is the view of Bechterew and other early objectivists.

2. Facts of conscious experience exist but are unsuited to any form of scientific treatment. This is the most common formulation of the behaviourist's position. It seems to have been Watson's view in his earlier writings , as is shown by the following statement:

   "Will there be left over in psychology a world of pure psychics, to use Yerkes' term? I confess I do not know. The plans which I most favor for psychology lead practically to the ignoring of consciousness in the sense that that term

> is used by psychologists today. I have virtually denied that this realm of psychics is open to experimental investigation. I don't wish to go further into the problem at present because it leads inevitably over into metaphysics. If you will grant the behaviourist the right to use consciousness in the same way that other natural scientists employ it — that is, without making consciousness a special object of observation — you have granted all that my thesis requires."

The supposedly unique facts of consciousness do not exist. An account of the behaviour of the physiological organism leaves no residue of pure psychics. Mind is behaviour and nothing else. This view is implied in much of Watson's writing, although it is not stated in so many words. For the most part he expresses a methodological behaviourism, but such statements as the following leave little doubt of his fundamental denial of the fact of consciousness, as described by the subjectivist. "It is a serious misunderstanding of the behaviouristic position to say, as Mr. Thompson does — 'And of course a behaviourist does not deny that mental states exist. He merely prefers to ignore them.' He 'ignores' them in the same sense that chemistry ignores alchemy, astronomy horoscopy, and psychology telepathy and psychic manifestations. The behaviourist does not concern himself with them because as the stream of his science broadens and deepens such older concepts are sucked under, never to reappear."

This is the extreme behaviouristic view. It makes no concessions to dualistic psychology and affirms the continuity in data and method of the physical, biological, and psychological sciences. "Consciousness is behaviour." "Consciousness is the particular laryngeal gesture we have come to use to stand for the rest." We shall speak of this doctrine as strict behaviourism, or for brevity simply as behaviourism, since methodological behaviourism is only a form of epiphenomenalism. Such a behaviourism has been called a materialism by several recent critics.

Perhaps it is such, to the extent that modern physics and physiology are materialistic, but the word materialism implies a metaphysical theory of reality, whereas these sciences are, at least in their systematic treatment, altogether phenomenological. Psychophysical dualism and epiphenomenalism do imply theories of the ultimate nature of mind and matter, but behaviourism claims to avoid this and to attempt nothing more than a logical and mathematical description of experience such as is presented by the physical sciences. To stigmatize this as materialism is to appeal against behaviourism to the prejudices aroused by a crude metaphysic which is nowhere implied in its doctrines.

When we examine the evidence upon which strict behaviourism is based, a weakness in its current formulations seems evident. The behaviourist denies sensations, images, and all other phenomena which the subjectivist claims to find by introspection or by some form of direct knowledge. This disagreement as to matters of fact is not necessarily fatal to behaviourism, although it is the most frequent ground for rejection of the system. But when we examine the evidence adduced in support of the denial of consciousness, the behaviourist seems to have failed to strike at the root of the dualistic systems. The arguments employed — they can scarcely be called evidence — fall into four chief classes.

(*a*) Appeals to the principle of parsimony to exclude consciousness because it is unnecessary for the explanation of behaviour. The inadequacy of this argument is evident. The gravitational effects of Jupiter are irrelevant to a physiology of digestion, yet they are none the less a fact. The behaviourist must show further that his system is adequate to explain the supposed phenomena of consciousness as well as of behaviour, before the argument becomes relevant. At best the argument in its present form can support only a methodological behaviourism.

(*b*) Reviews of the history of evolution or of superstition to show how the belief in the self may have arisen. This argument is beside the point. It may force the subjectivist to deny the universality of evolution or of historical sequence, but this he has already done in claiming the existence of a universe of non-material things as the subject of his study, and in refusing to admit their derivation from the physical phenomena of evolution.

(c) Redefining of mind in objective terms as when Bawden states that " . . . mentality or mind is a name for the fact of the control of the environment in the interest of the organism through the interaction of inherited capacities and acquired abilities." Such arguments likewise avoid the issue. They ignore the subjectivist's claim that he knows a unique mode of existence not definable in objective terms. At best from the standpoint of the subjectivist they constitute only a study of the physiological correlates of conscious processes.

(*d*) Attacks on the method of introspection. These are the behaviourist's big guns. In general, they take one of two forms. Introspection is inaccurate, unverifiable; the stuff revealed by it is variable and inconsistent. It is indeed so unreliable that we are justified in throwing out everything which it claims to establish. But much the same argument has recently been urged against the objective methods of mental testing. It may be a strong plea but it is not logically convincing. A method may be defective and yet reveal fundamentally important facts, as Loewenhoek's observations on infusoria.

The other form involves a theory of introspection. When one examines his own mental states he is really reacting to stimulation of his proprioceptors. Introspection is a physiological process and as such can reveal only other physiological processes. Even if mental states exist, they cannot be discovered by introspection. But the introspectionist may reply, "Your doctrine of introspection is only an hypothesis. You have not produced convincing proof of the homeodetic theory of introspection. Our claim taht ental states form a unique mode of existence is based on the nature of the material which introspection reveals. If it does reveal such phenomena, it must be more than a physiological process. It is only by showing that mental states do not exist that you can prove that you have given an adequate account of the introspective process."

Thus it appears that the current formulations of behaviourism have not made good their claim to exclusive possession of the field of psychology. Methodological behaviourism has all the faults of psychophysical parallelism plus that of intolerance. It admits the existence of certain phenomena called conscious, admits that it can not fit them into its system, and denies to others the right to study those phenomena and to seek to formulate them into a science. Or, it reverts to the early objectivism of Bechterew and admits the possibility of a subjective psychology, merely asserting that this psychology is irrelevant to behaviouristic explanation. It thus paves the way for the development of two cognate sciences, such as Fernberger has recently advocated.

Strict behaviourism is advanced as a theory, but the insistence upon methodological behaviourism at all costs has prevented the consideration of any supposedly subjective data and has left the theory undeveloped. Yet if behaviourism is to become a complete science, if it is to avoid becoming merely a coördinate system with subjectivism, it must subordinate questions of method, of objectivity, to the application of mechanistic or physiological principles to the whole of psychology. This point is emphasized by Dewey to whom the facts of consciousness appear as an experimental behaviouristic problem. "To recognize that the behaviouristic principle can make a place for them (the facts of consciousness) is important. For science is, after all carried on by men, and a seeming denial that such facts do exist and do come under the behaviouristic principle is sure to keep alive in the minds of some a futile introspectionist method, by setting to one side a realm of facts to which (so it is thought) it *must* be applied since the behaviouristic method confessedly does not apply."

It is possible to construct a physiological psychology which will meet the dualist on his own ground, will accept the data which he advances and show that those data can be embodied in a mechanistic system. A behaviourism will thus develop which will be an adequate substitute for the older psychology. Its physiological account of behaviour will also be a complete and adequate account of all the phenomena of consciousness. It will be methodological only in insisting that the concepts of the physical sciences are the only ones which can serve as the basis for a science, and in demanding that all psychological data, however obtained, shall be objected to physical or physiological interpretation.

Such a program demands that we face the issue squarely. We must accept tentatively the supposed data of introspection and test the validity of our system by its ability to deal with such data. We shall find but three alternatives: the data may be of such a character that we can not hope to embody them in any mechanistic system; they may even now fall into such a system; or we may be able to define the problem of consciousness as an experimental problem, unanswerable on the basis of existing data, but offering possibility of solution with the development of objective science. Indirect arguments and denials of facts which others consider verifiable will not suffice. The dualist advances specific data with certain definable attributes as evidence for the validity of his system. Perhaps we can not verify his findings objectively, but we can examine his claims and determine if and in what respects they are incompatible with the postulates of the natural sciences. The key to the development of behaviourism lies here.

When the behaviourist denies that consciousness exists, he denies, not the existence of the phenomena upon which the conception is based, but only the inference that these data constitute a unique mode of existence or that they are not amenable to analysis and description of the same sort as are 'physical' data. Unfortunately, the psychological terminology current today involves not only an enumeration of phenomena but also a definite theory of reality. It is this theory which behaviourism repudiates.

STRENGTHS AND WEAKNESSES BEHAVIOURISM

— *Weakness* -the learner may find themselves in a situation where the stimulus for the correct response does not occur, therefore the learner cannot respond. A worker who has been conditioned to respond to a certain cue at work stops production when an anomaly occurs because they do not understand the system.

— *Strength* - the learner is focused on a clear goal and can respond automatically to the cues of that goal. W.W.II pilots were conditioned to react to silhouettes of enemy planes, a response which one would hope became automatic.

5

Cognitive Approach to Learning

THE BASICS OF COGNITIVISM

As early as the 1920's people began to find limitations in the behaviourist approach to understanding learning. Edward Tolman found that rats used in an experiment appeared to have a mental map of the maze he was using. When he closed off a certain portion of the maze, the rats did not bother to try a certain path because they "knew" that it led to the blocked path. Visually, the rats could not see that the path would result in failure, yet they chose to take a longer route that they knew would be successful.

Behaviourists were unable to explain certain social behaviours. For example, children do not imitate all behaviour that has been reinforced. Furthermore, they may model new behaviour days or weeks after their first initial observation without having been reinforced for the behaviour. Because of these observations, Bandura and Walters departed from the traditional operant conditioning explanation that the child must perform and receive reinforcement before being able to learn. They stated in their 1963 book, *Social Learning and Personality Development*, that an individual could model behaviour by observing the behaviour of another person. This theory lead to Bandura's Social Cognitive Theory.

Cognitive theorists recognize that much learning involves associations established through contiguity and repetition. They also acknowledge the importance of reinforcement, although they stress its role in providing feedback about the correctness of responses over its role as a motivator. However, even while accepting such behaviouristic concepts, cognitive theorists view learning as involving the acquisition or reorganization of the cognitive structures through which humans process and store information.

As with behaviourism, cognitive psychology can be traced back to the ancient Greeks, Plato and Aristotle. The cognitive revolution became evident in American psychology during the 1950's. One of the major players in the development of cognitivism is Jean Piaget, who developed the major aspects of his theory as early as the 1920's. Piaget's ideas did not impact North America until the 1960's after Miller and Bruner founded the Harvard Center for Cognitive studies.

In the 1930s, Edward Tolman proposed a theory of learning called cognition. He did not accept the previous theory which stated that behaviour was an automatic response to an event. Tolman believed that behaviour was goal-oriented, and had both direction and purpose. What we do is motivated by a desire to achieve a goal or to avoid unpleasant circumstances. His theory also proposed that there are paths which we can follow, and tools that we can use to achieve our goals. One of Tolman's fundamental ideas was that we act as if a particular type of behaviour will lead to a certain goal.

Tolman's theory was partially based upon his belief that we expect specific outcomes to result from specific behaviour. For example, if you pay attention in class and study, you may expect your mark to be an A. If you do not get an A, you will continue working towards this goal and will not be satisfied with anything less.

What distinguished Tolman's theory of cognition from most others was that it stated that learning can occur without reinforcement. We can learn from experience, but only if we are motivated enough to turn our expectations into behaviour.

Motivation has two purposes: to allow internal tension to create a demand for the goal, and to establish the events that you will concentrate on. There are two main types of motivators: deprivation and incentives. Deprivation causes an internal desire to obtain the goal, and we are motivated more by a large reward than a smaller one. Incentives motivate behaviour based merely upon the adequacy of the reward.

Tolman's theory gained wide acceptance in the 1960s, and several other researchers began expanding upon his work, including Julian Rotter with his social-learning theory. Rotter proposed that our preference for an event is determined by its reinforcement value. For example, a well-kept classic car may be worth more to you than a new sports car. He believed that we each have subjective expectations concerning the likelihood of obtaining a reinforcer. For example, someone may not expect an event to occur and therefore not even try to accomplish it out of fear of failure. Rotter's theory also stated that our expectation of acquiring reinforcement is determined by the situation. Past experiences influence our expectations about whether we can achieve a particular goal or not. He believed that when we encounter new experiences, our generalized expectations from the past will guide our action.

KEY CONCEPTS OF COGNITIVE THEORY

— *Habit*: A habit is something that we learn to do over and over again without consciously thinking about doing it. Many of our actions are habits, such as the sequence of steps to tie a shoelace. All habits begin as an action that we are aware of, but the more times the action is performed, the easier and more automatic it becomes. Eventually an action that is constantly being repeated will become a "strong habit" that requires almost no thought.

It is believed that a particular stimulus must be present each time a habit is carried out. A red traffic light, for example, is a stimulus to an experienced driver. It triggers the driver to respond by pressing the brake pedal. Therefore learning this habit would require practice under normal driving conditions, which would make pressing the brake pedal more automatic.

Most psychologists agree that someone only learns a habit if it is beneficial to them. This idea is based upon the theory of operant conditioning, or goal-directed behaviour. If a positive reinforcement (or reward) is obtained, then the behaviour will be repeated more often. If a habit offers no reward or results in negative reinforcement, then the habit will probably be broken.

There are several types of habits. Some are simple and only require muscle movement, such as reaching for the doorknob when you approach a closed door. This movement is natural and automatic, but as a child you had to learn this habit. Other habits are more complex than simple muscle movement. They involve thoughts and attitudes about people and objects. These are termed "habits of adjustment", and often affect other people. Proper manners would be an example of a good habit of adjustment, while pencil tapping is a bad habit of adjustment. Bad habits are often annoying to others, and have limited personal benefit.

— *Schema* - An internal knowledge structure. New information is compared to existing cognitive structures called "schema". Schema may be combined, extended or altered to accommodate new information.

— *Three-Stage Information Processing Model* - input first enters a sensory register, then is processed in short-term memory, and then is transferred to long-term memory for storage and retrieval.

— *Sensory Register* - receives input from senses which lasts from less than a second to four seconds and then disappears through decay or replacement. Much of the information never reaches short term memory but all information is monitored at some level and acted upon if necessary.

— *Short-Term Memory (STM)* - sensory input that is important or interesting is transferred from the sensory register to the STM. Memory can be retained here for up to 20 seconds or more if rehearsed repeatedly. Short-term memory can hold up to 7 plus or minus 2 items. STM capacity can be increased if material is chunked into meaningful parts.

— *Long-Term Memory and Storage (LTM)* - stores information from STM for long term use. Long-term memory has unlimited capacity. Some materials are "forced" into LTM by rote memorization and over learning. Deeper levels of processing such as generating linkages between old and new information are much better for successful retention of material.

— *Meaningful Effects* - Meaningful information is easier to learn and remember. If a learner links relatively meaningless information with prior schema it will be easier to retain.

— *Serial Position Effects* - It is easier to remember items from the beginning or end of a list rather than those in the middle of the list, unless that item is distinctly different.

— *Practice Effects* - Practicing or rehearsing improves retention especially when it is distributed practice. By distributing practices the learner associates the material with many different contexts rather than the one context afforded by mass practice.

— *Transfer Effects*- The effects of prior learning on learning new tasks or material.

— *Interference Effects* - Occurs when prior learning interferes with the learning of new material.

— *Organization Effects* - When a learner categorizes input such as a grocery list, it is easier to remember.

— *Levels of Processing Effects* - Words may be processed at a low-level sensory analysis of their physical characteristics to high-level semantic analysis of their meaning. The more deeply a word is process the easier it will be to remember.

— *State Dependent Effects* - If learning takes place within a certain context it will be easier to remember within that context rather than in a new context.

— *Mnemonic Effects* - Mnemonics are strategies used by learners to organize relatively meaningless input into more meaningful images or semantic contexts. For example, the notes of a musical scale can be remembered by the rhyme: Every Good Boy Deserves Fruit.

— *Schema Effects* - If information does not fit a person's schema it may be more difficult for them to remember and what they remember or how they conceive of it may also be affected by their prior schema.

— *Advance Organizers* - Ausebels advance organizers prepare the learner for the material they are about to learn. They are not simply outlines of the material, but are material that will enable the student to make sense out of the lesson.

COGNITIVISM AND INSTRUCTIONAL DESIGN

Although cognitive psychology emerged in the late 1950s and began to take over as the dominant theory of learning, it wasn't until the late 1970s that cognitive science began to have its influence on instructional design. Cognitive science began a shift from behaviouristic practices which emphasised external behaviour, to a concern with the internal mental processes of the mind and how they could be utilized in promoting effective learning. The design models that had been developed in the behaviourist tradition were not simply tossed out, but instead the "task analysis" and "learner analysis" parts of the models were embellished. The new models addressed component processes of learning such as knowledge coding and representation, information storage and retrieval as well as the incorporation and integration of new knowledge with previous information.

Because Cognitivism and Behaviourism are both governed by an objective view of the nature of knowledge and what it means to know something, the transition from behavioural instructional design principles to those of a cognitive style was not entirely difficult. The goal of instruction remained the communication or transfer of knowledge to learners in the most efficient, effective manner possible. For example, the breaking down of a task into small steps works for a behaviourist who is trying to find the most efficient and fail proof method of shaping a learner's behaviour. The cognitive scientist would analyze a task, break it down into smaller steps or chunks and use that information to develop instruction that moves from simple to complex building on prior schema.

The influence of cognitive science in instructional design is evidenced by the use of advance organizers, mnemonic devices, metaphors, chunking into meaningful parts and the careful organization of instructional materials from simple to complex.

Cognitivism and Computer-Based Instruction

Computers process information in a similar fashion to how cognitive scientists believe humans process information: receive, store and retrieve. This analogy makes the possibility of programming a computer to "think" like a person conceivable, i.e.. artificial intelligence.

Artificial intelligence involve the computer working to supply appropriate responses to student input from the computer's data base. A trouble-shooting programs is one example of these programs. Below is a list of some programs and their intended use:

— *SCHOLAR* - teaches facts about South American geography in a Socratic method

— *PUFF* - diagnoses medical patients for possible pulmonary disorders

— *MYCIN* - diagnoses blood infections and prescribes possible treatment

— *DENDRAL* - enables a chemist to make an accurate guess about the molecular structure of an unknown compound

— *META-DENDRAL* - makes up its own molecular fragmentation rules in an attempt to explain sets of basic data

— *GUIDION* - a derivative of the MYCIN program that gave a student information about a case and compared their diagnosis with what MYCIN would suggest

— *SOPIE* - helps engineers troubleshoot electronic equipment problems

— *BUGGY* - allows teachers to diagnose causes for student mathematical errors

— *LOGO* - designed to help children learn to program a computer

— Individually Prescribed Instruction (IPI) Davis' math programs for the PLATO system - to encourage mathematical development through discovery.

PIAGET'S THEORY OF LEARNING AND COGNITIVE DEVELPOMENT

Over a period of six decades, Jean Piaget conducted a program of naturalistic research that has profoundly affected our understanding of child development. Piaget called his general theoretical framework 'genetic epistemology' because he was primarily interested in how knowledge developed in human organisms.

Piaget had a background in both Biology and Philosophy and concepts from both these disciplines influences his theories and research of child development. The concept of cognitive structure is central to his theory. Cognitive structures are patterns of physical or mental action that underlie specific acts of intelligence and correspond to stages of child development. There are four primary cognitive structures (i.e. development stages) according to Piaget:

— sensorimotor;

— preoperations;

— concrete operations; and,

— formal operations.

In the sensorimotor stage (0-2 years), intelligence takes the form of motor actions. Intelligence in the preoperation period (3-7 years) is intutive in nature. The cognitive structure during the concrete operational stage (8-11 years) is logical but depends upon concrete referents. In the final stage of formal operations (12-15 years), thinking involves abstractions.

The theory also postulates that cognitive structures change through the processes of adaptation: assimilation and accomodation. Assimilation involves the interpretation of events in terms of existing cognitive structure whereas accomodation refers to changing the cognitive structure to make sense of the environment. Cognitive development consists of a constant effort to adapt to the environment in terms of assimilation and accomodation. In this sense, Piaget's theory is similar in nature to other constructivist perspectives of learning.

While the stages of cognitive development identified by Piaget are associated with characteristic age spans, they vary for every individual. Furthermore, each stage has many detailed structural forms. For example, the concrete operational period has more than forty distinct structures covering classification and relations, spatial relationships, time, movement, chance, number, conservation and measurement.

Application

Piaget explored the implications of his theory to all aspects of cognition, intelligence and moral development. Many of Piaget's experiments were focused on the development of mathematical and logical concepts. The theory has been applied extensively to teaching practice and curriculum design in elementary education.

Example

Applying Piaget's theory results in specific recommendations for a given stage of cognitive development. For example, with children in the sensorimotor stage, teachers should try to provide a rich and stimulating environment with ample objects to play with. On the other hand, with children in the concrete operational stage, learning activities should involve problems of classification, ordering, location, conservation using concrete objects.

Principles

> Cognitive development is facilitated by providing activities or situations that engage learners and require adaptation (i.e., assimilation and accomodation).
>
> Learning materials and activities should involve the appropriate level of motor or mental operations for a child of given developmental stage; teachers should avoid asking students to perform tasks that are beyond their currrent cognitive capabilities.
>
> Use teaching methods that actively involve students and present challenges

GESTALT LEARNING THEORY

Gestalt became one of the main theories of learning. The three main Gestalt theorists (Wertheimer, Kohler, and Koffka) were all Germans, and received their training and did their early work in Germany, but all three ended their careers in the US. The term "Gestalt" was coined by Graf Christian von Ehrenfels. His ideas influenced the trio of theorists.

Gestalt was a holistic approach and rejected the mechanistic perspectives of the stimulus - response models. Numerous new concepts and approaches emerged from this different philosophical perspective. The Gestalt theory proposes that learning consists of the grasping of a structural whole and not just a mechanistic response to a stimulus.

A "Gestalt" is an integrated whole system with it's parts enmeshed. The whole is greater than just the sum of the parts.

The "PHI" phenomenon described a characteristic of things wherein they have a recognizability inherent in their nature. Examples include the recognizability of a melody, no matter how it is arranged or what instrument plays it, or the recognizability of a letter rendered in a wide variety of different fonts or type styles. Other examples include the apparent motion created by a rapid sequence of stills in motion pictures, and the sequences of illminating elements in neon signs which give the illusion of movement. Visual and auditory examples are numerous. This phenomenon leads to the conclusion that elements sensed are not the only reality.

"Phenomenology" is the acceptance of first hand experience as it is found in human consciousness.

Gestalt Learning Theory proposed several laws of organization, which are innate ways that human beings organized perceptions. A gestalt factor is a condition that aids in perceiving situations as a whole or totality. Isomorphism refers to the Doctrine of Psychophysical parallelism and depicts the cerebral cortex as "mapping these gestalt fields of stimuli.

The Factor of Closure suggests that perception tends to complete incomplete objects. When only part of an image, sound, thought or feeling is presented as a stimulus, the brain attempts to complete it to generate the whole.

The Factor of Proximity suggests that when elements are grouped closely together, they are percieved as wholes. This has relevance in reading, visual arts, and music.

The Factor of Similarity proposes that like parts tend to be grouped together in cognition. This has implications for instruction, suggesting that learning is facilitated if similar ideas are treated and linked together and then contrasted with opposing or complementary sets of ideas.

The Figure-Ground Effect suggests that the eye tends to see the objects, rather than the spaces or holes between them.

Trace Theory - This proposes a mechanism for learning in which neruological changes occur as connections are made in the brain. These changes, called traces, represent links between thoughts, ideas, concepts, images, etc. REpetition and uniqueness reinforce a trace. Thus, learning is the creation of traces. Traces group together to form maps. Instructional methods relating to repetition and to making items to be learned somehow distinctive to make learning (trace formation) quicker and more lasting.

From the early theorys of Gestalt, there also emerged a branch of therapeutic interventions, called Gestalt Therapy. Fritz Perls went through psychoanalytic training with Karen Horney and then with Wilhelm Reich. He also adapted existentialist philosophy along with Zen and Taoist views to therapeutic work, and was strongly influenced by Freud.

GESTALT-ANTECEDENT INFLUENCE OR HISTORICAL ACCIDENT

There has been relatively little appraisal of the antecedent influence of Gestalt psychology on Gestalt therapy. This section attempts to expand on the work of previous academic writers on the theoretical precursors of Gestalt therapy. Most of the relevant articles, monographs, or books which mention Gestalt psychology still refer to Wallen, whilst Perls in his books referred to the influence of Gestalt psychology, but gave little indication of the extent of that influence. Yontef highlighted the need for this type of exploration:

> Neither Gestalt psychology nor the connection with Gestalt therapy is adequately understood, even by most Gestalt therapists, and has not been adequately discussed in the Gestalt therapy literature. Unfortunately this very important subject must be reserved for a more technical paper.

Two Gestalt Psychologists' Attitudes

Henle in an article titled "The relations between Gestalt psychology and Gestalt therapy" was critical of Perls' use of the word "Gestalt." She quotes a number of Perls' statements out of context, or slants meanings in favor of her particular argument. The final conclusion that she drew was that " . . . the two approaches have nothing in common".

One Gestalt psychologist apart from Henle who has mentioned the relationship between the two approaches was Arnheim. The one paragraph letter to *Contemporary Psychology* was not sufficient to allow analysis of his position other than the consideration of Arnheim's own interpretation of what Wertheimer would have done — that is, ". . . fly into one of his magnificent rages at the use of the name 'Gestalt' in Gestalt therapy"

Only by critical analysis of certain quotations and extracts from early writings in the Gestalt literature can a meaningful conclusion be drawn as to the degree to which Perls adopted, developed and integrated certain notions and concepts from Gestalt psychology.

Perls' Use of Gestalt

The very fact that Perls called his method of therapy "Gestalt therapy" indicated that he saw significant links and connections between that therapy and the tradition of Gestalt psychology.

Perls regarded Gestalt therapy with its "dependence on the laws of Gestalt dynamics" as "the next step after Freud in the history of psychiatry". Simkin reported Perls as saying of Gestalt psychology:

> . . . the thing that fascinated me was the Gestalt approach. For the first time, the breaking away from the piecemeal consideration and getting perspective.

Gestalt therapists themselves appear not to be in agreement as to the theoretical precursors of Gestalt therapy, and particularly to Gestalt psychology. For instance, Enright argued that Gestalt psychology was probably the least important theoretical influence on Perls, but was possibly used to name the new therapy because it was the most recent influence, and " . . . was uppermost in his (Perls') mind". Yontef is more positive when enunciating the influence of Gestalt psychology:

> . . . the underlying holistic and phenomenological structure of Gestalt therapy is a clinical derivative of Gestalt psychology.

Perls noted that although he was an assistant to Professor Kurt Goldstein and aware of the Gestalt psychologists' work in the 1920's, he was primarily psychoanalytically oriented, both as a therapist/analyst and as a patient. It is significant that Perls did not use the word "Gestalt" in any title nor in any significant manner when he wrote *Ego, Hunger and Aggression*, his first major attempt to outline his theory. Rosenfeld commented on this point:

> There's not a lot in *Ego, Hunger and Aggression* that points to the really extensive development that he made of the whole metaphor of Gestalt.

Perls chose the title "Gestalt therapy" (in the title of *Gestalt Therapy: Excitement and Growth in the Human Personality*) over strong objections from his wife Laura, and his coauthors Paul Goodman and Ralph Hefferline. Laura Perls considered that the approach as outlined in the book had little relation to the academic Gestalt psychology she had studied, and wanted to use the name "Existential Therapy." Goodman thought the title too esoteric, while Hefferline wanted their work presented as "Integrative Therapy". It is perhaps not surprising that Enright suggested that the name Gestalt therapy was an historical accident, and that it is misleading to attach too much weight to it in understanding Perls' works.

This "historical accident" theory is not upheld, however, by Perls' own work. In his autobiography, Perls described his relation to Gestalt psychologists as a peculiar one, but in no way denied that such a relationship existed. He acknowledged his adoption of the fundamental idea of the unfinished situation, or incomplete gestalt, to Gestalt therapy. He also stated his admiration for their work, although disagreeing with their logical positivism.

Perls' feelings about his status as a "Gestaltist" are revealed in this quotation:

> The academic Gestaltists of course, never accepted me. I certainly was not a pure Gestaltist.

Perls' gratitude for the contributions made by classical Gestalt psychology to Gestalt therapy was reflected both in his dedication of his first book to the memory of Max Wertheimer, and in this poem which appeared in his autobiography:

> Reality is nothing but
> The sum of all the awareness
> As you experience here and now
> The ultimate of science thus appears
> As Husserl's unit of phenomenon
> And Ehrenfeld's discovery:
> The irreducible phenomenon of all
> Awareness, the one he named
> And we still call
> GESTALT.

The basic premise on which Gestalt therapy rests is that of holism. The greatest value in the Gestalt approach, according to Perls, Hefferline and Goodman:

> . . . lies in the insight that the whole determines the parts, which contrasts with the previous assumption that the whole is merely the total sum of its elements.

Latner stated: "The foundation of the first principle of Gestalt therapy is holism". This basic premise was not only adopted by Gestalt psychology, but also by Gestalt therapy, and in fact all of the humanistic and existential psychologies. Perls had largely credited the Gestalt psychologists with the formulation of the concept of holism and applied to his model of personality wrote that it was:

> . . developed by a group of German psychologists working in the field of perception, who showed that man does not perceive things as unrelated isolates but organizes them in the perceptual process into meaningful wholes.

It would appear that the term holism was most recently coined by Smuts in 1906 and alluded to by him as early as 1892-3, although this notion can he traced to Eastern philosophy and religions many centuries earlier.

Smuts formulated a number of basic concepts, the most important of which to Perls were the unity of the individual and integration. Smuts wrote:

> . . every individual form of life is a unity . . . it is this ultimate and internal unity that shapes the innumerable products of life into an orderly and harmonious whole . . . This distinct, single, indivisible unity of life in each individual I call the personality of that individual . .

This understanding of man regarded the physical, the emotional, thoughts, all mental events, and so on, as expressions of a unified being; of each individual. Holistically we cannot attain an adequate concept of self by merely summing up the individual component parts of self — the whole is greater than the sum of its parts. Gestalt therapy is a philosophy of life based on the holistic epistemology outlined above. It is descriptive, integrative, and structural, emphasizing phenomenology, the here and now as well as a positive wholeness which emphasizes our creating our lives and discovering our strengths.

The Organism-Environment Interaction

Basically, Gestalt therapy is concerned with the interaction between the organism and its environment. In the healthy organism, many needs are present at any one time. These organize themselves into a hierarchy of importance, as a natural process. The most dominant need forms, or becomes figure. In order to satisfy this need, the organism searches its environment for the desired object (sensory activity); when the object is found, the organism acts to assimilate it (motor activity). The concept of the connection between the sensoric and motor activities has been extensively discussed by the Gestalt psychologists for many years. When the needed object has been assimilated, the Gestalt is closed, and a state of equilibrium is reached. The formerly dominant need recedes from awareness (becomes ground), and the energy thus freed is directed towards the next most dominant need. Organisms are thus self-regulatory or homeostatic. In this way, the organism is regarded as being "born with the capacity to cope with life".

Figure-Ground Differentiation/Pragnanz/Closure

Perls had been influenced by Wertheimer, Koffka and Kohler through their writings. He had direct contact with Lewin and with Goldstein, working with the latter at the Goldstein Institute for Brain Damaged Soldiers in 1926. Goldstein expanded Gestalt psychology as a study of perception to Gestalt psychology as a study of the whole person. His views appeared in *The Organism*, and came to be known as "organismic theory."

Goldstein argued that the primary organization of organismic functioning is the figure-ground. He proposed three dynamic concepts — i) the equalization processes or tension) reduction systems that keep the organism centered or balanced; ii) the processes of "getting what one wants in the world" (a concept adapted by Perls extensively in psychotherapy); and iii) "the notion of self-actualization. In this theory, self-actualization is the "master motive." The satisfaction of any specific need becomes figure when it is the dominant need at that time for the whole organism. This notion was also incorporated almost verbatim from Goldstein. Perls wrote that whilst working for Goldstein, he had not understood the term self-actualization, although twenty five years later, coming from Maslow it acquired more meaning. It was not until much later that the concept was fully understood and acquired.

Perls stated that the first basic premise of Gestalt therapy is that

> . . . it is the organization of facts or perceptions and not the individual items of which they are composed, that defines them and gives them their specific and particular meaning.

Wheeler had recorded this notion as the first of his eight "organismic" laws, which hold that any item of reality is in its own right an integrated whole that is more than the sum of its parts. Fantz argued that academic Gestalt psychologists did not fully apply the principles of Gestalt formation to organic perceptions—e.g., feelings, emotions or body awareness, " . . . nor did they integrate the problems of motivation with those of perception". Fantz claimed that this integration was successfully introduced by Perls. It may be, however, that Fantz had overlooked the work of Goldstein and other Gestalt psychologists, which shows how the figure-ground and other principles can be applied to the total motivation and action processes of individuals, and how physical and mental pathologies may he viewed in terms of these principles. It is significant that Goldstein subtitled his book *A Holistic Approach to Biology: Derived From Pathological Data in Man.* In fact, Perls appears to be simply the first to apply such principles, and especially that of the figure-ground, to psychotherapy.

This figure-ground concept was quickly assimilated into the main body of Gestalt therapy and today it is almost synonymous with Gestalt. The figure-ground principle stated that every perception is organized into a figure which stands out from a background. However, these are not necessarily properties of the stimulus object, but rather of the psychological field. Koffka devoted five chapters to the environmental field, and to figure-ground differentiation. Although Koffka did attempt to incorporate memory, will, and action, and referred to the "silent organization" of human experience, figure remained limited essentially to inside-the-form visual phenomena, and ground to outside-the-form phenomena.

Perls et al., introduced the concept of needs into the "psycho-therapeutic" figure-ground concept (i.e., needs arise and the Gestalt recedes when the need is satisfied). Koffka, however, referred to a super sensory ground, from which all sensory figures arise, and to which all figures return once needs have been satisfied. It can be argued that in Gestalt psychology as in Gestalt therapy, Gestalt formation is considered a primary characteristic of organismic functioning.

Perls discussed the connection between needs and figure-ground differentiation:

> Formulating this principle in terms of Gestalt psychology, we can say that the dominant need . . . becomes the foreground, and the other needs recede. . . into the background.

A field that is poorly organized is still organized to the individual. The Gestalt psychologists' principle of pragnanz suggests that any psychological field is as well organized as conditions permit at that time. Thus it is possible, as was recognized by Koffka and Kohler years ago, that certain circumstances can interfere with the Gestalt formation process (e.g., stress, motivation). This concept was adopted by Perls, who went on to argue that in neurotic self-regulation, certain forces are prevented from having their full effect on the individual. Thus, the meeting or contact between the self and the environment may be less than optimal, resulting in a distorted perception of the contact process. Kohler stated: "To a degree, the organization of the field may yield to stress . . .," where stress referred to the particular valence associated with the parts of the field. This position was endorsed by Perls.

The impression that the Gestalt principle of figure-ground is merely the equivalent of "attention" in other systems is not implied here. The Gestalt psychologists emphasized figure-ground as a spontaneous and natural organization which does not depend on learning, but is an inevitable consequence of man's perceptual apparatus. Perls et al., criticized the Gestalt psychologists for not having sufficient interest in the meaning of "ground." To Perls, ground is everything that is progressively eliminated from attention in the experienced situation. This criticism may be seen as an overstatement, for it is contrary to the principle of "what is, is" (implying acceptance of the self); it is also contrary to the anti-analytic position generally espoused by Gestalt therapists and Gestalt psychologists. The later introduction of the concept of grooving shows how Perls' attitude to this concept changed. Both the Gestalt psychologists and Perls adopt the position that the figure is more impressive, it dominates consciousness and is usually mentioned before the ground.

One of the important laws in Gestalt psychology was that of closure. Once characteristic of perceptions is the individual's movement towards closure. Closure for Perls was achieved by concentrating on the now, by rejecting intellectualization and flights into the past or future, and by accepting responsibility for ourselves. Polster and Polster suggested that closure was more than a perceptual reflex. Rather, it is a personal reflex which is frequently thwarted by societal restraints and thus interrupts some processes which are forced into the background where they remain as "unfinished business." Perls stated the place of "closure" in Gestalt therapy:

> . . . one of the basic laws of Gestalt formation — the tension arising out of the need for closure is called

> frustration, the closure is called satisfaction . . . With satisfaction, the imbalance is annihilated, it disappears. The incident is closed.
>
> Just as balance and discovery are met on all levels of existence, so are frustration, satisfaction and closure.

Once closure has allowed the dominant need to recede from awareness, the individual returns to a state of equilibrium.

The Concept of Equilibrium

Many of the broad philosophical features of the Gestalt psychologists' work, such as the laws of pragnanz and closure, are related to a fundamental concept which runs through the whole of Gestalt therapy and Gestalt psychology — that of equilibrium. The perceptual field and its underlying isomorphic cortical field are said to be dynamic wholes, which, like a magnetic field of force in physics, tends towards equilibrium. When the psychological field is disturbed by the introduction of new forces, the whole undergoes a new alignment of forces until equilibrium is once more established. In short, it is a fundamental property of percepts to tend towards stability, and to remain as stable as conditions permit. Perls stated:

> Man seems to be born with a sense of social and psychological balance as acute as the sense of physical balance . . . difficulties spring not from the desire to reject such equilibrium, but from misguided movements aimed towards finding and maintaining it.

The Role of Attention, Awareness and Experience

Attention is important in Gestalt therapy because the therapist usually endeavors to facilitate the individual towards attending to cortical processes or phenomena. Ternus stated that attention

> . . . embraces the entire figure unless instructions to the contrary are given . . . and the center of attention typically coincides with the figural center of the presented object.

Attention for Perls is a deliberate way of listening or attending to the foreground, Fantz regarded perception as a function of the figure-ground relationship and a direct result of the focus of attention and activity is called the figure or Gestalt, and what does not become part of the focus remains background. Perls would probably have concurred with Henle when she stated that " . . .attention intensifies the process which underlies the perception of an object."

The role of awareness in Gestalt therapy is somewhat obscure, although it is of fundamental importance. Polster and Polster described awareness or experience as one of the three touchstones of all Gestalt therapy, the other two being contact and experiment. Enright described awareness in the following manner:

> . . . awareness is a state of consciousness that develops spontaneously when organismic attention becomes focused on some particular region of the organism-environment contact boundary at which an especially important and complex transaction is occurring.

A technique of Gestalt therapy is the development of the continuum of awareness — the therapist facilitating a person increasing awareness in himself/herself. Most people interrupt or block awareness if it is unpleasant, and avoid it, developing defense mechanisms such as intellectualization or flights into the past or future, anxiety, denial, deflection or other "coping" strategies. Kreuger had foreshadowed such techniques when reflecting that an emotional state tended to be dissipated by attention to it as such. When attention and awareness come together — the "fuzzy twin" — there is an experience of the "now".

The greater the experience of the now, the more choices become available to the person. And, although it is not apparently mentioned elsewhere, Baumgardner credited Perls with saying that the greater the awareness, the greater the chance of tracing — otherwise called a "grooving" process. This means that there is an after-image that links up the past and the acquisition of experience. This concept is firmly rooted in Gestalt psychology. Gottschaldt wrote that past experience is an explanatory concept in that such experience constitutes an independent force, capable of modifying subsequent perception in a specific manner. Baumgardner concurred to a large degree — the grooving always provides one part of the Gestalt — the background.

The Here and Now

Perls set out an equation of "now = experience = awareness = reality." The only awareness is here and now, whether it be the past (memories) or the future (anticipation) — past and future events are in the present, as they occupy present processes. Naranjo contended that Gestalt therapy " . . . aims at the sub-ordination of these thought forms to life."

Perls insisted that to stray from the present distracts from the living quality of reality. This emphasis on the "now" is consistent with the Gestalt psychologists' definition of psychology as the study of the immediate experience of the whole organism, the "now" as it is perceived. Asch in writing a brief outline of Gestalt psychology suggested that it " . . . assigns a place of crucial importance in psychological enquiry to the data of immediate experience."

Murphy and Jensen set out the Gestalt psychologists' position with regard to personality and present immediate experience, a position endorsed by Perls:

> Just as the parts fail to explain the whole, so the past fails to explain the present or the present the future . . . at the present instant the future seems simply non-existent . . .

The Concept of Boundaries and Neuroses

Hartmann referred to the work of Rubin who discussed the role of contours and boundaries between figure and ground. Koffka went further and distinguished between the self and others. Kohler referred to the process whereby the environment meets the self (or the individual). Every part of the organism is said to be constantly influenced both by the outside world and by other parts within. Kubler's concept of boundaries suggested:

> . . . the inner states of any finite system develop relative to more or less fixed conditions along its boundaries and its interior.

These then are boundary problems, the state of any region of the system at any particular time is also influenced — even determined by the state of every other region. This principle constitutes the fundamental thought underlying the theory of Gestalten. Gestalt therapy practically reiterates this principle when it states that neuroses occur at the boundary.

Perls has incorporated this concept and amplified it in most of his books:

> The study of the way in which a person functions in his environment is the study of what goes on at the contact boundary between the individual and his environment. It is at this contact boundary that the psychological events take place. Our thoughts, our actions, our behaviour, and our emotions are our way of experiencing and meeting those boundary events.

In fact, Perls did not make a clear distinction between the contact boundary and the ego boundary, which is the differentiation between the self and otherness. However, this concept of Koffka's has been largely incorporated, as shown by Perls' description of the identification and alienation functions of the ego-boundary. Inside the ego boundary there is a cohesion, love and cooperation, whilst outside the ego boundary is suspicion and strangeness.

Gestalt therapy regarded neuroses as disturbances of the contact boundary:

> All neurotic disturbances arise from the individual's inability to find and maintain a proper balance between himself and the rest of the world . . .

In the healthy individual, the process of Gestalt formation and recession flows smoothly. If Gestalten are not adequately fulfilled, blocked energy thus results in anxiety. Perls interpreted Goldstein's view of anxiety as implying that anxiety is the result of "catastrophic expectations." This can lead to detachment and isolation of organismic parts, or in other words, a "splitting" of the personality. Baumgardner suggested that anxiety indicates that the individual has left the present for an imaginary journey into fantasy or the future. Anxiety is regarded as a substitute emotion which blocks awareness of what is really going on inside the individual. This is the view of Baumgardner and other ,Gestalt therapists who have reiterated Goldstein's description of the manner in which neurosis can result from anxiety.

The Mind-Body Position

Perls adopted the "holistic doctrine," which stated that man is a unified organism — a fact Perls suggested was ignored by psychiatry and psychotherapy, which ". . . are still operating in terms of the old mind-body split" . However, we only need to refer back to Wertheimer, who, discussing the mind-body split stated: "The principle here, is that something mental is meaningfully coupled with something physical". Thus, to observe the physical is to infer the mental. It was further expanded by Wertheimer, who carefully explained how often it is that various physical processes are "Gestalt identical" with the mental processes.

Gestalt psychologists formulated the law of "psychophysical isomorphism" which began from the prima facie dualism of mind and body. This notion further expands:

> . . that molar events in experience are structurally identical to the corresponding molar physiological events in the brain.

This is, in fact, a dualist position. Perls' position on the body-mind debate is not entirely clear. A monist position is espoused in some places when he maintained that we do not have a body but rather: "We are a body, we are somebody" . *In Ego, Hunger and Aggression*, he suggested that " . . . body and soul are identical *'in re'* though not *'in verbo,'* the words 'body' and 'soul''denoted two aspects of the same thing". Further elaborations of Perls suggest that dualistic and parallelistic theories are based on an artificial split which has no existence in reality. Although Perls considered himself a monist, a number of extracts from his writings suggest that he was not entirely a monist, but rather an uncertain dualist because he referred to " . . . purely mental experiences which comprise " . . . wishes, phantasies and daydreams . . ."; hardly the words of a pure monist. On the whole, it would appear as though he adopted a double aspect theory.

The position as espoused by Pens was not dissimilar to that of Wertheimer who stated that when a man is timid, afraid or energetic, happy or sad, it can be shown often that the course of his physical process is "Gestalt identical" with the course pursued by the mental process. Perhaps such statements influenced Perls when he introduced ". . . the concept of the unified field" which stated that in psychotherapy, what a person does gives the therapist clues as to what (s)he thinks. Gobar in referring to psychotherapy, stated that . . the concept of "'psychological equilibrium' is analogous to the concepts of 'physical equilibrium' and 'physiological equilibrium.'" If Gobar is adopting the word "analogous" in the same way that the *Shorter Oxford Dictionary* explains its meaning, that is, "equality of ratios" or equivalency" then the respective positions of Gestalt psychologists' usage and that of Perls may be seen as somewhat confused.

Henle stated in her book *Documents of Gestalt Psychology* that Gestalt psychologists hold that expressive behaviour reveais its meaning directly in personality. The approach according to Henle, and one adopted by Perls, was based on the "principle of isomorphism", whereby processes in one medium are similar in their structural identity to those in a different medium. Applied to body and mind, this meant that:

> . . . if the forces which determine bodily behaviour are structurally similar to those which characterize the corresponding mental states, it may become understandable why physical meaning can be read off directly from a person's appearance and conduct.

Another direct quote from Henle is compatible with the views expressed by Perls in most of his works:

> The way a person dresses, keeps his room, handles the language . . . can be called expressive in that they permit conclusions about the personality or the temporary state of mind of the individual.

Kohler insisted strenuously on a "special type of parallelism" when he wrote:

> When someone experiences that flash by which a new idea or the solution of a problem comes to him, he will suddenly interrupt his walking or abruptly strike his head. Here both his inner experience and his outer aspect will exhibit the same interruption of continuity.

Henle's criticisms are somewhat diluted when considering one section of Hartmann's book *Gestalt Psychology*, published in 1935. Hartmann stated that: " . . . the monism of Gestalt is implied" when it is asserted that the psychological and the physical are " . . . one and the same reality (and) are expressed in two different conceptual systems". (It is a Zen notion that mind and body are not one, not two, but between one and two). Further, Gestalt psychology equated bodily with mental events since the same configuration is found in both. It is this concept which appears to be one of the most important in Gestalt therapy. The therapist can only ever be in touch with a client from various extrapolations and "interpretation" of physical processes from mental material. The total organism is not to be analyzed into parts. Perls stated that:

> We believe further that the "mental-physical" or "mind-body" split is a totally artificial one, and that to concentrate one either term in the dichotomy is to preserve neurosis, not to cure it. . .

This line of thought represents another direct influence of Goldstein on Perls. Goldstein suggested that loss of categorical thinking (inability to abstract and classify) results in a limitation of orientation and of action. In all his writings, Perls emphasized the importance of using words which express the precise meaning of what he wanted to convey. Pathology, he stated produces both distortion of word meaning (incorrect vocabulary) and wrong application of grammar (incorrect syntax). He (Perls) encouraged one to learn the value of each word, and to appreciate the power hidden in the "logos." Avoidance of ego language (use of "I" when speaking of oneself) and the avoidance of personal responsibility are closely related.

Psychotherapy and Integration

Gobar is one of the few authors to have discussed the role and purpose of psychotherapy in Gestalt psychology. He suggests that in Gestalt theory, all psychological disorders involve, in some form or other, the destruction of a basic psychological structure and a concomitant generation of a "bad configuration." This results in a pervasive disturbance of the equilibrium of the psychological makeup as a whole.

It is important to examine the rationale for therapist assistance/intervention with clients. Perls suggested that successful therapy " . . . frees the patient's ability to abstract and integrate . . . his/her abstractions". The long term goal of therapy:

> . must be to give him the means with which he can solve his present problems and any that may arise tomorrow or next year.

If successful therapy integrates the personality, then the approach described by Gobar has much in common with that of Perls. According to Gobar, the concept of "cure" in psychotherapy (cure comes from the Latin *cura* meaning care) can be seen as:

> . . . the process of the reconstruction of the psychological system and the resultant restoration of equilibrium."

For Gobar, the principle of equilibrium holds for all psychological processes including the perceptual and cognitive at all genetic levels. In addition, it also " . . . constitutes the explanatory principle for the fundamental process of adaptation of the organism-environment".

Goldstein is quoted as describing the process of integration in this way:

> All of a person's capacities are always in action in each of his activities. The capacity that is particularly important for the task is in the foreground; the others are in the background. All of these capacities are organized in a way which facilitates the self-realization of the total organism in the particular situation. For each performance there is a definite figure-ground organization of capacities . . .

One of the therapeutic tools that Perls adopts when a person cannot remember a dream is to request the person to fantasize what the dream would be if (s)he could remember it — a method which some regard as free association. Hartmann stated that: "Wertheimer actually won some repute as an authority on the diagnostic or detective use of the free association method." Once again, the influence of Gestalt psychology appears to have been present.

Perls adopts a position on awareness similar to that espoused by various writers on Gestalt psychology such as Hartmann. One of Perls' statements which has been popular in the literature gives us a clear insight into the nature of cure in psychotherapy: " . . . awareness per se — of and by itself — can be curative. Hartmann writes that " . . . an emotional state tends to be dissipated by attention to it as such". Kreuger also added to this concept of cure when stating:

> An emotional complex loses in its Intensity and plasticity of its emotional character to the degree that it becomes analyzed, so that its parts become relatively separated, or that the partial moments in it come out clearly as such.

Once again, the writings of early Gestalt psychologists appear similar to those of Perls.

COGNITIVE DISSONANCE

Cognitive Dissonance Theory, developed by Leon Festinger, is concerned with the relationships among cognitions. A cognition, for the purpose of this theory, may be thought of as a [3]piece of knowledge.[2] The knowledge may be about an attitude, an emotion, a behaviour, a value, and so on. For example, the knowledge that you like the color red is a cognition; the knowledge that you caught a touchdown pass is a cognition; the knowledge that the Supreme Court outlawed school segregation is a cognition. People hold a multitude of cognitions simultaneously, and these cognitions form irrelevant, consonant or dissonant relationships with one another.

Cognitive Irrelevance probably describes the bulk of the relationships among a person[1]s cognitions. Irrelevance simply means that the two cognitions have nothing to do with each other. Two cognitions are consonant if one cognition follows from, or fits with, the other. People like consonance among their cognitions. We do not know whether this stems from the nature of the human organism or whether it is learned during the process of socialization, but people appear to prefer cognitions that fit together to those that do not. It is this simple observation that gives the theory of cognitive dissonance its interesting form.

Two cognitions are said to be dissonant if one cognition follows from the opposite of another. What happens to people when they discover dissonant cognitions? The answer to this question forms the basic postulate of Festinger[1]s theory. A person who has dissonant or discrepant cognitions is said to be in a state of psychological dissonance, which is experienced as unpleasant psychological tension. This tension state has drivelike properties that are much like those of hunger and thirst. When a person has been deprived of food for several hours, he/she experiences unpleasant tension and is driven to reduce the unpleasant tension state that results. Reducing the psychological sate of dissonance is not as simple as eating or drinking however.

To understand the alternatives open to an individual in a state of dissonance, we must first understand the factors that affect the magnitude of dissonance arousal. First, in its simplest form, dissonance increases as the degree of discrepancy among cognitions increases. Second, dissonance increases as the number of discrepant cognitions increases. Third, dissonance is inversely proportional to the number of consonant cognitions held by an individual. Fourth, the relative weights given to the consonant and dissonant cognitions may be adjusted by their importance in the mind of the individual.

If dissonance is experienced as an unpleasant drive state,the individual is motivated to reduce it. Now that the factors that affect the magnitude of this unpleasantness have been identified, it should be possible to predict what we can do to reduce it:

— *Changing Cognitions*: If two cognitions ar discrepant, we can simply change one to make it consistent with the other. Or we can change each cognition in the direction of the other.

— *Adding Cognitions*: If two cognitions cause a certain magnitude of dissonance, that magnitude can be reduced by adding one or more consonant cognitions.

— *Altering importance:* Since the discrepant and consonant cognitions must be weighed by importance, it may be advantageous to alter the importance of the various cognitions.

6

CONSTRUCTIVISTIC APPROACH TO LEARNING

THE BASICS OF CONSTRUCTIVISM

Bartlett pioneered what became the constructivist approach. Constructivists believe that "learners construct their own reality or at least interpret it based upon their perceptions of experiences, so an individual's knowledge is a function of one's prior experiences, mental structures, and beliefs that are used to interpret objects and events." "What someone knows is grounded in perception of the physical and social experiences which are comprehended by the mind."

If each person has their own view about reality, then how can we as a society communicate and/or coexist? Jonassen, addressing this issue in his article *Thinking Technology: Toward a Constructivist Design Model,* makes the following comments:

— "Perhaps the most common misconception of constructivism is the inference that we each therefore construct a unique reality, that reality is only in the mind of the knower, which will doubtlessly lead to intellectual anarchy."

— "A reasonable response to that criticism is the Gibsonian perspective that contends that there exists a physical world that is subject to physical laws that we all know in pretty much the same way because those physical laws are perceivable by humans in pretty much the same way."

— "Constructivists also believe that much of reality is shared through a process of social negotiation..."

Constructivsm is recognized as a unique learning theory in itself. It however, may be associated with cognitive psychology because as a theory of learning it focuses on a learner's ability to mentally construct meaning of their own environment and to create their own learning. As a teaching practice it is associated with different degrees of non-directed learning. The term constructivsm is linked to Cognitive and Social Constructivsm.

Theorists associated with Constuctivism are:

— John Dewey

— Lev Vygotsky

— Jean Piaget

— Jerome Bruner

— Seymour Papert

— Mitchell Resnick

The merits of Bahaviourist learning theory and of their teaching practices are well documented. They have served well in teaching a growing North American population over the past six decades. Bahavioural learning theory manifested itself in creating a systematic approach to teaching.

Robert Gagne and Leslie Briggs, in their book, Principles of Instructional Design, combined Bahaviourist principles of learning with a cognitive theory of learning named Information-Processing. The focus of the latter theory in this combination was of the internal processing that occurred during a learning moment.

The design of instruction must be undertaken with suitable attention to the conditions under which learning occurs. With reference to the learner, learning conditions are both external and internal. These conditions are in turn dependent upon what is being learned. How can these basic ideas be used to design instruction ? How can they be applied to the design of single lessons, of courses, and of entire systems of instructions ?

Gagne and Briggs' principles of instructional design broke down the teaching process into a systematic process of nine steps. It is in effect, this type of systematic approach to teaching that acted as the catalyst for the creation of another view of the way humans learn.

Bahaviourist learning theory had served its purpose and its approach and goals were becoming outdated according to Constructivists like Seymour Papert. Constructivist learning theory sought to improve on what Bahaviourist learning theory had already established by focussing on the motivation and ability for humans to construct learning for themselves. It viewed Bahaviourism as being too teacher centered and directed. Constructivists regarded the educational system as a process of matching skill objectives with test items. It was void of meaningful learning. They also saw the teaching process focus too much on individual work rather than on group work.

The final critique of Bahaviourist learning theory from the Constructivist perspective helped define the core of Constructivism. To imply that knowledge is separate to the human mind and that it must be transferred to the learner in a teacher centered approach fundamentally was counter to the Constructivist theory of learning.

Constructivists believe that all humans have the ability to construct knowledge in their own minds through a process of discovery and problem-solving. The extent to which this process can take place naturally, without structure and teaching is the defining factor amongst those who advocate this learning theory.

Jean Piaget, a Swiss psychologist, observed human development as progressive stages of cognitive development. His four stages, which commence at infancy and progress into adulthood, characterize the cognitive abilities necessary at each stage to construct meaning of ones environment.

Seymour Papert, psychologist and contemporary critique of Bahaviourist teaching methods, writes in his book, The Children's Machine:

> Thus, constructionism, my personal reconstruction of constructivism has as its main feature the fact that it looks more closely than other educational -isms at the idea of mental construction. It attaches special importance to the role of constructions in the world as a support for those in the head, thereby becoming less of a purely mentalist doctrine.

As the inventor of LOGO, the programming tool for children, Papert too believed that children as learners have a natural curiosity to construct meaning of their world. The educational system as Papert saw it was too structured and it stifled this natural curiosity. The means by which children were being taught relegated them to a role of passive recipients of the teaching hence, they were not motivated to construct any learning for themselves. Learning according to Constructivists is a question of motivating an individual to attach new meaning to past cognitive experiences. According to Papert:

> It [constuctivsm] does not call in question the value of instruction as such. That would be silly: Even the statement (endorsed if not originated by Piaget) that every act of teaching deprives the child of an opportunity for discovery is not a categorical imperative against teaching, but a paradoxically expressed reminder to keep it in check. The constructionist attitude to teaching is not at all dismissive because it is minimalist - the goal is to teach in such a way as to produce the most learning for the least teaching. Of course, this cannot be achieved simply by reducing the quantity of teaching while leaving everything unchanged. The principle other necessary change parallels an African proverb: If a man is hungry you can give him a fish, but it is better to give him a line and teach him to catch fish himself.

Papert's desire to have children become motivated learners, critical thinkers, problem-solvers and metacognitionists is to be achieved through educational reform that provides the learner with the necessary tools to participate and to take ownership of the learning process. According to Papert, the computer is the appropriate tool to achieve such desired educational reform.

These desired objectives of Papert and others who share the Constructivist view of learning are coming closer to reality as more people discover the power of computer technology. From Donald Tapscott's perspective, Papert's desired reality is happening now, as a paradigm shift to more interactive learning due to the exploitation of the digital media is taking place in our learning institutions.

Tapscott cites eight shifts in learning today:

— From linear to hypermedia.

— From instruction to construction and discovery.

— From teacher-centered to learner-centered education.

— From absorbing material to learning how to navigate and how to learn.

— From school to lifelong learning.

— From one-size-fits-all to customized learning.

— From learning as torture as learning as fun.

— From the teacher as transmitter to the teacher as facilitator.

REALISTIC VS. RADICAL CONSTRUCTION

Realistic constructivism - cognition is the process by which learners eventually construct mental structures that correspond to or match external structures located in the environment.

Radical constructivism - cognition serves to organize the learners experiential world rather than to discover ontological reality.

MERRILL'S ASSUMPTIONS OF CONSTRUCTIVISM

- knowledge is constructed from experience
- learning is a personal interpretation of the world
- learning is an active process in which meaning is developed on the basis of experience
- conceptual growth comes from the negotiation of meaning, the sharing of multiple perspectives and the changing of our internal representations through collaborative learning
- learning should be situated in realistic settings; testing should be integrated with the task and not a separate activity.

CONSTRUCTIVISM AND INSTRUCTIONAL DESIGN

The shift of instructional design from bahaviourism to cognitivism was not as dramatic as the move into constructivism appears to be, since bahaviourism and cognitivism are both objective in nature. Bahaviourism and cognitivism both support the practice of analyzing a task and breaking it down into manageable chunks, establishing objectives, and measuring performance based on those objectives. Constructivism, on the other hand, promotes a more open-ended learning experience where the methods and results of learning are not easily measured and may not be the same for each learner.

While bahaviourism and constructivism are very different theoretical perspectives, cognitivism shares some similarities with constructivism, An example of their compatibility is the fact that they share the analogy of comparing the processes of the mind to that of a computer. Consider the following statement by Perkins:

> "...information processing models have spawned the computer model of the mind as an information processor. Constructivism has added that this information processor must be seen as not just shuffling data, but wielding it

> flexibly during learning — making hypotheses, testing tentative interpretations, and so on."

Other examples of the link between cognitive theory and constructivism are:

— schema theory

— connectionism

— hypermedia

— multimedia

Despite these similarities between cognitivism and constructivism, the objective side of cognitivism supported the use of models to be used in the systems approach of instructional design. Constructivism is not compatible with the present systems approach to instructional design, as Jonassen points out :

> "The conundrum that constructivism poses for instructional designers, however, is that if each individual is responsible for knowledge construction, how can we as designers determine and insure a common set of outcomes for leaning, as we have been taught to do?"

In the same article, Jonassen lists the following implications of constructivism for instructional design:

> "...purposeful knowledge construction may be facilitated by learning environments which:
>
> — Provide multiple representations of reality - avoid oversimplification of instruction by by representing the natural complexity of the world
>
> — Present authentic tasks - contextualize
>
> — Provide real-world, case-based learning environments, rather than pre-determined instructional sequences
>
> — Foster reflective practice
>
> — Enable context- and content-dependent knowledge construction

— Support collaborative construction of knowledge through social negotiation, not competition among learners for recognition

"Although we believe that constructivism is not a prescriptive theory of instruction, it should be possible to provide more explicit guidelines on how to design learning environments that foster constructivist learning"

Jonassen points out that the difference between constructivist and objectivist, (bahavioural and cognitive), instructional design is that objective design has a predetermined outcome and intervenes in the learning process to map a pre-determined concept of reality into the learner's mind, while constructivism maintains that because learning outcomes are not always predictable, instruction should foster, not control, learning. With this in mind, Jonassen looks at the commonalties among constructivist approaches to learning to suggest a "model" for designing constructivist learning environments.

"...a constructivist design process should be concerned with designing environments which support the construction of knowledge, which ..."

— Is Based on Internal Negotiation

— a process of articulating mental models, using those models to explain, predict, and infer, and reflecting on their utility (Piaget's accommodation, Norman and Rumelhart's tuning and restructuring.)

— Is Based on Social Negotiation

— a process of sharing a reality with others using the same or similar processes to those used in internal negotiation

— Is Facilitated by Exploration of Real World Environments and Intervention of New Environments

— processes that are regulated by each individual's intentions, needs, and/or expectations

— Results in Mental Models and provides Meaningful, Authentic Contexts for Learning and Using the

Constructed Knowledge

— should be supported by case-based problems which have been derived from and situated in the real world with all of its uncertainty and complexity and based on authentic realife practice

— Requires an Understanding of its Own Thinking Process and Problem Solving Methods

— problems in one context are different from problems in other contexts

— Modeled for Learners by Skilled Performers but Not Necessarily Expert Performers

— Requires Collaboration Among Learners and With the Teacher

— the teacher is more of a coach or mentor than a purveyor of knowledge

— Provides an Intellectual Toolkit to Facilitate an Internal Negotiation Necessary for Building Mental Models

The technological advances of the 1980s and 1990s have enabled designers to move toward a more constructivist approach to design of instruction. One of the most useful tools for the constructivist designer is hypertext and hypermedia because it allows for a branched design rather than a linear format of instruction. Hyperlinks allow for learner control which is crucial to constructivist learning; however, there is some concerns over the novice learner becoming "lost" in a sea of hypermedia.

To address this concern, Jonassen and McAlleese note that each phase of knowledge acquisition requires different types of learning and that initial knowledge acquisition is perhaps best served by classical instruction with predetermined learning outcomes, sequenced instructional interaction and criterion-referenced evaluation while the more advanced second phase of knowledge acquisition is more suited to a constructivist environment.

If a novice learner is unable to establish an "anchor" in a hypermedia environment they may wander aimlessly through hypermedia becoming completely disoriented. Reigeluth and Chung suggest a prescriptive system which advocates increased learner control. In this method, students have some background knowledge and have been given some instruction in developing their own metacognitive strategies and have some way to return along the path they have taken, should they become "lost".

Most literature on constructivist design suggests that learners should not simply be let loose in a hypermedia or hypertext environment, but that a mix of old and new (objective and constructive) instruction/learning design be implemented. Davidson's article, suggesting a criteria for hypermedia learning based on an "exploration of relevant learning theories", is an example of this method.

Having noted the eclectic nature of instructional design, it is only fair to point out that not all theorists advocate a "mix and match" strategy for instructional design. Bednar, Cunningham, Duffy and Perry wrote an article that challenges the eclectic nature if instructional systems design by pointing out that "...abstracting concepts and strategies from the theoretical position that spawned then strips them of their meaning." They question objectivist epistemology completely and have adopted what they consider a constructivist approach to instructional design. In the article they compare the traditional approaches of analysis, synthesis, and evaluation to that of a constructivist approach.

CONSTRUCTIVIST LEARNING

As a philosophy of learning, constructivism can be traced to the eighteenth century and the work of the philosopher Giambattista Vico, who maintained that humans can understand only what they have themselves constructed. A great many philosophers and educationalists have worked with these ideas, but the first major contemporaries to develop a clear idea of what constructivism consists in were Jean Piaget and John Dewey, to name but a few. Part of the discussion that ensues grapples with the major tenets of their philosophies, with a view to shedding light on constructivism and its vital contribution to learning. As a revealing gloss on this issue, it could be said that constructivism takes an interdisciplinary perspective, inasmuch as it draws upon a diversity of psychological, sociological, philosophical, and critical educational theories. In view of this, constructivism is an overarching theory that does not intend to demolish but to reconstruct past and present teaching and learning theories, its concern lying in shedding light on the learner as an important agent in the learning process, rather than in wresting the power from the teacher.

Within the constructivist paradigm, the accent is on the learner rather than the teacher. It is the learner who interacts with his or her environment and thus gains an understanding of its features and characteristics. The learner constructs his own conceptualisations and finds his own solutions to problems, mastering autonomy and independence. According to constructivism, learning is the result of individual mental construction, whereby the learner learns by dint of matching new against given information and establishing meaningful connections, rather than by internalising mere factoids to be regurgitated later on. In constructivist thinking, learning is inescapably affected by the context and the beliefs and attitudes of the learner. Here, learners are given more latitude in becoming effective problem solvers, identifying and evaluating problems, as well as deciphering ways in which to transfer their learning to these problems.

If a student is able to perform in a problem solving situation, a meaningful learning should then occur because he has constructed an interpretation of how things work using preexisting structures. This is the theory behind Constructivism. By creating a personal interpretation of external ideas and experiences, constructivism allows students the ability to understand how ideas can relate to each other and preexisting knowledge (Janet Drapikowski, personal communication).The constructivist classroom presents the learner with opportunities for "autopoietic" learning with a view to helping learners to build on prior knowledge and understand how to construct new knowledge from authentic experience—certainly a view in keeping with Rogers' experiential learning. C. Rogers, one of the exponents of experiential learning—the tenets of which are inextricably related to, and congruent with, those of constructivism—made the distinction between cognitive learning, which he deemed meretricious, and experiential learning, which he considered significant. For him, the qualities of experiential learning include:

— personal involvement;

— learner-initiation;

— evaluation by learner; and

— pervasive effects on learner

Rogers' humanistic approach to learning is also conducive to personal change and growth, and can facilitate learning, provided that the student participates completely in the learning process and has control over its nature and direction; it is primarily based upon direct confrontation with practical, social, personal or research problems; and, self-evaluation is the principal method of assessing progress or success.

Interestingly, contrasting this approach with the typical behaviourist classroom, where students are merely passive "receptacles" of information from the teacher and the textbook, is rather revealing. We will come to that later on in the study. At this juncture, it is important to briefly discuss the theories of John Dewey, Jean Piaget, and Jerome Bruner that have certainly influenced our stance toward the nature of learning and, concomitantly, teaching. For Dewey, knowledge emerges only from situations in which learners have to draw them out of meaningful experiences. Further, these situations have to be embedded in a social context, such as a classroom, where students can take part in manipulating materials and, thus, forming a community of learners who construct their knowledge together. Students cannot learn by means of rote memorisation; they can only learn by "directed living," whereby concrete activities are combined with theory. The obvious implication of Dewey's theory is that students must be engaged in meaningful activities that induce them to apply the concepts they are trying to learn.

Piaget's constructivism is premised on his view of the psychological development of children. Within his theory, the basis of learning is discovery: 'To understand is to discover, or reconstruct by rediscovery, and such conditions must be complied with if in the future individuals are to be formed who are capable of production and creativity and not simply repetition'. According to Piaget, children go through stages in which they accept ideas they may later discard as wrong. Understanding, therefore, is built up step by step through active participation and involvement. However, applying Piaget's theory is not so straightforward a task as it may sound.

According to Bruner, learning is a social process, whereby students construct new concepts based on current knowledge. The student selects information, constructs hypotheses, and makes decisions, with the aim of integrating new experiences into his existing mental constructs. It is cognitive structures that provide meaning and organization to experiences and allow learners to transcend the boundaries of the information given. For him, learner independence, fostered through encouraging students to discover new principles of their own accord, lies at the heart of effective education. Moreover, curriculum should be organized in a spiral manner so that students can build upon what they have already learned. In short, the principles that permeate Bruner's theory are the following:

— Instruction must be commensurate with the experiences that make the student willing and able to learn (readiness).

— Instruction must be structured so that it can be easily understood by the student (spiral organization).

— Instruction should be designed to facilitate extrapolation (going beyond the information given).

It could be argued that constructivism emphasizes the importance of the world knowledge, beliefs, and skills an individual brings to bear on learning. Viewing the construction of new knowledge as a combination of prior learning matched against new information, and readiness to learn, this theory opens up new perspectives, leading individuals to informed choices about what to accept and how to fit it into their existing schemata, as well as what to reject. Recapitulating the main principles of constructivism, we could say that it emphasises learning and not teaching, encourages learner autonomy and personal involvement in learning, looks to learners as incumbents of significant roles and as agents exercising will and purpose, fosters learners' natural curiosity, and also takes account of learners' affect, in terms of their beliefs, attitudes, and motivation. In addition, within constructivist theory, context is accorded significance, as it renders situations and events meaningful and relevant, and provides learners with the opportunity to construct new knowledge from authentic experience. After all,

Learning is contextual: we do not learn isolated facts and theories in some abstract ethereal land of the mind separate from the rest of our lives: we learn in relationship to what else we know, what we believe, our prejudices and our fears. On reflection, it becomes clear that this point is actually a corollary of the idea that learning is active and social. We cannot divorce our learning from our lives. What is more, by providing opportunities for independent thinking, constructivism allows students to take responsibility for their own learning, by framing questions and then analyzing them. Reaching beyond simple factual information, learners are induced to establish connections between ideas and thus to predict, justify, and defend their ideas.

Having expatiated upon the main tenets of constructivism, let us now content ourselves with juxtaposing constructivism with other theories, objectivist theories that is, and, more specifically, contiguity theory. Byrnes and Arseneau and Rodenburg contrast objectivist and constructivist approaches to teaching and learning.

Objectivist View	Constructivist View
Knowledge exists outside of individuals and can be transferred from teachers to students.	Knowledge has personal meaning. It is created by individual students.
Students learn what they hear and what they read. If a teacher explains abstract concepts well, students will learn those concepts.	Learners construct their own knowledge by looking for meaning and order; they interpret what they hear, read, and see based on their previous learning and habits. Students who do not have appropriate backgrounds will be unable to accurately "hear" or "see" what is before them.
Learning is successful when students can repeat what was taught.	Learning is successful when students can demonstrate conceptual understanding.

Amongst the din of shifting paradigms, a theory that used to dominate the field but is not well-known is contiguity theory, an exponent of which is E. Guthrie. The classic experimental paradigm for contiguity theory is cats learning to escape from a puzzle box. Guthrie used a glass box which allowed him to photograph the movements of cats. These photographs showed that cats learned to repeat the same movements associated with the preceding escape from the box. In this vein, improvement comes about when irrelevant movements are unlearned or not included in successive associations.

Drawing upon behaviouristic principles, contiguity theory sets out to show that, in order for conditioning to occur, the organism must actively respond; inasmuch as learning involves the conditioning of specific behaviours, instruction boils down to presenting very specific tasks; exposure to variations in stimulus patterns is necessary in order to produce a generalized response; and the last response in a stimulus-response situation should be correct since it is this one that will be associated.

Within a positivistic tradition, so to speak, under which come the theories of behaviourism, contiguity theory, and many others, the learner was, and still is, seen as relatively passive, 'simply absorbing information transmitted by a didactic teacher'.

In the universe created by these paradigms, the powerless learner is "worlds apart" from the omniscient and powerful teacher, whose main concern is to 'deliver a standard curriculum and to evaluate stable underlying differences between children' . Against this background, the cognitive paradigm of constructivism has been instrumental in shifting the locus of responsibility for learning from the teacher to the learner, who is no longer seen as passive or powerless. The student is viewed as an individual who is active in constructing new knowledge and understanding, while the teacher is seen as a facilitator rather than a "dictator" of learning. Yet, despite its "democratic" nature, many contemporary philosophers and educationalists have tried to demolish or vitiate some of its principles. Such a discussion is outside the remit of this study, of course. We will only briefly mention George Hein, who voices some reservations about constructivist learning.

For Hein, constructivism, although it appears radical on an everyday level, 'is a position which has been frequently adopted ever since people began to ponder epistemology' . According to him, if we align ourselves with constructivist theory, which means we are willing to follow in the footsteps of Dewey, Piaget and Vygotsky, among others, then we have to run counter to Platonic views of epistemology. We have to recognize that knowledge is not "out there," independent of the knower, but knowledge is what we construct for ourselves as we learn. Besides, we have to concede that learning is not tantamount to understanding the "true" nature of things, nor is it akin to remembering perfect ideas, 'but rather a personal and social construction of meaning out of the bewildering array of sensations which have no order or structure besides the explanations...which we fabricate for them'.

It goes without saying that learners represent a rich array of different backgrounds and ways of thinking and feeling. If the classroom can become a neutral zone where students can exchange their personal views and critically evaluate those of others, each student can build understanding based on empirical evidence. We have no intention of positing methods and techniques for creating a "constructivist classroom." After all, classrooms are, and should be, amenable and sensitive to a whole lot of approaches to teaching and learning, and a slavish adherence to the letter rather than the spirit of education is bound to prove detrimental. It should be borne in mind that the theory of constructivism, with which we have been concerned, is not yet another "educational decree." Like philosophy, constructivism can lead to its own de-construction, in the sense that it forges the very structures and associations that could possibly demolish it. It is a meta-theory, in that it fosters a meta-critical awareness. A constructivist orientation to learning is unique because at its heart lies the individual learner in toto, rather than dimly perceived "apparitions" of her essence. Constructivism is a modern version of human anatomy, in the sense that it is based on, and provides insights into, brain mechanisms, mental structures, and willingness to learn.

CONSTRUCTIVIST STRATEGIES IN VIRTUAL LEARNING ENVIROMENT

Learning can be considered as a conjunction of a number of factors, both of internal and external origins. This section offers a reconcilement of these factors in an interdependent unity, building a "total learning environment", adding up emotional, sensorial, motivational and intellectual aspects. It also approaches the use of this reconcilement in virtual learning environments, seeking for technological tools for a permanent and renewing quest of knowledge, in contrast with the bahaviourist model of repetition of content and stimulus-response conditioning.

The history of the psychology of learning retraces, pertaining to the study in question, to the IV century a.C., specifically to the school of philosophy established by Plato to spread out the ideas of Socrates. In the book VII of "the Republic", Plato displays the myth of the cave, an alegory according to which the world that we know is nothing but a shade in a wall of the cave of reality projected by the pure ideas that are planted, since birth, in our soul. In other words, knowledge is always the projection of our innate ideas. This doctrine resurged in the racionalist and idealistic thoughts of Descartes, Leibniz or Kant, being revisited by authors representing the current cognitivist movement, like Fodor and Chomsky.

Aristotle, disciple of Plato, developed another doctrine: the *tabula rasa*, according to which the knowledge comes from the senses that endow the mind with pictures, interlinked according to three laws: proximity, similarity and contrast. Aristotle's influence will be felt in the psychology of learning through its consequences in both the estruturalism and, mainly, in the bahaviourism of Skinner. Regarding bahaviourism, it is a form of response to subjectivism. For the bahaviourists, the study of higher mental processes for the understanding of human bahaviour is unnecessary: one learns through conditioning and repetition.

The impulse given by diverse external factors to psychology, especially the technological evolution, the new theories of communication, linguistics and cybernetics, brought a new paradigm, represented by information processing, that enables the study of the mental processes denied by bahaviourism. These new studies, supported in technological bases and searching an interdisciplinarity in such fields as philosophy, computer science, medicine and psychology itself, had generated the cognitive school. The relevance of these two doctrines to the learning process is significant. Historically, as well as in the present, there is a predominance of the bahaviourist approach in educational methodologies used in schools of practically all levels.

Theorists like Chi and Rees, Gagné Glaser, Mandler Shuell ,among others, support that there are reasons enough to believe in the possibility that the cognitive approach may be adopted as the model of learning in a near future. Actually, some experiments are already being carried out in such direction, but they are embryonic studies and do not really represent a clear movement towards the adoption of the cognitive psychology of learning. Lakatos developed an application of the bahaviourist theory of learning which attempts to conciliate the issues of conditioning and repetition as bases for scientific research as a learning factor

One of the main criticisms to bahaviourism is its incapacity to produce original theoretical responses. As a consequence, new programs are being elaborated, whose basic difference consists of a release of the bahaviourist conceptual core, eliminating, mainly, the rejection of cognitive processes and increasing information gathering. The central concept of cognitive psychology, the basis of this new program, is broader than the concept of information processing itself. According to Rivière, "the most general and ordinary things we can say of Cognitive Psychology refers to the explanation of bahaviour, mental entities, states, processes and definitions of mental nature, all which demand an unique level of speech". This means, therefore, that the actions of the individual are determined by his mental representations, according to some authors like Piaget and Vigotsky.

Thus, learning capacity would be determined by the way that the individual represents his knowledge, together with his memory capabilities and his causal cognitive processes. To acquire these representations, the human being uses his mechanisms of assimilation as channels, understood here "as a broad sense of an integration to the previous structures" and uses, therefore, his senses as a door towards the perception of the external world together with the mental processes of information handling. The greater or minor effectiveness of this assimilation depends on learning factors, varying from person to person, and constituting learning strategies. These strategies take in account emotional, motivational, sensorial, and intellectual factors (or, using a computer era terminology, logical-mathematical factors).

Emotional Factors

Goleman, places the issue of emotional intelligence as a new type of ability, requiring a development of aptitudes natural to the "human heart". His theory appears in the context of a society with a rising increase of violence in practically all its forms (crime, suicides, drug abuse and other indicators of social distress); individualism, even as a consequence of social pressures, reaches an unprecedented exaggeration, causing, therefore, a growing competitiveness, mainly in the job market and academic fields. This conjunction of factors brings the isolation and deterioration of social relations, generating a slow disintegration of community life and the need for self-confidence.

Placing this scenario under a learning perspective, it is inferred that emotional education - or, in other words, emotional learning - urgently needs to be rethought. The human brain has mechanisms to deal with emotions, but such mechanisms come from a biological evolution that goes back to the origin of life itself . Our mental apparatus is prepared to face "wild" situations, as the ones experienced in a forest, but it has little power to confront rush hour traffic. Under the educator's point of view, it is important to be in harmony with the student's emotions and work the totality of the emotional repertoire. "In our emotional repertoire, each emotion plays a specific function, as disclosed by its distinct biological signatures (...). Using the new technologies that allow the exploration of the brain and the body as a whole, the researchers are discovering physiological details that enable the verification of how different types of emotions prepare the body for different types of responses:

— In *anger*, the blood flows to the hands, making it easier to draw a weapon or to hit the enemy; the cardiac beats speed up and a wave of hormones, like adrenalin, among others, generate a pulsation, a strong enough energy for a vigorous performance.

— In *fear*, the blood runs to the muscles of the skeleton, like those in your legs, facilitating the escape; the face is livid, since the blood is taken from there. At the same time, the body is paralyzed, even if for a brief moment, to perhaps allow the person to consider the possibility of, instead of reacting, running away to hide. Existing circuits in the emotional centers of the brain trigger the torrent of hormones that puts the body in general alert state, making it uneasy and ready to act. The attention is focused in the immediate threat, to better calculate the response to be given.

— The feeling of *happiness* causes one of the main biological alterations. The activity of the cerebral center is triggered, inhibiting negative feelings and favoring the increase of existing energy, silencing those that generate concern thoughts. But no particular physiological change occurs, except for a sense of tranquility, which makes the body recoup quickly from the stimulation caused by disturbing emotions. This pattern gives the body total relaxation, as well as energy and enthusiasm for the execution of any task and to achieve a great variety of goals.

— *Love*, and the feelings of affection and sexual satisfaction, implies parasympathic stimulation, which constitutes the physiological opposite that mobilizes one to "fight-or- run away" which occurs when the feeling is of fear or anger.

The parasympathic standard, called "relaxation response", is a set of reactions that cover the whole body, causing a general state of calm and satisfaction, facilitating recovery.

— The rising of eyebrows, in *surprise*, provides ampler visual sweepings, and also more light for the retina. This allows us to get more information on unexpected events, making it easier to perceive accurately what is happening, and to elaborate the best plan of action.

— Around the world, the expression *repugnance* is similar and sends the same message: some thing is unpleasant to the taste or smell, in actuality or metaphorically. The face expression of repugnance suggests, as Darwin observed, a primeval attempt to cover the nostrils to prevent a harmful odor or to spit out deteriorated food.

— One of the main functions of *sadness* is to propitiate an adjustment to a great loss, like the death of somebody or some major disillusionment. Sadness causes a loss of energy and enthusiasm towards life's activities, in particular for diversions and pleasures. When sadness is deep, approaching depression, the metabolic speed of the body is reduced. It is possible that this loss of energy was caused to keep the vulnerable human beings in sadness state so that they remained close to home, where they felt safer."

This emotional diversity shown by Goleman demonstrates that there are moments and situations that propitiate more effective learning. An educational methodology that would provoke a feeling of happiness, or, at the very least, respect moments of sadness or anger, would have better conditions to form new mental structures and to more efficiently relate all acquired knowledge.

Motivational Factors

Motivation brings inlaid the concept of impulse for action and the maintenance of such action. Schank states that learning is a natural process that happens in the form of a " waterfall":

first, the apprentice creates a goal, then generates a question and, finally, answers the question. This process brings implicitly the importance of motivational factors in learning: when there is a desire to learn to ride a bicycle, for example, a goal was created. During the process of "riding a bicycle", the apprentice will fall, loose balance or feel foolish, and all this will make him question exactly, even if internally, what he is doing wrong - why can't he succeed in riding a bicycle? He will then look for answers to this questioning, and will learn.

However, Schank doesn't expose the initial motivational role: why would someone want to ride a bicycle? Also, following the same reasoning, why didn't the apprentice give up when he fell for the first time? This motivation "to continue trying" is a consequence of the internal pressures generated by curiosity or challenge, both feelings of inadequacy. So, for the learning to occur entirely, a constant stimulation of the student's motivation is necessary.

To successfully keep the motivation, researchers develop new educational proposals, like self-orientation and personal effectiveness as educational goals. This way, the students can make their own learning decisions, cultivating an existing desire in all human beings: independence. Another important motivational factor is the relevance of learning. Students learn more effectively when what they are being taught has direct relation with their reality, offering them a chance to become agents of their own lives. "When professors add new information to the previous knowledge of the student, they activate his interest and curiosity, and apply their teachings with a sense of intention". It is not enough, therefore, to simply adopt the "natural waterfall" proposed by Schank. The teacher needs to show the student that it is good to get your feet wet, "to climb the waterfall".

Sensorial Factors

Senses are open doors to information in the world. All our knowledge comes directly from the mechanisms that we possess to absorb reality and to represent it. As a biological phenomenon, a human being has systems of perception capable of stimulating the brain to interact with the outside world, to understand it or to modify it, as a way to guarantee the adaptation of the species. The quality of this perception varies from person to person, and from culture to culture. To perceive is to know, through the senses, objects and situations the act of perceiving can also be characterized by the limitation of information. It is perceived according to a perspective. The possibility of apprehending the totality of the object only occurs in the imagination, which constitutes, on the other hand, a form of organization of the conscience internally protected against error.

Under this definition, there are some hidden basic aspects of learning. One of them is the limitation on the amount and the quality of information that can be perceived. This can easily be understood when we study, for example, Classic History. No matter how hard we read about the subject, no book will be able to transmit the feelings, the odors, the colors accurately, the social tensions and politics that existed at the time. Another aspect poses the question of perspective: one perceives what one wishes to perceive. In practical learning, this means that it is of little value to insist on teaching a pupil whose basis of knowledge differs from the professor's, since his perspective of the subject is another - it would be like trying to talk with a Chinese person without knowing how to speak Chinese. In this case, according to the concept of perception by Penna, there is no real perception of the object of study, but an inadequate mental construction that shelters the mind against error. In other words, no human being can dominate presented elements under a way not manageable by the nervous system.

Intellectual Factors

For Piaget, all learning derives from mental relations of abstraction and balance. In other words, the human being is constantly seeking the improvement of his higher reasoning capabilities. Thus, using mechanisms of assimilation, adjusting and adaptation, people learn through their mistakes and victories, analyzing them through mental operations and grouping relations. This process is what Piaget calls balancing mechanism.

It can also be included in the intellectual factors, the operations, the relations, the groupings, the construction of schemes and the structuring, all according to Piaget. In fact, such mental manipulations derive from the representation of reality that each one has. For Piaget, intelligence is constructed in continuous form, through processes of mental abstraction resulting from the relations between the individual and the object. These relations happen, in a higher form, as abstract operations that perceive reality associating mental structures and creating projects of assimilation of reality. That is where the denomination of intellectual factors comes from: its effectiveness depends on the logical-mathematical mental coordination, influenced by all the other factors, such as perception, emotion and motivation.

The importance of intellectual factors is as essential to determine the quality of learning as all other factors. Some educators tend to place too much emphasis in the intellectual aspects, forgetting, however, that these same factors depend upon a series of external circumstances. In other words, it is important to think, but the world is not only made of thoughts.

The Virtual Environment

The optimization of such learning factors in an educational program with technological bases facilitates a better exploitation of the student's cognitive capabilities. For this to occur, it would be necessary to build a virtual environment where the pupil was motivated to join; where he could show initiatives and feel good about it; where he would interact, through his senses, with the object of study; and where he would be allowed to guess the object's rules, patterns of bahaviour, and its relations with his reality. Also it would be important to let him make mistakes, and to construct his own "base of knowledge" on the subject.

Schank suggests several learning environments that make use of various cognitive strategies striving to construct these ideal conditions for learning. His architecture uses features that: a) explore the perceptive realm; b) work with emotions, trying to motivate the student; c) let the student himself determine his own rhythm of learning; d) lead the pupil to thinking and to making up rules about the situations just experienced; e) bring the object of study closer to the pupil's own reality through simulations; and f) guide the student into exploring diverse possibilities, so he may build different perspectives on what is being studied.

For an effective use of all the cognitive learning strategies, it is necessary to develop an environment that permits interactions between factors as described in fig. 3. Such environment needs to take in consideration not only the factors themselves, but also their interactions, and to allow emotional, sensorial feedback or both, giving motivational continuity to the learning process. It is important to remember that, as Piaget defends, change is the natural state of the human being - we are in constant balancing process, perceiving it as "a succession of the subject's active compensations in response to exterior disturbances and to certain regulating factors, at the same time, of retroactive (ring systems or feedback) and anticipatory nature, constituting a permanent system of such compensations".

An environment of such nature can also be constructed in the Internet, using technologies of artificial intelligence and of broadband data communication. Today's Internet's interactive nature allows the environment to supply the student with real feedback, creating challenges, stimulating curiosity and offering perspective (motivational factors). It also enables the creation of complex problems pertinent or adjacent to the student's object of study, leading him to use his logical-mathematical faculties and to establish relations between premises (intellectual factors).

The possibilities of contacting other people, or intelligent tutors themselves - something a virtual environment necessarily would have - gives the pupil the option of relaxation, of focusing on other areas, exchanging experiences, and relief of any emotional tension inherent to the solution of particularly difficult problems (emotional factors). Finally, the ample scope of available multimedia features makes the exchange of information possible between the environment and the pupil using different senses, complementing and strengthening all important content, calling for the use of several mental abilities (sensorial factors). The creation of a complete environment is already possible with the tools currently available by simply forming a multidisciplinary team and having appropriate financial support for the project.

Cognitive learning strategies can be understood as a conjunction of factors that define a variety of interactive ways responsible for the amplitude of an individual's knowledge. The knowledge of such factors (emotional, motivational, sensorial and intellectual) allows the educator to prepare all pedagogical content more efficiently and to offer his students, effectively, a much better learning process. These factors are also important in the creation of virtual environments.

The experiences of Schank demonstrate the potential of a natural educational approach, but maintain the existence of these factors implicit. The realization of their existence could define a new methodology of work in the construction of such environments, focused not only on natural learning, but also in the interaction between emotional, sensorial, motivational and intellectual factors in the formation of a permanent learning cycle, where the individual would be continuously motivated, moved, challenged, and sensorially interpellated, in a learning space full of stimuli and feedback.

CONSTRUCTIVISM IN TEACHER EDUCATION

Constructivism is an epistemology, a learning or meaning-making theory, that offers an explanation of the nature of knowledge and how human beings learn. It maintains that individuals create or construct their own new understandings or knowledge through the interaction of what they already know and believe and the ideas, events, and activities with which they come in contact. Knowledge is acquired through involvement with content instead of imitation or repetition. Learning activities in constructivist settings are characterized by active engagement, inquiry, problem solving, and collaboration with others. Rather than a dispenser of knowledge, the teacher is a guide, facilitator, and co-explorer who encourages learners to question, challenge, and formulate their own ideas, opinions, and conclusions. "Correct" answers and single interpretations are de-emphasized.

As an approach to teaching, constructivism may be examined as much for what it is NOT as for what it is. It challenges what Oldfather, Bonds, and Bray characterize as the default mode in education—an empiricist/reductionist approach to teaching and learning. They cite Freire who considers this approach to be a "banking" model—the teacher fills students with deposits of information considered by the teacher to be true knowledge, and the students store these deposits, intact, until needed. Cannella & Reiff label these traditional models didactic, memory-oriented transmission models. Constructivists generally maintain that when information is acquired through transmission models, it is not always well integrated with prior knowledge and is often accessed and articulated only for formal academic occasions such as exams. Constructivist approaches, in contrast, are regarded as producing greater internalization and deeper understanding than traditional methods.

While there are commonly accepted attributes of constructivism, there are also different interpretations of it. Vadeboncoeur identifies three significant strands within these interpretations—Piagetian, sociocultural, and emancipatory constructivism—strands differentiated primarily by

(1) the subject of study,

(2) views about how cognitive forms develop, and

(3) "the liberatory power of the pedagogical approaches derived".

In general, two broad interpretations can be found among contemporary educators—psychological constructivism, most notably articulated by Piaget, and social constructivism, associated with Vygotsky. Two major issues shape these interpretations:

(1) education for individual development versus education for social transformation and

(2) the degree of influence that social context has on individual cognitive development.

Psychological Constructivism

Psychological or Piagetian constructivists generally regard the purpose of education as educating the individual child in a fashion that supports the child's interests and needs; consequently, the child is the subject of study, and individual cognitive development is the emphasis. Learning is primarily an individualistic enterprise. This is a child-centered approach that seeks to identify, through scientific study, the natural path of cognitive development.

This approach assumes that students come to classrooms with ideas, beliefs, and opinions that need to be altered or modified by a teacher who facilitates this alteration by devising tasks and questions that create dilemmas for students. Knowledge construction occurs as a result of working through these dilemmas. Characteristic instructional practices include "discovery learning" and hands-on activities, such as using manipulatives; student tasks that challenge existing concepts and thinking processes; and questioning techniques that probe students' beliefs and encourage examination and testing of those beliefs. To a large extent, this approach assumes that development is an ingrained, natural, biological process that is pretty much the same for all individuals, regardless of gender, class, race, or the social or cultural context in which learning and living take place. Internal development is the focus of the teaching environment, and the social and historical context, as well as issues of power, authority, and the place of formal knowledge in the learning environment are not emphasized. It is essentially a decontextualized approach to learning and teaching. Critics of the psychological constructivist approach deprecate its lack of attention to "the influence of the classroom culture and the broader social context, as well as disregard for power issues, particularly power issues related to knowledge production.

Social Constructivism

Social or Vygotskian constructivism emphasizes education for social transformation and reflects a theory of human development that situates the individual within a sociocultural context. Individual development derives from social interactions within which cultural meanings are shared by the group and eventually internalized by the individual. Individuals construct knowledge in transaction with the environment, and in the process both the individual and the environment are changed. The subject of study is the dialectical relationship between the individual and the social and cultural milieu.

Schools are the sociocultural settings where teaching and learning take place and where "cultural tools," such as reading, writing, mathematics, and certain modes of discourse are utilized. This approach assumes that theory and practice do not develop in a vacuum; they are shaped by dominant cultural assumptions. Both formal knowledge, the subject of instruction, and the manner of its presentation are influenced by the historical and cultural environment that generated them. To accomplish the goals of social transformation and reconstruction, the context of education must be deconstructed, and the cultural assumptions, power relationships, and historical influences that undergird it must be exposed, critiqued, and, when necessary, altered Variants of social constructivism include situated constructivism, social reconstructivism, sociocultural constructivism, sociohistorical constructivism, and emancipatory constructivism.

Constructive Framework in Teacher Education

While it may inform and influence practice, constructivism is a theory of learning, not a theory of teaching, and translating theory to practice is both difficult and imprecise. However, education literature documents several large- and small-scale efforts to do so. For example, as part of a statewide education reform initiative, University of Louisville faculty, supported by funding from the Kentucky Department of Education, developed 11 guiding principles and possible indicators of constructivist teaching. The venerable Foxfire Project devised 11 core practices that reflect the constructivist underpinnings of the Foxfire approach to teaching and professional development, which has evolved over a 30-year period.

Constructivist teacher education generally reflects two major traditions—the developmental and social reconstructionist traditions. Programs influenced by the developmental tradition attempt to teach students how to teach in a constructivist, generally Piagetian, manner. They are typically characterized by substantial direct instruction in theory and practice, often without complementary opportunities for inquiry, discovery, or self-examination. This approach can easily become overly prescriptive. If this occurs, the teacher educator models an approach to teaching that is essentially antithetical to the approach students are intended to employ in their future classrooms. Programs influenced by social reconstructionist tradition attempt to help teacher education students deconstruct their own prior knowledge and attitudes, comprehend how these understandings evolved, explore the effects they have on actions and bahaviour, and consider alternate conceptions and premises that may be more serviceable in teaching. Critical analysis and structured reflection on formal course knowledge and everyday practical experience are incorporated.

Richardson identifies two factors that appear to affect the approach teachers and teacher educators take in forming constructivist settings—the extent to which the social is acknowledged as a critical factor in learning and individual cognitive development and the specific content, subject matter, or discipline. Some subjects, such as mathematics, are more "bounded" than others by rules, formulae, and procedures. They are more likely to be regarded by teachers as producing problems and tasks to which there are "correct" answers. Individual interpretations and construction of ideas and concepts are less likely to be encouraged by teachers than in subjects such as literature and writing.

Challenges

The overarching challenge constructivism presents to teachers and teacher educators is the formidable task of translating a learning theory into a theory of teaching, which in turn raises questions about what teachers need to know and be able to do. For teacher educators, among other tasks, this involves balancing the need to acknowledge the different discipline-specific requirements of teaching with the need to model constructivist methods in teacher education courses and practicums. Richardson also notes the limits of a perspective on teaching that values students' understandings at the expense of "right" answers. Student knowledge becomes idiosyncratic; 30 different students may arrive at 30 different understandings or interpretations of a concept, all of which are not equally appropriate. Inappropriately applied, constructivist approaches may lead to the "abandonment" style of teaching.

Several authors cite the importance of teacher educators' modeling constructivist approaches that engage students in interdisciplinary exploration, collaborative activity, and field-based opportunities for experiential learning, reflection, and self-examinationif future teachers are to be able to employ these strategies in schools.

To derive culturally relevant and socially just pedagogy and practice from constructivist epistemologies, Martin and Vadeboncoeur urge teacher educators to deconstruct and scrutinize cultural assumptions that underlie various interpretations of constructivism to expose how social beliefs have influenced the development of theory and practices. Without such scrutiny, societal inequities and historical forms of oppression may be perpetuated in supposedly constructivist classrooms, and the very constraints on individual development constructivists seek to remove or ameliorate will be reinforced.

A final challenge faced by educators is the pitfall of regarding constructivism as the only viable theoretical framework for teaching and learning. It is one way of thinking about how knowledge and understanding are formed, but it is not the only way. Nor are various interpretations of constructivism necessarily incompatible with one another. Prospective teachers should be exposed to varying perspectives and given opportunities to develop the discretion needed to choose most appropriately and the skills to implement their choices.

STRENGTHS AND WEAKNESSES CONSTRUCTIVISM

— *Weakness* - in a situation where conformity is essential divergent thinking and action may cause problems. Imagine the fun Revenue Canada would have if every person decided to report their taxes in their own way - although, there probably are some very "constructive" approaches used within the system we have.

— *Strength* - because the learner is able to interpret multiple realities, the learner is better able to deal with real life situations. If a learner can problem solve, they may better apply their existing knowledge to a novel situation.

7

Humanistic Approach to Learning

THE HUMANISTIC APPROACH

The Humanistic approach began in response to concerns by therapists against perceived limitations of Psychodynamic theories, especially psychoanalysis. Individuals like Carl Rogers and Abraham Maslow felt existing (psychodynamic) theories failed to adequately address issues like the meaning of behavior, and the nature of healthy growth. However, the result was not simply new variations on psychodynamic theory, but rather a fundamentally new approach.

There are several factors which distinguish the Humanistic Approach from other approaches within psychology, including the emphasis on subjective meaning, a rejection of determinism, and a concern for positive growth rather than pathology. While one might argue that some psychodynamic theories provide a vision of healthy growth (including Jung's concept of individuation), the other characteristics distinguish the Humanistic Approach from every other approach within psychology (and sometimes lead theorists from other approaches to say the Humanistic Approach is not a science at all).

Most psychologists believe that behavior can only be understood objectively (by an impartial observer), but the humanists argue that this results in concluding that an individual is incapable of understanding their own behavior—a view which they see as both paradoxical and dangerous to well-being. Instead, humanists like Rogers argue that the meaning of behavior is essentially personal and subjective; they further argue that accepting this idea is not unscientific, because ultimately all individuals are subjective: what makes science reliable is not that scientists are purely objective, but that the nature of observed events can be agreed upon by different observers (a process Rogers calls intersubjective verification).

The issues underlying the Humanistic Approach, and its differences from other approaches, are discussed more fully in the text, but the sources below provide useful supplementary information. One point worth noting: if you want to fully grasp the nature of the Humanistic Approach, you cannot consider it in abstract terms. Instead, you must consider if and how the ideas connect to your own experience—for that is how the meaning of behavior is derived!

CARL ROGERS

Carl Rogers was not only one of the founders of the Humanistic Approach, but also arguably the most influential therapist in the 20th century: a number of surveys, including several done after his death, found that more therapists cited Rogers as a major influence on their thinking and clinical practice than any other person in psychology (including Freud). To understand this, one must know something about Rogers as a person, as well as his theoretical ideas.

In terms of his theory, there are two fundamental ideas which are particularly worth noting. First, Rogers talked about healthy development in terms of how the individual perceived their own being. A healthy individual will tend to see congruence between their sense of who they are (self) and who they feel they should be (ideal self). While no one tends to experience perfect congruence at all times, the relative degree of congruence is an indicator of health. Some researchers have tried to measure congruence by using a self-assessment technique called a Q-Sort.

The second fundamental idea is Rogers's concept of the conditions for healthy growth, and the role of a therapist in fostering healthy growth. Through a process Rogers called person-centered therapy, the therapist seeks to provide empathy, openness, and unconditional positive regard. These conditions for growth are discussed further in the text; for information on person-centered therapy.

ABRAHAM MASLOW

Like Carl Rogers, Abraham Maslow is widely regarded as one of the founders of the Humanistic Approach. While less influential among therapists than Rogers, Maslow may actually be better known to the general public, because of his interest in applying psychological principles to areas like behavior in business settings. In this regard, his hierarchy of needs has been a basic concept in human resources and organizational behavior for several decades.

Maslow coined the term "the Third Force" to describe the Humanistic Approach, to emphasize how it differed from the Psychodynamic and Behaviorist Approaches, which dominated psychology (at least in North America) in the 1950's. His theory emphasizes motivation as the key to understanding human behavior (an emphasis which is somewhat reminiscent of Freud's theory, though the two models focus on very different types of motives). Nonetheless, it becomes the basis of a theory of personality, and ends up describing the characteristics of healthy growth in ways that are very similar to Rogers's "fully functioning person".

One difference between Maslow and Rogers is the emphasis that Maslow gave to peak experiences. Peak experiences are moments in life which take us beyond our ordinary perceptions, thoughts, and feelings. Typically, the individual feels energized, more "alive". In some ways, peak experiences are similar to the Zen concept of satori (literally "enlightenment"), which, like a peak experience, comes unexpectedly, and transforms the individual's understanding of themselves and the world.

Because of the "mystical" nature of peak experiences, some psychologists are less comfortable with Maslow's theory than with Rogers's, which uses concepts more easily related to "mainstream" psychology. Possibly, this accounts for Maslow being viewed as less influential among therapists. In any case, there is no doubt that Maslow's ideas about motivation have become widely known and used.

EXISTENTIAL PSYCHOLOGY

As in many areas of psychology, there are close linkages between the Humanistic Approach and philosophy. For example, Rogers's concept of the phenomenal field as the basis of defining the self can be linked to the ideas of phenomenological philosophers like Edmund Husserl. Similarly, the existentialist tradition began with European philosophers like Soren Kierkegaard and Jean-Paul Sartre.

While its roots extend back to the turn of the 20th century (and some would say even earlier), it really gained momentum as a result of World War II, whose devastation and destruction gave a sense of immediacy to questions about the purpose of living. (For example, Albert Camus, a leading existentialist writer, was a member of the French Resistance.)

Existentialists start from the premise that there is no absolute meaning to life, and hence that life in a purely rational sense is without purpose. Interestingly, however, from this bleak beginning, many arrive at interpretations that nonetheless affirm a value to life.

Asking about what life means to an individual provides an overlapping area of concern between existentialism and humanistic psychology, since the humanists seek to identify a positive model for human growth. As a result, while some psychologists prefer one term over the other, the theories often share a focus on similar kinds of issues, especially the questions of what an individual finds meaningful in life, and how individuals deal with the prospect of death.

Among the psychologists who have developed theories related to existential ideas are Rollo May, Ernest Becker, and Viktor Frankl. Of these, Frankl is arguably the best known to the general public; his best-known book, Man's Search for Meaning, went through multiple editions and reprintings, and was translated into dozens of languages.

Frankl, who began as a doctor and therapist in Vienna, was a prisoner in various Nazi concentration camps during the war, and it was partly his exposure to the horrors of the camps that contributed to his existentialist orientation. To learn more about him and other existential psychologists, and how their ideas relate to humanistic theories more generally.

MASLOW'S HIERARCHY IN THE WORKPLACE

Several researchers in the 1950s recognized the practical importance of Abraham Maslow's hierarchy of needs to the working world. It was not difficult to establish that for nonmanagement workers, jobs mainly fulfilled the basic physical and security needs of the individual: if the work is done, the worker is paid and more-or-less assured of being paid for subsequent work.

Higher order needs, such as social, esteem and self-actualization needs were not considered. Lyman Porter at the University of California at Berkeley, suggested that higher needs might be of more concern on the management level of an organization. He saw that people in most organizations received promotions from one job to another based on their technical qualifications, but nothing else. That is, it was assumed that because an individual could do the job, that job was the best one for him or her.

There was no indication that anyone regarded the psychological satisfaction with a job as being an important factor. Consequently, people might sometimes be promoted out of jobs that gave them satisfaction into jobs that were less satisfying for them, potentially rendering them less effective in their work. Porter realized that for individual satisfaction and for organizational efficiency, it was necessary to discover how people perceived their jobs in terms of need satisfaction, as Maslow had outlined. Knowing this might allow organizations to match people to jobs that they were not only qualified for, but which would give them the most satisfaction as well.

In order to study this, Porter sent a fixed alternative survey to 228 people in three companies. These people worked at different managerial levels, from bottom level supervisors or foremen up to middle level management who were just below vice presidency or major department head. The survey studied 15 characteristics or qualities that Porter thought were connected with management positions and were relevant to Maslow's need hierarchy.

For example, to determine whether esteem needs were being met by the job, Porter asked about the prestige of a managerial position; to determine whether social needs were being met by the job, he asked about the opportunities to develop friendships on the job; to determine whether self-actualization needs were being met by the job, he asked about feelings of self-fulfillment derived from the individual's working position.

The respondents to the survey were asked to indicate on a 7-point scale (with 1 indicating the lowest amount and 7 indicating the highest amount) first, how much of that quality was connected with the individual's management position; second, how much of that quality should be connected with the individual's management position; and third, how important that quality was to the respondent. So questions on the survey might look like this:

The feeling of self-esteem a person gets from being in my management position:

a) How much is there now? (min) 1 2 3 4 5 6 7 (max)

b) How much should there be? (min) 1 2 3 4 5 6 7 (max)

c) How important is this to me? (min) 1 2 3 4 5 6 7 (max)

Of the 228 people who were given the survey, 139 (61%) filled it out. While Porter attempted to give the surveys to a representative sample of low to middle management personnel, it cannot be claimed that the individuals who actually returned the survey constitute such a sample, so the results of this study must be interpreted with caution. Porter found that among these respondents, there was no difference in the amount of fulfillment of social needs, and that esteem needs are more often satisfied in middle management than in low management levels, not surprisingly.

But in both low and middle management, the respondents indicated that self-actualization needs are of great importance to them, but there were few opportunities for these needs to be fulfilled at work. It seems, then, that among the people who answered this survey, at least, their work did not offer them a sense of self-fulfillment, or an opportunity for personal growth and development or a feeling of worthwhile accomplishment. It would be expected that in higher management, the level at which policy decisions are made, there may be a greater chance to find areas of self- actualization.

What are the implications of this study? While we must be careful in making conclusions since a survey cannot demonstrate a causal relationship and since we have no way of knowing whether the sample was indeed representative of the population, we may still make some tentative conclusions. Most of us spend almost 30% of our lives at work, and yet this work may not give us the opportunity to pursue what we find important: self-actualization. Our deficiency needs may be met to a greater or lesser extent, but our growth needs may not.

What if our work gave us opportunity to fulfill growth needs, though? What if the organization we work for allowed us to help make the policy decisions that would affect the well-being of ourselves and others, for example? Orpen has found that among the respondents to his survey, job satisfaction is indeed greater when there is more opportunity for such decision-making. Did his respondents feel greater satisfaction because this gave them a chance to pursue self-actualization? We don't know, but maybe.

HUMANISTIC ORIENTATIONS TO LEARNING

A great deal of the theoretical writing about adult education in the 1970s and 1980s drew on humanistic psychology. In this orientation the basic concern is for the human potential for growth. As Mark Tennant notes, the concern with 'self' is 'a hallmark of humanistic psychology'. There was a reaction against 'scientific' reductionism – people being treated as objects and rationalism. Instead the affective and subjective world was to be reaffirmed. Personal freedom, choice, motivations and feelings had to have their place.

Perhaps the best known example is Abraham Maslow's hierarchy of motivation. At the lowest level are physiological needs, at the highest self actualization. Only when the lower needs are met is it possible to fully move on to the next level. A motive at the lower level is always stronger than those at higher levels. Tennant summarizes these as follows:

— *Level one*: *Physiological needs* such as hunger, thirst, sex, sleep, relaxation and bodily integrity must be satisfied before the next level comes into play.

— *Level two*: *Safety needs* call for a predictable and orderly world. If these are not satisfied people will look to organize their worlds to provide for the greatest degree of safety and security. If satisfied, people will come under the force of level three.

— *Level three*: *Love and belonginess needs* cause people to seek warm and friendly relationships.

— *Level four*: *Self-esteem needs* involve the desire for strength, achievement, adequacy, mastery and competence. They also involve confidence, independence, reputation and prestige.

— *Level five*: *Self-actualization* is the full use and expression of talents, capacities and potentialities.

Self actualizers are able to submit to social regulation without losing their own integrity or personal independence; that is they may follow a social norm without their horizons being bounded in the sense that they fail to see or consider other possibilities. They may on occasion transcend the socially prescribed ways of acting. Achieving this level may mean developing to the full stature of which they are capable.

Learning can, thus, be seen as a form of self-actualization, it contributes to psychological health. Yet while self actualization may seen as the primary goal, other goals are also around. These include a sense of accomplishment and the controlling of impulses.

Much criticism has been levelled at this model. For example,

— Do lower needs really have to be satisfied before higher ones come into play? People may well put physiological needs on one side to satisfy the need for love, for example.

— Are we all propelled to the sorts of qualities that Maslow identifies with 'self actualization'? To what extent are these qualities culturally-specific?

The idea of a hierarchy of needs, the identifying of different needs, and the notion of self-actualization did, however, exert a powerful hold over adult education writers like Malcolm Knowles. Humanistic psychology's positive view of people and their ability to control their own destiny, and the seemingly unlimited possibilities for individual development provided some hope for educators.

Perhaps the most persuasive exploration of a humanistic orientation to learning came from Carl Rogers. His passion for education that engaged with the whole person and with their experiences; for learning that combines the logical and intuitive, the intellect and feelings; found a ready audience. 'When we learn in that way', he said, 'we are *whole*, utilizing all our masculine and feminine capacities'. He saw the following elements as being involved in significant or experiential learning.

— *It has a quality of personal involvement*—the whole person in both feeling and cognitive aspects being *in* the learning event.

— *It is self-initiated.* Even when the impetus or stimulus comes from the outside, the sense of discovers of reaching out, of grasping and comprehending, comes from within.

— *It is pervasive.* It makes a difference in the behaviour, the attitudes, perhaps even the personality of the learner.

— *It is evaluated by the learner.* She knows whether it is meeting her need, whether ***it*** leads toward what she *wants* to know, whether it illuminates the dark area of ignorance she is experiencing. The locus of evaluation, we might say, resides definitely in the learner.

— *Its essence is meaning.* When such learning takes place, the element of meaning to the learner is built into the whole experience.

Abraham Maslow has been considered the Father of Humanistic Psychology. Maslow's theory is based on the notion that experience is the primary phenomenon in the study of human learning and behavior. He placed emphasis on choice, creativity, values, self-realization, all distinctively human qualities, and believed that meaningfulness and subjectivity were more important than objectivity. For Maslow, development of human potential, dignity and worth are ultimate concerns.

Maslow rejected behaviorist views and Freud's theories on the basis of their reductionistic approaches. He felt Freud's view of human nature was negative, and he valued goodness, nobility and reason. Also, Freud concentrated on the mentally ill, and Maslow was interested in healthy human psychology.

Maslow and his colleagues came to refer to their movement as "third force psychology," the first two being psychoanalysis and behaviorism. The third force is based on philosophies of existentialism and humanism. He is famous for proposing that human motivation is based on a hierarchy of needs. The lowest level of needs are physiological and survival needs such as hunger and thirst. Further levels include belonging and love, self-esteem, and self-actualization. From Maslow's perspective, the drive to learn is intrinsic.

The purpose of learning is to bring about self-actualization, and the goals of educators should include this process. Learning contributes to psychological health. Maslow proposed other goals of learning, including discovery of one's vocation or destiny; knowledge of values; realization of life as precious, acquisition of peak experiences, sense of accomplishment, satisfaction of psychological needs, awareness of beauty and wonder in life, impulse control, developing choice, and grappling with the critical existential problems of life.

Maslow's theory of learning highlighted the differences between experiential knowledge and spectator knowledge. He regarded spectator, or scientific, knowledge to be inferior to experiential.

Properties of experiential learning include:

— immersion in the experience without awareness of the flow of time

— momentarily not being self-conscious

— transcending time, place, history, and society by being beyond and unaffected by them

— merging with that which is being experienced

— being innocently receptive, as a child, uncritical

— suspending temporarily evaluation of the experience in terms of its importance or unimportance

— lack of inhibition, subsiding of selfishness, fear, defensiveness

— experience unfolds naturally without striving or effort

— suspending criticism, validation, and evaluation of the experience

— trusting experience by passively letting it happen; letting go of preconceived notions

— disengaging from logical, analytical, and rational activities.

According to humanistic theory, learning results from an individual's need to express creativity. Almost any activity, whether academic, business, or leisure oriented, can serve as a creative outlet. An individual must engage in creative activities to gain a sense of control, growth, and knowledge. An inner drive encourages them to learn and express themselves.

Humanists believe that the individual is responsible for his life and actions, and that he can creatively change his behavior at any time through personal awareness and desire. Behavior must satisfy the needs of the total self as the individual strives for self-actualization, self-maintenance, and self-enhancement.

Instinct

Instinct is behavior that is inherited rather than learned. The terms instinct and instinctive behavior refer to activities that involve neither experience nor learning. To be instinctive, a behavior pattern must be typical of almost all the members of that population. Occasionally, some individuals have a slightly different depiction of an instinctive behavior pattern. For example, goldfinches may use different amounts of certain materials in building their nests, or carry the materials in different manners.

Most instinctive behavior occurs due to a stimulus. The stimulus affects one or more glands of the individual's body. For example, the amount of daylight determines the amount of hormones released by some species of birds. A particular change in the amount of hormones being secreted stimulates the birds to migrate. If the hormones are not secreted in the proper amount, then the bird would not be able to enact this instinctive behavior.

All animals perform both instinctive and learned behaviors. Other creatures, such as insects and spiders, have limited capacities for learning, so their survival depends on their instinctive behavior patterns. Higher animals, including fish, reptiles, birds, and mammals, are capable of learning a lot more. They are also capable of modifying their instinctive behavior via learning. The higher the animal, the more it learns and the less it depends on instinct. Fish are more instinctive than birds, and birds are more instinctive than mammals. Human infants and young children display substantial amounts of instinctive behavior, such as smiling and sucking, but as we grow older we rely less on instinct and more upon learning.

HUMANIST THOUGHTS IN ADULT LEARNING

The roots of modern humanist thought can be traced to the ideas of such individuals as the Chinese philosopher Confucius, Greek philosophers such as Progagoras and Aristotle, Erasmus and Montaigne from the Renaissance period, and the Dutch philosopher Spinoza from the seventeenth century.

Humanism generally is associated with beliefs about freedom and autonomy and notions that "human beings are capable of making significant personal choices within the constraints imposed by heredity, personal history, and environment". Humanist principles stress the importance of the individual and specific human needs. Among the major assumptions underlying humanism are the following:

(a) human nature is inherently good;

(b) individuals are free and autonomous, thus they are capable of making major personal choices;

(c) human potential for growth and development is virtually unlimited;

(d) self-concept plays an important role in growth and development;

(e) individuals have an urge toward self-actualization;

(f) reality is defined by each person; and

(g) individuals have responsibility to both themselves and to others.

Principles of humanist thought have served as a foundation for major developments in both psychology and education. In psychology, the humanist paradigm emerged as a response to both the determinism inherent in Freudian psychoanalysis and the limited place of affect and free will found in behaviorism. While many individuals have made important contributions to humanistic psychology, two of the most noteworthy contributors were Abraham Maslow and Carl Rogers.

Maslow discussed the concept of "self-actualization," which he described as "the full use and exploitation of talents, capacities, potentialities, etc." He identified a number of characteristics of self-actualizing people, three of which are tolerance for ambiguity, acceptance of self and others, and "peak experiences" that lead to personal transformation through new insights.

Rogers, through the approach he referred to as "client-centered therapy," noted that the major goal of therapy is to help clients foster greater self-direction. According to Rogers, self-direction "means that one chooses - and then learns from the consequences"

Humanistic education is based on similar ideas. Patterson has stated that "the purpose of education is to develop self-actualizing persons". According to Valett, humanistic education is a lifelong process, the purpose of which "is to develop individuals who will be able to live joyous, humane, and meaningful lives". Priorities of humanistic education should include "[t]he development of emotive abilities, the shaping of affective desires, the fullest expression of aesthetic qualities, and the enhancement of powers of self-direction and control (emphasis added)". Essential characteristics of the humanistic educator are empathic understanding, respect or acceptance, and genuineness or authenticity

Humanism is not without its critics. One of the most frequent criticisms, usually emanating from fundamentalists on the religious right, is that humanism runs contrary to basic tenets of Christian and other theological orientations. In fact, humanism does emphasize the "here and now" and frequently is viewed as denying existence of the supernatural, although as Elias and Merriam point out not all humanists see incompatibility between affirming autonomy and existence of a god. As Lamont puts it, "[h]umanism is the view-point that men [sic] have but one life to lead and should make the most of it in terms of creative work and happiness; . . . that in any case, the supernatural, usually conceived of in the form of heavenly gods or immortal heavens, does not exist".

While this assumption may dissuade some individuals from fully embracing humanism, we believe that teachers, trainers, or administrators do not have to abandon traditional theologies in order celebrate the good of humanity and to engage in practices designed to facilitate self-direction.

A second criticism is that humanism is sometimes believed to be a highly self-centered, or selfish, approach to life. Typically, the argument goes something like this: "If an individual is concerned primarily with personal growth and development, how can that person truly be concerned with what is good for all of society?" Humanists are quick to refute this misunderstanding. Lamont, for instance, states that the individual can find one's "highest good in working for the good of all".

Similarly, one of the characteristics of self-actualizers discussed by Maslow is the tendency for individuals to focus on problems that lie outside of themselves. Within the realm of adult education, one of the most powerful reflections of how humanists look at the relationship between individual and social concerns is offered in this observation made by Lindeman in 1926:

> "Adult education will become an agency of progress if its short-time goal of self-improvement can be made compatible with a long-time, experimental but resolute policy of changing the social order".

Comparisons between Philosophical Beliefs of Instructional Procedures

Several sources, including Merriam and Caffarella represents a continuum between humanist and behaviorist views. We cover an extensive time range, too, starting from Plato and Aristotle and continuing forward until very recent attempts at research on adult learning and cognitive psychology. Table 1 displays the comparative information.

Presenting comparisons in a dichotomous manner is always difficult because ideas, attitudes, and movements seldom fall neatly into an either-or configuration. There usually are various ways ideas or statements can be viewed and the interpretations we have made regarding the views of others may not reflect their reality. Establishing one side or view of the world versus another side or view can create unexpected or undesired emotions, too. It is even difficult to say that many of the items presented in the comparison are "absolutely" attached to one side or the other.

Table1. Comparison of key differences in beliefs and approaches between adult education and instructional design

Adult Education Humanism Views	-vs-	Instructional Design Behaviorism Views
Plato	-vs-	Aristotle
Rationalism/emotionalism	-vs-	Empiricism
Reflection	-vs-	Sensory impression
Gestalt psychology	-vs-	Behavioral psychology
Search for whole patterns	-vs-	Search for single events or parts
Information processing	-vs-	Information acquisition
Separation of mind and body	-vs-	Innate mental abilities
Right brain hemisphere	-vs-	Left brain hemisphere
Memory	-vs-	Accumulation of knowledge
Learning how to learn	-vs-	Acquiring knowledge
Learning as a process	-vs-	Learning as an end product
Instruction as a process	-vs-	Instruction broken into manageable parts
Meaningful learning	-vs-	Rote learning
S - O - R (O = human organism)	-vs-	S - R
Dynamic view	-vs-	Mechanistic view
Perceptions	-vs-	Observable behavior
Internal thoughts	-vs-	Behavioral change
Liberal studies for adults	-vs-	Programmed learning

Maslow/Rogers	-vs-	Skinner/Thorndike
Cross/Knowles/Mezirow/Tough	-vs-	Ausubel/Bruner/Gagne/Piaget
Individual determines learning	-vs-	Environment shapes learning
Individual locus of control	-vs-	External locus of control
Personal control and evaluation	-vs-	Imitating and observing others
Role of experience	-vs-	Reinforcement/operant conditioning
Interactive needs assessment	-vs-	Task analysis
Facilitator	-vs-	Trainer
Qualitative methods predominate	-vs-	Quantitative methods predominate
Process evaluation	-vs-	Product evaluation
Goal free evaluation	-vs-	Criterion/normative/goal referenced evaluation
Learner controlled verification	-vs-	External testing
Affective learning	-vs-	Cognitive/mechanistic/psychomotor learning
Individuals control own destiny	-vs-	Predetermination
Andragogy	-vs-	Pedagogy
Self-directed learning	-vs-	Expert directs learning/expert models
Crystallized intelligence	-vs-	Fluid intelligence
Internal motivation	-vs-	External motivation
Relative ends	-vs-	Fixed ends

There is some overlap, some items may fit both sides, and some comparisons may be better understood as representations of representations of continua rather than dichotomies. There is even considerable debate in the literature as to how definitive the related research and thinking has been on some of the items. For example, right -vs- left brain hemispheric and crystallized -vs- fluid intelligence research both have been discussed and critiqued in various ways. So, Table1 should be viewed in light of these possible limits.

The instructional design field during the past decade also has become increasingly involved with cognitive science and psychology, producing considerable information on learning analysis and cognitive strategies. Many researchers in cognition have sought to move beyond the strictures of any behaviorist schools of thought in various ways:

(a) attempting to understand the physical makeup of human memory;

(b) trying to discern the way information is stored, coded, and utilized by the human brain;

(c) researching properties of short term memory; and

(d) considering the needs, desires, emotions, attitudes, motivations, and values of learners in terms of cognitive change.

Some scholars refer to instructional design based on cognitive assumptions and the structuring of knowledge as second generation instructional design theory, although Duffy and Jonassen suggest that both behaviorism and cognitive psychology are girded by objectivist epistemologies where structured knowledge rather than a learner's experience or need is a basis for instruction.

Some of the current instructional design theories reflect changing views of how to work with learners most effectively. For example, Merrill's component display theory draws from the multiple perspectives of behavioral, cognitive, and humanistic beliefs. Likewise, Reigeluth's elaboration theory of instruction incorporates a great deal of learner control into the instructional design process.

Currently, debates within the instructional design field are also going on pertaining to the desires of some to recast the field in terms of constructionist views. Constructivism makes a decidedly different set of assumptions about learning and corresponding instruction. It is concerned with the way people construct knowledge based on experiences, mental structures, and beliefs. In essence, this means learners build their own meaning from new knowledge rather than having that meaning built by someone else. Instruction is then based on past experience and aims to develop a learner's skill at constructing meaning from new knowledge and experiences. Both the May and September, 1991, issues of Educational Technology are devoted to pro and con discussions of constructivism.

Thus, the complementary roles of experience, feeling, and cognition in learning are impacting on the ways instructional designers think about their tasks. Many of the views may no longer fit neatly into Table 1's right column descriptors

Adult education, too, has undergone several changes in the past two decades in addition to considerable scholarship on adult learning, self-direction, and instruction described earlier. Brookfield and Mezirow have been two of the scholars helping the field become more aware of critical thinking, transformative dimensions of adult learning, and emancipatory learning. Jarvis has encouraged adult educators to better understand sociological perspectives pertaining to the teaching and learning process. Smith has been instrumental in helping educators of adults understand more about learning how to learn concepts. Peters, Jarvis, and Associates even describe how the field's development in the past two decades has been informed by various interdisciplinary dimensions. All of these changes do not always fit neatly within the humanistic side of the comparison figure.

However, we have initiated this comparison as a mechanism to suggest that many adult educators and instructional designers (and even educators who devote most of their research and energy toward the education of youth) have been approaching several of the problems pertaining to learning and instruction from different ideological points of view and often different research methodologies. It is our contention that many of the tenets, beliefs, and views of the world that may appear to fit when dealing with youth or young adults with few life experiences may not work well for educators working with adults as learners.

Humanising the Instructional Process

In the previous section, we made some general comparisons between what is often found in the fields of adult education and instructional development. Our intent was not to dichotomize the two fields into a right -vs- wrong status, nor did we intend to enter into what Tobias calls a perennial controversy between advocates of tailoring instruction to learners' unique attributes versus instruction that steers learners toward certain curricular standards. Rather, our goals was to show that although there are differences in the concepts and people representing the two fields, there is nonetheless much potential for exchange.

There are several shared elements between the humanist orientation and the behaviorist paradigm:

1. Learning should focus on practical problem solving.
2. Learners enter a teaching-learning setting with a wide range of skills, abilities, and attitudes, and these need to be considered in the instructional planning process.
3. The learning environment should allow each learner to proceed at a pace best suited to the individual.
4. It is important to help learners continuously assess their progress and make feedback a part of the learning process.

5. The learner's previous experience is an invaluable resource for future learning and thus enhancing the value of advanced organizers or making clear the role for mastery of necessary prerequisites.

Several years ago, Miller and Hotes presented a series of strategies for humanizing the systems approach to individual instruction. While stressing the use of "accurate measurable behavioral objectives," "appropriate practice opportunities," and "task analysis," Miller and Hotes pointed out that one way to humanize the system "is to make it responsive to the needs of the individual student". They believe the three strategies that can be useful are learning by example (modeling), learning by doing, and positive reinforcement. We believe there is considerable value in examining the ways humanist and behaviorist approaches to adult learning might be linked.

In our own work on self-direction in learning, we have presented a framework for understanding key dimensions of the concept. We developed what we call the Personal Responsibility Orientation (PRO) model. This model starts with the notion of personal responsibility, in which "individuals assume ownership for their own thoughts and actions". This, we believe, is central to an understanding of self-direction in learning, especially when working with adults as learners.

We assert that only by assuming primary responsibility for personal learning is it possible for an adult to take a proactive approach to the teaching-learning process. Obviously, we believe that an adult learner's proactivity is desirous because from our experiences the ability to be self-directed regarding learning pursuits benefits everyone. Further, personal responsibility is not an either/or characteristic; rather it exists within each of us to a greater or lesser degree.

A humanistic orientation to the instructional process can help learners increase their levels of responsibility. We do recognize there may be times when self-directed opportunities are minimal, such as when involved in collaborative learning or when learning entirely new content, but believe that the assumption of personal responsibility is possible in ways not tied to the type of learning or content. We also recognize that various social, political, and organizational factors may inhibit the employment of humanistic techniques, but urge that as much attention as possible be given to the potential of learners taking charge of their own learning.

For example, in the PRO model, we make an important distinction between "learner self-direction" and "self-directed learning." Learner self-direction refers to those characteristics within an individual "that predispose one toward taking primary responsibility for personal learning endeavors". It is probably best understood in terms of personality. To a great extent, the characteristics of learner self-direction are found in basic tenets of humanistic philosophy and psychology.

Self-directed learning, in the PRO model, refers specifically to the teaching-learning process, and centers on the planning, implementation, and evaluation of learning activities where learners assume primary responsibility for the process. For purposes of the current discussion, we would like to elaborate a bit on this notion, as this is where it is possible for educators and trainers to actively implement strategies that will allow them to humanize the instructional process.

Both Patterson and Valett present a host of useful strategies designed to humanize education. While many of their ideas can be adapted to adult learning settings, these works tend to stress elementary and secondary education. More recently, Hiemstra and Sisco have presented an approach to individualizing instruction derived from principles of humanism and designed specifically for working with adult learners.

The individualizing instruction (II) process model consists of six steps, which are related to each other in a circular rather than linear format). The six steps are:

(a) activities prior to the first session (e.g., developing a rationale, preplanning);

(b) creating a positive learning environment (physical, social, and psychological);

(c) developing the instructional plan (with active involvement of participants in assessing personal and relevant group needs, ascertaining the relevance of past experience, and prioritizing knowledge areas to be covered);

(d) identifying the learning activities (determining learning activities and techniques);

(e) putting learning into action and monitoring progress (formative evaluation); and

(f) evaluating individual learning outcomes (matching learning objectives to mastery).

In the II process, the instructor's role is to manage and facilitate the learning process; "optimum learning is the result of careful interactive planning between the instructor and the individual learners"

There are some very important differences between humanist and more behavioral approaches. For instance, an instructor in the II process serves more as a facilitator, while an instructor operating within a behavioral framework is more a manager or director of the process and delivery system. In addition, the II model places great importance on affective aspects of the teaching-learning transaction. Concern for interpersonal relationships and active involvement of learners in determining both process and content of the learning experience are two examples. Furthermore, while behaviorist models tend to focus on the outcomes of learning, the II approach also places great importance on "the process that enables mastery to occur".

One final element of the PRO model needs to be discussed. In the model, we stress the need to recognize the social and political context in which learning takes place. For example, while we believe that self-direction is vital to the teaching-learning process, we also recognize that the individualized emphasis of this approach may run contrary to values held in some cultural settings. In addition, there are times when the pragmatic requirements of a given training need may prevent learners from taking much or even any personal responsibility.

We do not wish to "impose" our approach on individuals or groups whose perceptions of reality (particularly with regard to individuality, autonomy, and personal responsibility) run contrary to ours; at the same time, we do feel obligated to share our views with such people to promote awareness of alternative ways of thinking and acting. It also is not our wish to seem like evangelists trying to convert others to a particular way of thinking. Rather, based on our experiences and knowledge bases, we believe in promoting learner self-direction as the most appropriate instructional approach when working with adults as learners.

The increasing use of computer technology for individualized instruction and for distance learning is further reason for humanists, constructionists, and behaviorists to learn from each other. For example, humanistic, self-directed learning activities are important components of many of computer mediated conferencing distance education courses. As humanism undergirds much of the understanding about self-direction, it is important that such a case be made. Here are some initial ideas for those adhering to humanist views on how to promote a better understanding:

— Engage in dialogue with those not understanding or even dismissing humanist views through articles, papers, books, and even co-authored writing.

— Model effective adult instruction that is grounded in humanistic views.

— Recruit instructional design students into adult education courses where humanistic views are described and employed in the instructional process.

— Encourage adult education students with a humanistic orientation to learn about behaviorist or cognitive models of instructional development and to become able to analyze and, where appropriate, adapt elements from such models into their own practices.

— Determine or explore various ways that instructional design theories and approaches can better inform self-directed learning practices.

— Encourage all educators of adults to explicate their personal instructional philosophy, delineate their actual beliefs in terms of a humanist to behaviorist continuum, and determine how such beliefs inform their instructional efforts.

Humanism embraces the goodness of humanity and the virtual limitlessness of human potential. Self-direction is one of many ideas from educational practice that is tied to these basic values.

8

FACTORS INFLUENCING LEARNING

CONDITIONS REOUIRED FOR LEARNING

Motivation

Motivation is anything that affects the state of the nervous system to determine behavior. It is the driving force for the activation and persistence of behavior, and helps explain why some behavioral patterns occur more frequently or at certain times. Motivation generally relates to a psychological drive or need which pressures us into behaving accordingly. There may also be external stimuli or incentives that contribute to motivation by rewarding appropriate behavior.

There are two main aspects of motivated behavior: the provocation of behavior and the direction of behavior. Provocation of behavior includes anything that causes a behavioral reaction, resulting from internal or external stimuli. Direction of behavior is the response to whatever provokes a behavioral response. The response may be either instinctive or purposeful. For example, heat that causes pain is an external provocation of behavior, and pulling away from the heat is instinctive direction of behavior.

Motives themselves also direct behavior in that different motives cause us to act in different ways. There are three types of motives: homeostatic, nonhomeostatic, and learned motives. Homeostatic motives include things such as hunger, thirst, and breathing. They work to keep the body in the state of homeostasis (internally balanced). Nonhomeostatic motives include required activities, such as seeking shelter, and curiosity. Learned motives include the desire for novelty, achievement, power, and approval. These motives develop through experience, and once developed, they continue to influence behavior throughout life. The three types of motives may also overlap. For example, the desire for new experiences or challenges may be homeostatic as well as learned. Since people differ as to the level they are affected by homeostatic mechanisms, some people are always looking for something new to try while others are content with the familiar.

Several general unifying theories have been present to explain motivation. Early theorists, including Clark Hull, proposed that motivation is fundamentally an attempt to reduce drives. Donald Hebb and Daniel Berlyne proposed a more flexible theory, which said that all motivational states are an attempt to maintain an optimal level of action. This theory took into account that a certain behavior is reduced when it is too high and will increase it when it too low, and that we purposely expose ourselves to exciting stimuli (such as skydiving, bungy jumping, or watching scary movies).

More recently, Richard Solomon developed the process theory. The process theory states that acquired motivations involve a primary motivational state that is either intensely positive or intensely negative, and a secondary state that is opposite to the primary state and outlasts it. With repeated exposure to the stimulus, the secondary state becomes stronger.

Although these theories help account for certain behaviors, they do not address the role of motivation in the cognitive processes that are characteristic to humans. These processes were first considered by Sigmund Freud, who believed that behavior is driven by a biological drive for pleasure. He suggested that morality and social reality regulate the expression of motivation, and that the typical response to these motives becomes socially acceptable behavior. Abraham Maslow proposed that behavior is motivated by seven needs arranged in a hierarchy, with the highest being self-actualization (the need to realize one's full potential).

Research has also shown that approval and achievement are important factors. In social situations, people with a need for approval tend to agree with other people's suggestions and opinions even if they disagree with them. Achievement motivation is affected by the desire for personal reward or success. People with a high need for achievement tend to choose tasks that are intermediately difficult, for a moderate probability and higher degree of success.

People with a low need for achievement tend to select either very easy or very hard tasks, since the completion or outcome of the task is not important. People with the need for high achievement attribute their success and failure to internal factors, whereas people with little need for achievement attribute success to external factors and failure to internal factors. This explains why people with a high need for achievement persist even in the face of difficulty and failure, while people with a low need for achievement give up relatively easily.

Interest

Interest is important to learning, since it facilitates thinking and attention. We cannot effectively think about a topic that we find boring and purposeless, nor can we learn something that seems tedious. Interest guarantees that we will focus on what we are supposed to be learning. We think and learn when we read the newspaper or a novel, watch television or a movie, or solve a problem - but only if we are interested in it.

When we are not interested in something, we tend to think of something else or"daydream". These distractions shield us from boredom while allowing us to try to find something else to think and learn about. Not understanding something also tends to lead us away from critical thought, and eventually destroys our interest in that topic.

Thinking and learning are inseparable because our brains strive to think all the time, meaning that learning occurs whenever there is meaningful thought. Only rote learning involves little thought, but it is also inefficient and uninteresting.

Interest does not guarantee that we will think efficiently, but it does ensure that we will put ourselves in situations where relevant thought occurs. When we find something interesting, we try to involve ourselves with that topic or activity. We will read books or watch movies about the topic, and talk to experts in the field. These activities help facilitate effective learning.

Transfer of Training

The recognition that new learning can profit from old learning because learning one thing helps in learning another, is called transfer of training.

By the end of the nineteenth century, many educators believed that a student's learning ability could be strengthened. They believed that Latin strengthened the mind, and math strengthened reasoning ability. However, today this belief is rejected due to many studies which have shown that reasoning ability did not significantly differ between students who had studied math and those who had not. Furthermore, students who had learned similar processes did not show transfer of training from one task to another (for example, learning to add did not help the students learn multiplication).

Currently, the viewpoint regarding transfer of training is that both concrete and abstract knowledge can be transferred from one situation to another. Recent studies have shown that the most important factor in transfer of training is the quality of the person's organization of prior knowledge.

Transfer of training can be either positive or negative. If someone is trying to learn two tasks, after learning the first task, the second one may be easier or harder. If the second task is easier, then the previous learning was useful, and therefore positive transfer of training occurred. If it is more difficult, then the old learning was a hindrance and negative transfer of training occurred.

Whether a particular transfer of training is positive or negative depends on the relationship between the two (or more) tasks. Positive transfer of training occurs when the tasks have similar stimuli that elicit the same response. Negative transfer of training occurs when the tasks have similar stimuli, but elicit different responses, making the last task harder to learn.

New learning can profit from old learning because of three main factors:

1. Positive transfer of training.
2. General principles that are learned from one task and can be applied to another task.
3. Good study habits that are learned from one task which help us learn another task.

Environment

Research with laboratory animals has revealed that exposure to sensory-enriched environments can change the structure and chemistry of the brain. Rats raised in environments containing toys, stimulating objects, and other rats exhibited increased thickness of their neocortex. Their cell bodies and neuron nuclei were larger, dendrites were longer, and the area of synaptic contacts were greater. These rats also had more protein, more glial cells, larger capillaries, and an increased ratio of RNA to DNA.

The most prominent change in the stimulated animals was in the visual association. However, most areas of the cortex were affected, including the cerebellum and hippocampus. Except for the frontal cortex, where the right hemisphere is affected more than the left, both brain hemispheres appear to be almost equally influenced by an enriched environment.

The more varied the enriched environment and the longer the rat stayed in the environment, the longer it retained its increased cortical dimensions after being moved to a less stimulating environment. These effects were found in both young and old rats. Research also showed that the rats exposed to enriched environments performed tasks such as maze running significantly better than those raised in less stimulating environments.

FACTORS DETERMINING EFFECTIVE LEARNING

Attention

Attention is the focusing of your consciousness on a specific activity. There are different types and levels of attention, which can be focused on one or more things. Sometimes attention is involuntary, being drawn from an intensive stimulus. Intensive stimuli usually elicit an orienting response (sudden captivation and the switching of attention towards the stimulus). However, if the stimulus is repetitive or continuous, attention will slowly be turned away from it and towards something else, due to habituation. Attention is not required for some types of activities, such as registering the general features of your surroundings. Also, over time, some activities that initially required your full attention may become so automatic that they no longer require you to focus your attention on them.

Research into which sections of the perceptual process are influenced by attention culminated in Donald Broadbent's Filter Theory. This theory proposed that a large amount of sensory information can be absorbed at once, and that a selective "filter" reduces the input for one source while the brain is processing the information from another source. The information placed on hold may later be perceived if it is deemed to be important. Broadbent showed that an unfocused state of mind allows some learning to take place, but that motivation or interest may be required to activate these memories.

Dividing attention between multiple tasks becomes more difficult when the tasks involve the same abilities. For example, most people can listen to music and read at the same time, while few people can listen to two people talking to them at the same time. It is believed that this is due to the anatomical separation of the brain centers that perceive different types of sensations.

Concept Formation

A concept is any idea that includes a description of the important properties of a category. Someone who has formed or attained a concept can easily fit new ideas into a category, thereby acquiring an effective thinking device. While on the surface it appears as though things in our world form natural groups and categories, concepts are simply the names that people learn to associate with them. This summary of concepts does not address the fact that concepts can be false, and neglects that the human mind may impose as well as discover it.

Traditionally, everything in a category must have some characteristics in common. Thus, concept formation and attainment is learning what these defining characteristics are. However, categories do not always need to have something in common, but rather may have a resemblance structure, where the category members share similar properties but are not sufficient to firmly place them in the same category. For example, most birds fly, sing, and build nests in trees. However, ostriches do none of these things, yet they are still birds. So while ostriches belong in the "bird category", they are not necessarily put into this category when someone bases their "bird category" purely on resemblance structure.

Research into cognitive psychology has suggested that concepts are more than just lists of characteristics. An individual's knowledge and theories in the organization of concepts are also important. People may demonstrate a bias by assuming that categories have defining properties and then theorize about what exactly those properties are. Theories such as these may fall between the ideal properties and the actual properties, leaving the structure of that person's concepts to be imposed and discovered via the interaction of the mind and world.

Habituation

Habituation is a decrease in responsiveness to unimportant stimuli or stimuli that do not provide appropriate feedback. In other words, habituation is learning not to respond to a certain stimulus. Sometimes when a stimulus is first encountered, the response is immediate and vigorous. However, if the stimulus is presented many times, the elicited response to it gradually decreases and may eventually disappear altogether. If the stimulus is withheld for a period of time after habituation, the response may reappear if the stimulus is later presented. This is called sensitization.

Habituation is an important aspect of learning since it increases efficiency. Birds learn not to waste energy by taking flight at the sight of every leaf blowing in the wind. Squirrels learn not to respond to the alarm calls of other animals if these calls are not followed by an actual attack. This may also help us understand why animals avoid predators (since they are rarely seen), while ignoring common, harmless species.

Imprinting

Imprinting is an aspect of learning which occurs at an early age. An example of imprinting is how young geese follow their mothers. But how do the young geese know whom to follow? Konrad Lorenz addressed this question in several experiments which led him to discover that newly hatched goslings would follow whatever moving object they saw first, and would continue to identify with this object throughout their lives. Lorenz divided a nest of goose eggs, leaving half with the mother and putting the rest in an incubator. The geese raised by their biological mother showed normal behavior, following her around during their youth and growing up to interact with other geese.

When the incubated eggs hatched, the goslings spent their first few hours with Lorenz instead of their mother. From then on, these goslings followed Lorenz around, showing no recognition of their own mother or even adults of their own species. As adults, these geese continued to prefer humans over members of their own species. Lorenz's experiment showed that geese have no instinct telling them who their mother is, or who is of their species. Instead, they respond to and identify with the first moving object they encounter.

There are two features that distinguish imprinting from other aspects of learning. First, what is learned from imprinting is irreversible. Second, imprinting must occur within a critical period, which is a limited phase in an animal's development during which learning a particular behavior can occur. For example, Lorenz discovered that goslings isolated from any moving object for the first two days after hatching failed to imprint on any parent figure afterwards. So for these geese, the critical period for parent imprinting was two days.

Imprinting has traditionally been thought of as only involving very young animals rather than short critical periods. However, it is now known that similar learning processes occur in older animals, and that critical periods may be of various durations. Not only do young birds require imprinting to recognize their parents, but the adults also require imprinting to recognize their young. For the first day or two after their young hatch, adult herring gulls will accept and defend another chick introduced to their nest, even if it is of a different species.

Memory

Memory is the ability to remember something that has been learned or experienced. It is also a vital part of the learning process, since if you were unable to remember anything from the past you could not learn anything new.

Little is known about how memories are stored in the brain. Storing memories seems to involve chemical changes in the brain's nerve cells as well as changes in their physical structure. Research has shown that these changes seem to occur in a small area of the brain called the hippocampus. The hippocampus is part of the cerebral cortex, which controls most higher brain functions (such as problem solving and language). It is believed that memory is acquired via a series of event in the brain which consolidate and then store the information.

Although there are many types of memory, they are usually divided into three main groups: sensory memory, short-term memory, and long-term memory.

Sensory memory is our instantaneous memory, which is only held for an instant as something is experienced. For example, when looking at a photograph, sensory memory occurs as the image of the picture enters your eyes and is transmitted to the brain. This entire process takes less than a second.

Short-term memory can hold a piece of information for as long as you actively think about it. For example, short-term memory is used when looking up and dialing a telephone number. As long as you are focusing on this information, you are utilizing short-term memory. However, about twenty seconds after you stop repeating this information to yourself, it will begin to fade unless it is transferred to long-term memory.

Long-term memory can last a lifetime. Information enters long-term memory due to either repetition or intense emotion. So, for example, friends and family will be remembered for a long time, while someone you only meet once will not. Similarly, the events surrounding a traumatic experience are remembered, while the typical day-to-day events leading up to it are usually not.

Memory is accessed by recall, recognition, and relearning. Recall involves thinking of a past event and trying to list as many details of it as you can. Recognition is isolating accurate details from more facts than are relevant. Most people tend to recognize more facts than they can recall, which is why students tend to perform better on multiple-choice tests than on long-answer tests. Relearning involves memorizing details after you supposedly forgot them. People tend to relearn information faster than they learned it the first time, depending on how much of the original learning they actually remember.

There are many reasons why people forget things over time. The primary explanations include interference, retrieval failure, motivated forgetting, and constructive processes.

Interference occurs when remembering certain facts block the memory of other facts. For example, if one of your friends moves, initially you may not be able to remember his new telephone number. The old phone number may keep coming to mind, interfering with your ability to remember the new number. However, after you have thoroughly learned the new number you may not even be able to remember the old one. When previously learned information hampers the ability to remember new material, it is called proactive interference. On the other hand, learning new facts may interfere with old memories, and is called retroactive interference.

Retrieval failure is the inability to remember facts that have been stored in long-term memory. A prime example is when you are unable to think of a name, place, or event, even though it seems to be "on the tip of your tongue". Often later, when you are no longer thinking about it, the information will suddenly come to you.

Motivated forgetting is the loss of memory due to conscious or unconscious desire. We forget many things simply because we want to forget them. Motivated forgetting is also called repression if it involves forcing unpleasant feelings or experiences into the unconscious mind.

Constructive processes involve the unconscious invention of false memories. When trying to remember an event from several months or years ago, only a few details may be recalled. The gaps in those facts are filled with details that seem logical, but may be untrue. Constructing facts to tell a complete story is called refabrication. Refabricated memories often seem real, and are almost impossible to distinguish from the memories of the events that actually occurred.

Perception

Perception is the way we receive and interpret the information we are presented with. Understanding of our surroundings is perceived by our sense organs. Light and radiation stimulate our eyes; sound waves and air vibrations stimulate our ears; tastes stimulate our tongues; and smells stimulate our noses. Our skin is also a sense organ, perceiving pressure, pain, and temperature.

Through perception, we learn to associate certain things as being known objects, events, or people. However, perception does not tell us about the objects, events, or people themselves. Our brains must organize and interpret what our sense organs perceive, converting environmental stimuli into information about the world. There are three factors that make up perception:

1. *Detection:* Sensing the stimulus.
2. *Recognition*: Identifying the stimulus.
3. *Discrimination:* Differentiating between stimuli (such as different musical notes).

Receptors are important to perception. Sensory systems (such as vision and hearing) each have specialized receptors which are sensitive to certain types of stimuli. They receive the environmental stimuli, and send information to the brain via nerve impulses. For example, the human eye has two types of receptors in the retina: rods and cones. The rods respond to the intensity of light, resulting in detailed black-and-white vision. The cones respond to the frequency of light, perceiving color. Rods allow us to have detailed vision even in dim light, while the cones enable us to perceive color and vivid detail in bright light.

Many factors (including experience, expectations, and physical, emotional, and psychological influences) affect what we perceive. Personal experience, emotion, and motivation are also important in determining our perception. Experiments have shown that the perception of form, color, pain, and touch differ between cultures and age groups. Therefore habits, customs, and education also influence perception. Emotions can prevent perception entirely, such as when an emotional shock causes someone to temporally lose their hearing. We are also more likely to perceive stimuli that are related to our motivation. Motivation affects the characteristics we observe in people, objects, and events, such as when a highly anticipated day seems to take forever to arrive while the day of an exam seems to rapidly approach.

While many people believe that an illusion is a false perception, it is actually defined as anything that is inconsistent with other perceptions. Since perceptions do not impart information about objects or events themselves, no sensory system is better than another at receiving truthful perceptions.

Closure is a general principle of perception that allows us to perceive general or incomplete things as being complete. Our experience and knowledge allows us to use closure to fill in parts of a perception that may be missing, or associate a general perception with a known one. On the other hand, constancy is the principle stating that despite changes that may occur, we tend to perceive objects as being constant in their physical properties (such as size, shape, and color). For example, under different kinds of light, we tend to perceive an apple as being red despite not actually seeing that color. The opposite of constancy can also occur, when an object stays the same but we begin to perceive it differently. M C Escher's art involving optical illusions is a prime example of this.

Problem-Solving

A problem exists when someone has a goal and an idea as how to solve it, but does not know how to proceed. Problem-solving deals mainly with intellectual problems: those which can be solved mentally or by manipulation. Problem-solving uses three main methods:

1. Examining what has been said about the problem.
2. Experimenting with the problem.
3. Working through the problem.

Research into problem-solving has shown that this process is not entirely open to consciousness. A person may begin by using conscious reasoning, but the solution is often found suddenly, as if it came out of nowhere. Graham Wallas described the general problem-solving sequence as containing four distinct stages:

1. *Preparation* - The problem is defined and possible ways to approach it are explored.
2. *Incubation* - Attention is turned away from the problem, and towards other things.
3. *Illumination* - The solution suddenly become apparent.
4. *Verification* - The solution is checked to confirm that it works.

The first studies into problem-solving were carried out by Gestalt psychologists, who emphasized the difference between solving a problem by understanding its structure and finding the solution by a blind application of known rules. Karl Duncker applied this type of analysis to multiple-step problems. He discovered that every phase of a solution tends to be a slight variation of the original problem. Duncker coined the term "functional fixedness" to describe a common source of difficulty: if the solution to a problem requires a concept to be used in an unfamiliar way, a fixation on the familiar usage may prevent the new one from being discovered.

Mathematician Gyorgy Polya introduced the idea that there are general techniques which can be applied to solving problems. He called these techniques heuristics: procedures that can help solve a problem, but cannot guarantee success. One well-known heuristic technique is working backwards when the answer is known.

Since the 1960s, computers have been an important contribution to problem-solving. A recent computer approach involved memory-based reasoning, in which a program compared new data to previously solved problems and tried to make decisions based on similar cases. Although computer systems examine the possible solutions more quickly, even the most complex computer system cannot match the complexity of human reasoning or incorporate human experience into their problem solving methods.

Reasoning

Reasoning is a process of directed thinking. We may reason with a specific goal in mind (such as finding the solution to a problem) or more generally (such as to deal with inconsistencies in thought).

Reasoning is often treated as a process that follows the rules of logic, building formal arguments from fixed conditions in order to reach a valid conclusion. Reasoning can be viewed as a loose combination of mental processes which are focused towards finding a more coherent view of an issue. Feelings and sensation may contribute to this process, and the underlying logical structure can be abandoned if required. Such reasoning is referred to as cognition, concept formation, problem solving, or thinking. The approach to reasoning can be divided into three main categories: clinical, learning, and developmental.

The clinical approach to reasoning studies the ways in which people reason. Sigmund Freud is well known for distinguishing between the two thought processes believed to be involved: the primary process (which responds to internal and biological interactions) and the secondary process (which responds to social and environmental interactions). This conscious and rational approach to psychoanalysis served to approach the principles of predicting events and understanding the world.

The learning approach to reasoning studies apparent behavior and stimulus-response connections. These behaviorists believe that problem solving involves gradual, continuous, and automatic behavior changes, and that these general processes form the basis of intelligence and creativity.

The developmental approach is based upon four stages. The first stage is sensory-motor thought, characterized by physical interactions with objects and the idea that objects exist independently of one's perception of them. The second stage is pre-operational thought, where the thought process is based upon an internal representation involving symbols that are limited to the interpretation of appearance. Concrete operational thought, the third stage, is characterized by reasoning based upon logic and independence from appearance. The fourth stage, formal operational thought, is based upon systematic, formal, deductive thinking fully independent from appearance.

FACTORS AFFECTING COMPUTER ASSISTED LEARNING

The advent of Computer Assisted Learning (CAL) in the mid 1980s coincided with an increase of small group activities with some primary school classrooms undoubtedly changing in this respect, both as a result of and alongside the introduction of computers. For some, the introduction of small group work has occurred simply to make use of a relatively scarce resource - the classroom computer; for others, group work has been introduced as a central feature of new pedagogy, often to engineer a change in the locus of control in learning environments, orientating control towards the learner. There is also growing evidence to suggest computer use can have considerable impact on students' learning in groups.

Significant amounts of research have been done into small group learning, although there has been rather less investigating verbal interactions within groups. The greater proportion of small group learning research has been in non-computing environments. However, there has long been a concern to compare the impact of cooperative learning in CAL on learning outcomes, with individual learning this concern continues today.

Different software encourage different types of interactions and learning outcomes amongst students. For example, Johnson & Johnson and Sherwood have suggested that verbal interactions between students when using simulation software facilitate higher-order thinking, as students readily interact with their peers to solve problems.

In the context of word processing it has been reported that collaborative writing environments encourage students to find solutions to a range of writing problems, largely through extensive discussion; whilst others have reported that students are able to work longer, and develop a better understanding of the writing process when working cooperatively on a writing task. Indeed, significant research in this area has revealed that the word processing environment is an ideal one to motivate students to discuss, reflect upon and edit their work within cooperative groups; and that there is increased participation and collaboration among students when grouped to use computers to write.

Indeed, Clements and Nastasi have suggested that it is these 'richer CAI environments' (e.g. simulation and word processing) that are likely to produce a greater frequency of quality interactions.

Simulation and word processing software are chosen by many teachers as the focus for computer-based learning and at least one major evaluation of computer use in primary and high schools, lists these software amongst the most frequently applied. For these reasons, simulation and word processing software have been chosen as the focus for this study.

Cognitive styles

Cognitive styles refer to the preferred way an individual processes information and describe a person's typical mode of thinking, remembering or problem solving. Furthermore, styles are usually considered to be bipolar dimensions whereas abilities are unipolar (ranging from zero to a maximum value). Having more of an ability is usually considered beneficial while having a particular cognitive style simply denotes a tendency to behave in a certain manner.

Cognitive style is a usually described as a personality dimension which influences attitudes, values, and social interaction. A number of cognitive styles have been identified and studied over the years. Field independence versus field dependence is probably the most well known style. It refers to a tendency to approach the environment in an analytical, as opposed to global, fashion.

Learning styles specifically deal with characteristic styles of learning. For example, Kolb proposes a theory of experiential learning that involves four principal stages: concrete experiences (CE), reflective observation (RO), abstract conceptualisation (AC), and active experimentation (AE). The CE/AC and AE/RO dimensions are polar opposities as far as learning styles are concerned and Kolb postulates four types of learners (divergers, assimilators, convergers, and accommodators) depending upon their position on these two dimensions. For example, an accommodater prefers concrete experiences and active experimentation (AE, CE). Pask has described a learning style called serialist versus holist. Serialists prefer to learn in a sequential fashion, whereas holists prefer to learn in a hierarchial manner (i.e. top-down). Theoretically, cognitive and learning styles could be used to predict what kind of instructional strategies or teaching methods would be most effective for a given individual and learning task.

Constructivism versus instructivism

There are a whole range of theories concerned with the way in which students learn which together inform what is usually meant by ' constructivism'; some theories emanate from a cognitivist tradition , others from a social psychological, interactionist or experiential perspective (and the list could go on). However, in much of the current and recurring debate about the role of educational and learning theory in instructional technologies (especially multimedia), there seems to be a readiness to polarise one theory of learning (behaviourism) with a metatheory (constructivism), and, further, to present the former as grossly deficient and the latter as the only credible explanation of student learning.

The difficulty here is that such a polarisation is entirely philosophical, and as such represents fundamentally different views on what is meant by knowing, the role of education and the nature of learning. The polarisation, outside of a philosophical debate, is certainly not helpful in determining effective instructional design. For example, even although the main components of behaviourism (or at least the behavioural theory of Skinner) were largely discredited as general truths in the 1970s, the principles of contiguity, repetition, reinforcement through feedback and motivation are still recognised as important in processes of learning

Indeed, there are various dimensions in different theories of learning, and not all fit along an imaginary continuum connecting two supposed extremes—this is where Reeves' work on the evaluation of instructional technologies is misleading. If we need a metaphor to represent learning or educational theories as a whole, a series of corresponding and opposing objects, each with its own attributes, some common, some unique, is ultimately a more accurate and useful metaphor than a simple, linear path connecting two poles or extremes.

Perhaps the overriding point is that, in designing and evaluating instructional software, we must be prepared to refer to explanations of student learning to describe the most appropriate way of addressing a particular learning situation. Also, that all theories or explanations of learning, be they psychometric, humanistic or behaviouristic, are each credible in helping to understand certain kinds of learning; but that each theory is also partial in that it refers to a limited range of learning situations and that it is often based on a limited set of data.

Context and situation

It is often argued that context and situation are all important in providing for learning at all levels, and should influence in particular, the design of instructional software. Collins describes situated learning thus, 'situated learning is the notion of learning knowledge and skills in contexts that reflect the way the knowledge will be useful in real life'. In the same context, Collins, Brown and Newman argue strongly for the effectiveness of cognitive apprenticeship models of pedagogy, where, it is suggested, 'teaching methods should be designed to give students the opportunity to observe, engage in, and invent or discover expert strategies in context' so that they might best learn both cognitive and metacognitive skills.

Cognitive apprenticeship models of instruction are current in much multimedia software development for schools where such software builds easily onto the demonstrated effectiveness of experiential and activity-based education found in subjects such as science.

It is not clear, however, that the concept of situated learning allows for the levels of abstraction required for understanding in many domains of knowledge, particularly those studied by older students. For example, Laurillard argues cogently that learning in situated contexts does not, by itself, allow for a learner to make abstractions from the particular context and therefore be able to generalise or even be able to apply what is learnt to new situations or contexts. This has, in particular, an important implication for learning what Laurillard classifies as 'academic knowledge'—she considers academic knowledge to be different to everyday knowledge, drawing a distinction between learning 'percepts' in everyday life and learning 'precepts' in education, implying that learning precepts necessitates students building understanding in a deeper (abstract) sense, a level of understanding which cannot be provided for simply by situating the learning experience.

Feedback/reinforcement

Feedback and reinforcement are two of the most pivotal concepts in learning. Feedback involves providing learners with information about their responses whereas reinforcement affects the tendency to make a specific response again. Feedback can be positive, negative or neutral; reinforcement is either positive (increases the response) or negative (decreases the response).

Feedback is almost always considered external while reinforcement can be external (extrinsic) or instrinsic (i.e. generated by the individual). Information processing theories tend to emphasise the importance of feedback to learning since knowledge of results is necessary to correct mistakes and develop new plans. On the other hand, behavioural theories focus on the role of reinforcement in motivating the individual to behave in certain ways. One of the critical variables in both cases is the length of time between the response and the feedback or reinforcement.

In general, the more immediate the feedback or reinforcement, the more learning is facilitated. The nature of the feedback or reinforcement provided was the basis for many early instructional principles, especially in the context of programmed instruction. For example, the use of 'prompting' (i.e. providing hints) was recommended in order to 'shape' (i.e. selectively reinforce) the correct responses. Other principles concerned the choice of an appropriate 'step size' (i.e. how much information to present at once) and how often feedback or reinforcement should be provided. These principles are often used in CAL drill and practice software.

Imagery

According to dual coding learning theory, it is considered that learners are much more likely to learn effectively if information is presented both verbally (or in written form) and visually, similtaneously. CAL software often provides for the representation of images but usually only as an illustrative medium, and not as an application of dual coding theory. It is only with the application of interactive multimedia that the power of sophisticated and realistic images is being exploited. But even with the advent of this new technology, very few multimedia software products deliberately apply dual coding of information. Thus, even with today's more sophisticated software, the role of images in the cognitive processes in learning, are often not exploited.

Individualised learning

Individualised instruction or learning, does not necessarily mean independent working but rather, the involvement of each student working with learning plans designed to meet individual needs, interests and abilities. Usually, there are thought to be five aspects of individualised instruction;

— the pace of learning;

— instructional objectives;

— learning activities or materials;

— reading level of materials;

— methods by which students are requested to demonstrate learning.

Alterations in any of these aspects may provide for individualised instruction/learning. With some CAL software, particularly that which locates substantial control over the learning experience with the learner, there is a high level of variation provided in the pace of learning, thereby facilitating individualised learning. However, in most other aspects, CAL does not provide well for individualised learning—which is perhaps ironic given that computers were first touted as 'individualised learning machines'. More recently, there have been moves to provide individualised learning environments—sometimes called ' natural learning environments ' supported by computer technologies.

In the context of CAL, learning it is suggested, should be seen largely in terms of cognitive change. That is not to suggest that other learning of an affective or psychomotor sort is not of importance, or that CAL does not provide for such learning—but rather, in a majority of educational contexts at least, cognitive development in learners is perhaps the central aim of *most* instructional software.

FACTORS AFFECTING EDUCATIONAL REFORM

Successful schools help young people learn the skills to succeed in a personal way within the framework of society. However, society today is rapidly changing, and in some aspects that change is accelerating.

Technologies and philosophies taking advantage of technology are becoming widely dispersed and often fundamental to many aspects of western society, such as business, research and home life. However, Schank and Cleary have argued strongly that up to now our educational systems have not been developing these essential skills. Technology skills have been left mostly to post-secondary schooling and "learning on the job". However, recognition of the problem is growing there has been many calls for educational reform from business, government, parents and students. There is strong evidence that the situation is improving as these calls are slowly being acted upon, and that the lag in recent decades of educational systems behind other areas of society will be reduced. Against a background of technological change, this essay will examine the factors that have been preventing educational reform in the recent past, the factors that are now promoting educational reform in our schools, and their relationships.

Factors holding back development of schools

Limited funding

During the last few decades, while business was forging ahead with development and utilisation of technology, school education was constrained by limited funds. The purchase of a mainframe and terminals, or a multimedia computer, costing hundreds of thousands of dollars was simply not as cost-effective for small schools as it was to hire several new teachers. The situation is worse for schools situated in remote and sparsely populated areas. These small schools are usually further behind in technology than their city counterparts because of reduced funding and increased costs due to the distances.

Established school attitudes

During the eighties, the potential of computers for education was beginning to be glimpsed by pioneering teachers, and many of them introduced early computers to their schools. However, despite initial optimism, these early computers did not radically change the school culture in any way. They were invariably forced into specific computer labs, where "computer studies" could be taught in computer classes. Papert describes it like this: "The system, the administration, the ministries now began to take charge, so the computers were no longer in the hands of the visionary teacher but were in the hands of the administration. And, in principle, the bureaucratic administration has a deep, vested interest in maintaining the status quo."

Lack of professional development

During the late eighties and early nineties, computers began to infiltrate more and more into workplaces, homes and school computer labs. Yet use of them was still constrained. One of the main reasons for this was, and is, a lack of knowledge among the majority of teachers about using the new technologies for teaching.

Cultural attitudes

Almost all adults today have been to school. As a result we all have ingrained ideas about what a school is and what it should be for our children. Not everyone has the luxury of being able to research competing educational theories in detail or even to realise that schools are struggling to keep up with societal changes — they understandably assume the schools know what they're doing.

These attitudes are reflected in voting behaviour in elections, which affect governments and thus school funding. They are also reflected in the choices of schools that parents make, and the types of support they give children at home.

Even early attempts at educational computer software reflected these attitudes, centering on drill-based programs, quizzes or page turning exercises.

Factors promoting the development of schools

Countering the depressing effect of the factors outlined above, are a number of factors pushing for educational reform in schools, including business, technology, methodology and use in the home.

Business in the information age

Highly competitive and complex global business environments and the compound effects of education developments of the past century are pushing our evolving technologies to be cheaper, more effective and ubiquitous in the workplace, the home, and now the school.

The percentage of employees dealing almost solely with the analysis and manipulation of symbols is rising rapidly while the percentage of people working in primary industries and production is dropping due to technological effects such as automation and economies of scale. Toffler has written persuasively about the "Information Age" as a third wave after the Agricultural Age and the Industrial Age. In addition, employees at every level are being asked to demonstrate advanced levels of problem-solving skills to retain their level of employment. Crucial skills include learning to think critically, to analyse and synthesise information to solve problems in a variety of contexts and to work effectively in teams.

Increasingly, work can be defined in terms of constructing a solution to a problem. Work that is repetitive and requires no problem solving (aspects of primary and secondary industry, as well as many forms of service) is often seen as an opportunity to implement automation and gain competitive advantage through efficiency.

To be successful, our educational systems need to change to keep up with the business of our society and allow new generations to develop the skills they will need to be successful in a dynamic and rapidly changing environment. The people of tomorrow's society should be able to look upon new technologies as an opportunity, not a problem. Schools are feeling the pressure of this demand from society, and business is increasingly looking at school education as an opportunity for sales and development.

Technology costs are dropping, capabilities are rising

As a primary result of research and development by government and business, technology costs for any given capability are coming down dramatically. Capabilities that would have cost hundreds of thousands of dollars in 1985 are available today for hundreds and thousands: and continue to drop. Networks, servers, mainframes, groupware, and today's personal computer all started off being well out of the reach of educational institutions and home users. At the same time, these systems are proving their value above traditional classroom and paper-based technologies.

The cheaper technology also allows students the opportunity to own their own hardware, which is important. Not only does this save costs for the school, and allow them to spend 'computer lab' money elsewhere, but it also allows some important changes in methodology.

One particular interesting area of technology is software. While many commercial packages are still expensive, equivalent versions are emerging as "free software" or shareware. This can happen for two reasons: first, the increasing development of well-written modular software (for example, Linux, and World Wide Web), and secondly, software delivered over the internet has zero manufacturing costs, zero distribution costs and a global marketplace. The final factor in producing software is software design, which is an extremely competitive area and getting cheaper all the time.

The new technologies allow people to do more work in less time. They can also do new work that never existed before, almost exclusively in the growing fields of symbolic manipulation. This ensures their further development in a competitive workforce. It seems likely that a large number of today's small children will grow up to do work that hasn't been designed yet.

New methodologies

Ubiquitous information technologies allow effective implementation of methodologies that would be much harder without the technology, such as learner-centred models, curriculum reform, tool personalisation.

Learner-centred education

A growing number of theorists and practitioners agree that it is the learning models based on constructivism which best optimises the potential of technology in the learning experience. These theories have been in development for many years, yet so far have not made great inroads into school education.

Constructivism is the belief that knowledge is actively constructed by learners on the basis of their existing knowledge (with the corollary that knowledge is not transmitted directly from teacher to learner). von Glasersfeld's 'radical constructivism' adds the idea that knowledge about the world serves an adaptive function, rather than yielding objective truth about an observer-independent external reality - a perspective shared by the many other forms of constructivism.

Constructionism is an educational method based on constructivismwhich says that students will be more deeply involved in their learning if they are constructing something that others will see, critique, and perhaps use.

Hannafin writes:

> Constructional design focuses on the creation of environments that enable and support individual construction or building by engaging in design and invention tasks; the design task is to provide a learning environment within which individual construction is facilitated, not one in which concepts are explicitly taught. [..]

Similarly, problem-based learning activities require learners to draw upon technological, cognitive, and social resources in order solve complex, open-ended problems which serve as orienting contexts for interpretation as understanding and skills are constructed and refined through use.

This was always possible, using libraries and teachers, but computer networks combined with the content of the Internet provide an environment that is not only richer, but more current, faster, and cheaper than previous solutions — making it feasible to implement in schools on a wide scale. Successful implementations of new systems based on these philosophies are described at Trinity Kew College and Brewster College in the U.S.

Other examples can be found in the business world, particularly those areas with ubiquitous technology access for the past twenty years or more, where they have been developing for decades. One of the leading examples, due to its innately high level of symbol manipulation, is IT systems development. In developing such systems, for example, employees frequently work on a project basis with specific or open-ended goals. There are usually many different ways to achieve the same goal, depending on changing technologies and the current environment. Effective employees are able to work with others in a team, yet also act autonomously to research new techniques and tools to complete a project. In these cases, the Internet has proven itself as a rich and useful resource and communications tool to support the self-learner.

Examples of other professions that benefit from access to large amounts of information include teachers, financiers, lawyers, managers, researchers, technical support. Such highly symbolic professions benefit from a good general understanding of systems to guide on-the-spot research that enables appropriate decision-making exactly when and where it is needed.

Curriculum Reform

India is currently undergoing a reform of the state-wide curriculum with the recent design of a new complete curriculum framework for K-12 education. The framework brings together statements of key principles and desired learning outcomes in eight broad learning areas, based on five desired core values.

It sets out what all students should know, understand, value and be able to do as a result of the programs they undertake in Indian schools. In general it encourages more learner-centered methodologies as outlined above, and sets a clear and forward-thinking path for educational reform in this state.

All schools are obliged to modify their activities to achieve the framework's learning outcomes over the next five years. How a school structures learning opportunities in terms of time and the range of courses and programs provided remains the school's responsibility, but this is still obviously a great pressure on the schools to reform.

Personalised Tools

Technology that is cheap enough to become truly "personal", such as lap-top computers or smaller information appliances allows further benefits to the information-literate individual — both as a personal information manager and as a "tool to think with". Papert talks about two sides of personal technology, the constructional side (project and goal-based learning) as the driving force that motivates a student to use the informational side (resources and communication). Computer labs operate under the implicit assumption that every computer is the same, rather than a project to be worked on.

In the past decade, educational software often focussed on custom-designed drill-based software to teach specific outcomes. Now, the trend is moving toward using open-ended packages and non-content specific applications such as "office" applications, databases and programming languages, in order to stimulate "higher-order thinking" and problem solving.

An adaptable and powerful computer that is with you all the time truly becomes a tool to think with, if you can you develop and construct it to your own needs. Again, in business, this has been the norm for a long time. Many workplaces supply each employee with their own personal computer that is used all day long. Over time the employee will customise the machine to suit their needs.

Modern computers are becoming increasingly portable, customisable, and open, consisting of many pieces of software, some bought, some written by the user and some downloaded from the Internet. The current growing trend of open software development delivers and promises free access to world-class software by anyone. In the near future these systems will probably evolve more agent-like abilities so that they themselves learn from their owner and configure themselves more automatically.

Compare this scenario with current computer labs in many schools where each computer must be refreshed nightly from backup to actually remove customisations by students so that different students can use them the next day, and you can see schools will be under pressure to develop further, no matter how many computer labs they have.

In addition to computer literacy, the idea of using a computer on an ongoing basis as a thinker's toolkit promotes information literacy. A good description of information literacy is published as part of the IT policy document at John Paul College, in Queensland. In part, it reads:

> Information literacy is the critical thinking process necessary to seek, gather, evaluate and apply information in all formats; to look beneath the surface of the visual, the auditory, and the textual; to solve problems; and to identify possible solutions.

An information literate person:

— recognises the need for information

— recognises that accurate and complete information is the basis for intelligent decision-making

— formulates questions based on information needs

— identifies potential sources of information

— develops successful search strategies

— accesses print and technology based sources of information

— is a competent reader

An information literate person evaluates information:

— establishes authority

— determines accuracy and relevance

— recognises point of view and opinion versus factual knowledge

— rejects inaccurate and misleading information

— creates new information to replace inaccurate or missing information as needed

An information literate person uses information and:

— organises information for practical application

— integrates new information into the existing body of knowledge

— applies information in critical thinking and problem solving

This type of critical thinking combined with today's technology allows a student to make real use of resources like the Internet to solve whatever problem they may have. For children growing up with the Internet as a ubiquitous fact, they will need very strong critical skills to deal with the wide amount of conflicting and possibly dangerous information available.

INDEX